Journeys of Faith

Journeys of Faith

Religion, Spirituality, and Humanistic Psychology

Second Edition

MIKE BROCK

WIPF & STOCK · Eugene, Oregon

JOURNEYS OF FAITH
Religion, Spirituality, and Humanistic Psychology

Second Edition

Wipf & Stock
An Imprint of Wipf and Stock Publishers
199 W. 8th Ave., Suite 3
Eugene, OR 97401

www.wipfandstock.com

PAPERBACK ISBN: 978-1-6667-7401-6
HARDCOVER ISBN: 978-1-6667-7402-3
EBOOK ISBN: 978-1-6667-7403-0

06/19/23

I dedicate this book to Dr. John Morgan—
scholar, teacher, mentor, friend, man of peace.

"When the student is ready, the teacher will appear."

The human being needs a framework of values, a philosophy of life, a religion or religion-surrogate to live by and understand by, in about the same sense that he needs sunlight, calcium, or love.

—Abraham Maslow, *Toward a Psychology of Being*

Contents

Introduction

Humanistic psychology rose to prominence in America during the post-World War II years and continued to influence the national conversation—psychologically, culturally, socially, and spiritually—throughout the remaining decades of the twentieth century. During those years, it attracted a wide and diverse following, becoming a cultural phenomenon that affected everything from counseling and education to parenting, religion, and business management. Its influence continues to be felt today, though often unrecognized and uncredited.

This book examines the role and contributions of the leading figures of the humanistic psychology movement with particular attention to their spiritual journeys, which developed alongside their newly emerging psychology in a unique, symbiotic relationship. The key players—Abraham Maslow, Carl Rogers, Erich Fromm, and Rollo May—hailed from different sociocultural and religious backgrounds and followed dissimilar, though interconnecting, professional paths. They all rejected the orthodoxy of their religious inheritance in favor of a more humanistic approach and, in the process, discovered a renewed spirituality that, they hoped, would address the concerns of a world yearning for something to believe in.

While Maslow, Rogers, Fromm, and May confronted the world's problems through the lenses of psychology and psychotherapy, other thinkers approached them from different, though equally humanistic, perspectives. Among those others, the evolutionary biologist Julian Huxley will receive special attention as one with particularly useful insights into the intersection of science and spirituality.

Humanistic psychology arose as an antidote to the spiritual shock that followed a second world war on the heels of the first, a genocide designed and perpetrated by a modern European nation-state, atomic bombs over Japan, the rise of the Soviet Union as a rapidly developing threat, and the growing fears of massive, mutual nuclear destruction. American psychology itself mushroomed in response to the war, particularly its aftermath, as soldiers returned to their families and the workforce after having experienced the worst that humanity can do to itself.

But it wasn't just the trauma of the postwar years that led to the rise of humanistic psychology; it was the manner in which the American political, business, and social communities responded to the war—through denial, distraction, and the promises of American know-how and material prosperity for all. In unison, America appeared to be saying, "Let's forget the war, the horror, and the continuing threats and embrace happiness through more and better material comforts." And many did—even some in the Freudian camp concentrated more on personal adjustment and conformity to societal norms, a cultural corollary to the reconciliation of id and superego, rather than toward the transformation of self and society. For budding humanists, who would come to place societal transformation on a par with personal self-actualization, adjustment and conformity fell flat.

Two distinctly different approaches dominated the psychological scene when humanistic psychology began to assert itself: B. F. Skinner's behaviorism and Sigmund Freud's psychoanalysis. With its roots in animal studies, its emphasis on the prediction and control of behavior, its reduction of the person to a soulless, stimulus-and-response entity, and its unwillingness to engage the spiritual, behaviorism had little to say to a postwar generation seeking a more meaningful response to what ails the self and the world. Abraham Maslow, who spent his early years in behavioral psychology and learned invaluable research tools as a result, abandoned it as he became more conscious of the need for a more encouraging, affirming, transcendent response to the world's challenges.

At a behavioral parenting presentation I attended in the early 1990s, a fellow participant turned to me at the close of the speaker's words and said, "I can do all those things he's talking about. Positive reinforcement, negative reinforcement—I can do all that. But I wouldn't feel *ennobled* by it." It wasn't ennobling in the 1990s, and it wasn't ennobling in the 1950s. Behaviorism had failed to provide any meaningful answer to the psychologists, social scientists, pastoral counselors, and others who sought a deeper response to what the world needed and, hence, were asking the more significant questions, what Rollo May, following his mentor, theologian Paul Tillich, called "the ultimate questions": *Why is there something rather than nothing? Is the urge to destroy intrinsic to humanity? Are the distractions of consumerism and materialism the only responses available to us? What is the human person? What are our common values?*

If behaviorism offered little in response to the postwar generation's need for something uplifting, something ennobling, the Freudian alternative, with its Old World aura and esoteric ambience, failed to attract anything but a limited audience in an America ready to turn its back on the old and fully embrace the new—an "America on the move." Further, Freud's characteristic pessimism offered little in the way of inspiration to those seeking more hopeful responses. In *Civilization and Its Discontents*, published in 1930, nine years before his death, Freud elaborated on how the process of development that led us from our primitive beginnings to the civilization we now experience (a process that parallels the id-ego-superego development) has led to the discovery that civilization is less an achievement than the very source of our struggle. In words that could hardly be called encouraging, he wrote,

> If the development of civilization has such a far-reaching similarity to the development of the individual and if it employs the same methods, may we not be justified in reaching the diagnosis that, under the influence of cultural urges, some civilizations or some epochs of civilizations—possibly the whole of mankind—have become "neurotic"?[1]

Just as the conflict between the id and the superego results in neurosis, so too does that between our aggressive impulses, which Freud decries, and the demands of civilization. Freud saw these demands as unrealistic, citing the commandment to love your neighbor as yourself (and the even more troublesome "love thy enemy") as particularly untenable and in conflict with the need to restrict our love to those closest to us. Less humanistic words could hardly have been spoken.

What were the philosophical antecedents to this new movement? As noted, its contemporary form as a psychological movement arose from the ashes of World War II in response to the need for a new vision of the person in opposition to the perceived negativism and reductionism of Freud and the spiritual sterility of behaviorism. What was needed was a vision that emphasized growth, health, potentiality, creativity, subjective experience, and values that are definable not in terms of an external source but as discoverable within humanity itself.

Were these strivings unique to mid-twentieth-century Americans? Although care must be taken to avoid conflating humanistic psychology, which began at a certain time and place, with the larger word *humanism*, we can appreciate their relatedness and are able to identify strands of thought

1. Freud, *Civilization and Its Discontents*, 109–10.

throughout the ages that reach into our own times and in which the heart and soul of humanistic psychology participates.

References to moral decision-making, the moral character, and the human soul found throughout the writings of Plato and Aristotle often surface in the humanist literature and are frequently highlighted in the movement identified with Maslow, Rogers, Fromm, and May. So too are the teachings of Socrates, who, in the words of philosopher Andy Norman in *Mental Immunity*, "helped others give birth to healthy ideas . . . [while] exposing 'false' and 'unhealthy' ideas,"[2] thereby laying the foundation through which Maslow and others might discern and identify a set of universal values, as we will learn in a later chapter. The Golden Rule, espoused by Jesus and other religious figures before and after, highlights the relational dimension of values, a key humanist emphasis.

Erich Fromm often hearkened back to the Hebrew prophets and his talmudic Jewish upbringing in his call to identify an ethical response to current struggles, to embrace freedom rather than escape it, to discover within the person the source of an ethical life, to live a life of being rather than possessing, and to eschew authoritarianism. He also frequently referenced the medieval mystic Meister Eckhart and the seventeenth-century Dutch philosopher Baruch Spinoza as antecedents to his thought. Immanuel Kant's categorical imperative, which highlights an approach to identifying universal values that emphasizes the person as the starting point, is occasionally noted by various humanistically oriented thinkers as contributive to their work.

Closer to our own century, William James is credited for his philosophical approach to psychology, one that emphasizes the human experience, as in *The Varieties of Religious Experience*. Likewise, John Dewey's *A Common Faith* must be noted for identifying a more naturalistic and humanistic approach to religion, a perspective shared across the ocean by Julian Huxley. Both modern existentialism and phenomenology influenced the development of humanistic psychology, the former defined in terms of "the *existing* person . . . as he is *emerging, becoming*,"[3] and the latter as "the disciplined effort to clear one's mind of the presuppositions that so often cause us to see in the patient only our own theories or the dogmas of our own systems, the effort to experience the phenomena instead in their full reality as they present themselves."[4] Both definitions are from Rollo May, the most philosophically oriented of the five theorists studied.

2. Norman, *Mental Immunity*, 20.
3. May, *Existential Psychology*, 16.
4. May, *Existential Psychology*, 26.

Central to this book is identifying the spiritual element as fundamental to humanistic psychology as it developed at the time. The openness to the spiritual on the part of each of those examined here came as a surprise when I first read their biographies and studied their books. It also came as a surprise to some of them. It was a spirituality that focused initially on the person, broadened to address both the interpersonal and the communal, and eventually provided the movement with a universal message that attracted the attention of religious and political figures at the highest levels.

This second edition of *Journeys of Faith* would not have been possible—or even considered—had it not been for the 2021 publication of *Psyche and Soul in America: The Spiritual Odyssey of Rollo May*, by Robert H. Abzug, Audre and Bernard Rapoport Regents Chair of Jewish Studies and professor of history and American studies at the University of Texas. While writing the first edition, I learned that a new biography of May was being written by Dr. Abzug and immediately wrote to him for advice related to my chapter on May. He responded promptly with the information I needed, and we had a warm exchange.

Psyche and Soul in America led to a major revision of my chapter on May, as would be expected, but it offered much more: because Abzug so successfully weaved the story of May into the larger story of American humanism—psychological, spiritual, and sociocultural—the imprint of his book can be discerned in every chapter. Further, the author got to know May during the last years of his life, earning his trust at such a level that he was granted unrestricted access to his papers and encouraged "to present his life in full—his ideas, accomplishments, shortcomings, obsessions, and fragilities."[5] I am deeply indebted, and I hope this new edition is worthy of his contributions.

Three other books written after publication of the first edition of *Journeys of Faith* deserve mention here as well. Through *Transcend: The New Science of Self-Actualization*, psychologist Scott Barry Kaufman has reintroduced Maslow to contemporary audiences, who more often than not know Maslow solely in terms of the hierarchy of needs. Andy Norman's timely *Mental Immunity: Infectious Ideas, Mind-Parasites, and the Search for a Better Way to Think* imagines a world in which healthy and honest dialogue through an updated version of the Socratic method might serve to root out toxic ideas and lead to a greater incidence of identifying and promoting healthy ones. And John Morgan's *The Damaged Self: Exploring the Psychopathology of a Diminished Life* examines how the development of a healthy self-concept—as explored through the writings of psychologists

5. Abzug, *Psyche and Soul*, xvii.

and social scientists such as Carl Rogers, Abraham Maslow, Karen Horney, Anna Freud, and others—might guide us today as we seek to provide a more affirming, encouraging, and humanistic environment for generations yet to come. All three of these books added significantly to this new edition.

As noted in the first edition, this book emerged from a doctoral dissertation under the direction of John Morgan, Karl Mannheim Professor of the History and Philosophy of the Social Sciences and past president of the Graduate Theological Foundation. It could not have been written without his teaching, guidance, mentoring, and encouragement. I cannot express my gratitude enough. My gratitude is extended also to Wipf and Stock Publishers, particularly Rebecca Abbott, for her copyediting, and Savanah Landerholm, for her typesetting and design. *Journeys of Faith: Religion, Spirituality, and Humanistic Psychology* would not have been possible without their proficiency, professionalism, guidance, and patience throughout the manuscript-to-book process. Thank you. I take full responsibility for any gaffes that might remain.

Although certainly not intended, nor even considered, the writing of *Journeys of Faith* has become for me a personal spiritual journey, a journey through which I have been forced to confront numerous assumptions about religion, faith, spirituality, God, and how one's understanding of all that translates, or should translate, into ethical responses to the world's challenges. I have learned immensely from the theorists studied, and those learnings have translated—I hope—into a more mature and healthy faith life. I am much indebted to all of them.

Finally, I extend my deepest appreciation to Jennifer Malloy, who reviewed the book at a critical time in the process and offered both creative and substantive suggestions, along with unceasing encouragement. Someone once said that although parents indeed give birth to their children biologically, children often give birth, or rebirth, to their parents spiritually. This has certainly been my experience: Jennifer's spiritual maturity and authenticity over the years have often forced me to confront my inherited belief system and hold it up to the light of reason. I hope that has made me a better person and a better dad.

Chapter 1

Something in the Air

An Ode to Humanistic Psychology

Very early, I understood that growth was life force revealing itself, a manifestation of spirit. I looked at the tiny seeds I planted and watched them grow into big plants. My reverence for life was set early in life. . . . No plants ever grew because I demanded that they do so or because I threatened them. Plants grew only when they had the right conditions and were given proper care. . . . Finding the right place and the proper nourishment for plants—and people as well—is a matter of continual investigation and vigilance.

—Virginia Satir, *The New Peoplemaking*

Something was in the air as America entered the 1960s, a decade destined to become iconic. The birth of a new psychology is rarely the kind of event that captures the public imagination, but it was about to happen. This new psychology was originally called the "third force" because it was posited as an alternative to the two dominant psychologies of the day—B. F. Skinner's behaviorism and Sigmund Freud's psychoanalysis. It would soon embrace the more descriptive label of *humanistic psychology*. Suggesting an association that reached back through the history of Western civilization to at least the eighteenth-century Enlightenment, with stirrings several centuries earlier during the early Renaissance, humanistic psychology offered a fresh approach to understanding and working with the individual. Taking its first tentative steps in the late 1930s, the movement's pace quickened after the horror of the Second World War and began to soar during the 1950s, reaching a place of prominence just as the 1960s were dawning.

In 1954, Carl Rogers, who redefined the counseling relationship with the simple yet profound substitution of the word *client* for *patient*, offered his groundbreaking *On Becoming a Person: A Therapist's View of Psychotherapy*, which cemented the art of counseling as a legitimate course of study. Within five years, existentialist psychologist Rollo May published *Existence*, signaling both his own philosophical orientation and the affinity between existentialism and the newly emerging humanistic psychology. And Abraham Maslow, of "hierarchy of needs" fame, published *New Knowledge in Human Values*, a cry for the identification and affirmation of a set of universal values that might serve as a template for a troubled world.

In 1956, Erich Fromm, part of the generation of German Jews who left Europe in the wake of Hitler and transported their devotion to scholarship to their newly adopted land, wrote *The Art of Loving*, a paean to humanistic relationships that sold over twenty-five million copies. And across the ocean in London, Julian Huxley—an evolutionary biologist whose insights on "religion without revelation," the title of one of his books, serve as an introduction to the larger humanist world—published *The Humanist Frame*.

Like Maslow's *New Knowledge in Human Values*, published two years previously, *The Humanist Frame* presented a host of theorists from a broad span of disciplines, all proposing the identification of universal human values as the one cure for a fractured world. And it was no coincidence that on January 25, 1959, amid all this psychological reawakening, a seventy-five-year-old pope, whom no one thought would do much but serve as a placeholder in the Vatican during a time of uncertainty, first used the word *aggiornamento*, "bringing up to date," to describe the modernization of a 1900-year-old Church. Something was very much in the air.

Before the humanistic psychologists, there was William James, whose foundational *The Principles of Psychology* served to unravel the secrets of the human mind. The early nineteenth-century psychiatrists focused on medical responses to various psychoses and conducted their work in hospitals and asylums. There were the behaviorists who directed their attention toward that which could be accurately observed and measured and who busied themselves with the task of improving human behavior through reinforcement and conditioning. And there was Freud. Strategically positioned behind his patients as they reclined on his iconic couch, Freud made possible the free flow of dreams and associations that would lead to an approach to healing—psychoanalysis, the "talking cure"—that would change much more than just the narrow world of psychology. But it would fall to the humanistic psychologists to abandon the couch (and the desk that, for many, continued to separate doctor from patient) and face their clients free of physical boundaries, one person to another. It would take a while for that word *client* to replace the medically suggestive word *patient*, but when it did, counseling was born.

What is humanistic psychology, and who were these pioneers of the counseling profession? Jessica Grogan, in *Encountering America: Humanistic Psychology, Sixties Culture & the Shaping of the Modern Self*, recognizes the difficulty of defining the movement best represented by thinkers such as Maslow, Rogers, Fromm, and May. She settles on four key points:

- A focus on an innate tendency toward growth, represented by words such as *self-actualization* and *self-realization*
- A redirection of psychology toward human subjectivity and complexity, areas previously rejected as unobservable by the more positivistic approaches to psychology that focused solely on that which can be derived from sensory experience
- A return to the more philosophical and theological roots of psychology represented in America by William James, John Dewey, and others, and a movement away from the dry, biomedical approach that has taken on a new form in the present day
- A populist appeal, resulting in the dissemination of its principles to the broader public through books by leading humanistic thinkers, the sales of which routinely reached into the millions, suggesting that humanistic psychology had something to say to an audience beyond academia

The German developmental psychologist Charlotte Bühler, another of the many European émigrés who brought their academic gifts to America during the turbulent years between the two world wars, offers a philosophical approach to a definition in her 1972 *Introduction to Humanistic Psychology*, emphasizing

- The experiencing person as the center of psychological inquiry
- The distinct qualities that define and differentiate the human being, such as freedom of choice, creativity, and values
- Meaning as a legitimate area of study
- The person's inherent dignity, worth, and potential

Ten years previously, Bühler had published *Values in Psychotherapy*, in which she explored contrasting views regarding the source and significance of values, differentiating them around the larger philosophical question of immanence (intrinsic to the person) versus transcendence (outside or beyond the person). She compared, for example, humanistic psychologists like Maslow and Rogers, for whom values emerged through natural organic processes, with existentially oriented thinkers like Rollo May and Viktor Frankl, who argued for the personal identification of meaning in one's life, through which one's unique values would be revealed—a challenge that Bühler understood as transcending the individual person. The more existentially oriented thinkers eschewed words like *self-actualization* and *self-realization* (for our purposes here, those words are used interchangeably), with their assumption of an immanent, directional, and creative striving. Summarizing her thoughts, Bühler observes that "while the self-realization theorist's solution of life is immanent and experienced as the life process itself, the existentialist's solution of life is transcendent and becomes real in the product or result of life."[1]

Bühler's words deserve our attention not only because she expressed a core distinction between various theorists at the dawn of humanistic psychology—one, broadly speaking, between the secularly oriented (the *immanents*) and the religiously oriented (the *transcendents*)—but because that distinction remains significant in the present day. *Values in Psychotherapy* serves well as a prelude to the larger debate today between, for example, the more secularly oriented in the scientific community who would argue against any role for religion in matters related to societal improvement and those found largely in the more fundamentalist churches, who push back against what they perceive as secular threats to their religious beliefs and traditions. We will revisit this discussion throughout this study, most notably in the chapters on Maslow and Huxley.

For the proponents of self-actualization, who were largely secular thinkers (though, as we will discover, often deeply spiritual), "the life process itself"—the innate tendency in all life toward growth and fulfillment—reveals our fundamental human values, much as, for example, the process of deep therapy reveals a more expansive sense of the self to the client. For Frankl and May, on the other hand, who were largely religious in their orientation, values exist beyond the subjective self and are revealed through the identification of meaning and purpose in life. Having an objective reality of their own, values transcend the personal dimension and therefore demand a more transcendent, perhaps spiritual, response.

1. Bühler, *Values in Psychotherapy*, 59.

Disagreements about the source and identification of values notwithstanding, the humanistic psychologists were united in their recognition of the importance of their work, whether it was in the counseling office or on the world stage. The world desperately needed new values; the first half of the twentieth century had made that clear. The challenges facing humanity, not the least of which was spiritual emptiness, were formidable, and humanistic psychology would set before itself no greater task than creating a world in which those challenges might be met.

A third synopsis of humanistic psychology is suggested by Maslow, perhaps the most passionate—some would say "messianic"—of this emerging movement. Each of the six chapters of *Toward a Psychology of Being*, published at the cusp of the formation of the American Association of Humanistic Psychology in 1962, highlights a specific characteristic of this new direction in psychology, this alternative to the prevailing behaviorism and psychoanalysis of the times:

- An orientation toward health rather than sickness
- The promotion of growth and motivation
- The recognition of the experiencing person as a valued subject of research
- The celebration of individual creativity
- The promotion of the study of values
- A future orientation toward personal self-actualization

Drawing on the seminal work of those thinkers, as well as on humanistic psychologists who have built upon their work in subsequent years, a composite definition that may serve us well as we study their lives and works follows: *Humanistic psychology is a holistic, health- and growth-oriented approach to working with and learning about persons in their unique, subjective, experiencing states that has as its goal the promotion of innate human potential. Critical to the success of this goal is the personal identification of healthy values, especially those that inspire us to take action for the greater good.*

But if that sounds a bit dry and lifeless, Carl Rogers, in *A Way of Being*, offers a more vivid and picturesque definition, one that echoes "the life process itself" noted by Bühler. He presented the analogy of potatoes stored several feet below a window in a cold, dark storage cellar on his Illinois farm. He observed that despite the less-than-optimum conditions, sprouts were growing on the potatoes and, following an internal, organic striving, were winding their way toward the window above. He noted that they were white, spindly sprouts, not the healthy green sprouts one would observe in a potato given adequate light and nutrition. But they were there nonetheless, striving for the faintest beam of sunlight through the storage cellar window. That light-seeking potato, propelled by its own internal organismic valuing process, its own striving to become the potato plant it was designed to be, might well serve as an apt metaphor for the humanistic psychology movement.

Since this book's overarching theme explores the spiritual domain within the humanist movement in psychology, spirituality also deserves definition. Today, it has become fashionable for persons disaffected by their particular religious inheritance to say that they are spiritual but not religious, and we seem to grasp their meaning readily. Broadly speaking, the word *religion* refers to the organizational and the proscriptive, *spirituality* more to the personal and the experiential; and, like people, they often work best when working together.

In *Beyond Religion*, David Elkins, psychology professor at Pepperdine University, defines spirituality in terms of components such as transcendence, longing, mystery, connectedness, meaning, and purpose. He suggests that it is best understood in relation to two other words, *soul* and *sacred*. Spirituality, he writes, "is rooted in the soul and cultivated by experiences of the sacred; it feeds on poignancy, wonder, and awe."[2] Also: "Where the soul is stirred, nurtured, and moved by the sacred, there is spirituality."[3] These themes will repeatedly surface in our review of the work of Maslow, Rogers, Fromm, May, and Huxley.

John Morgan, the author of *Clinical Psychotherapy*, a study of the modern schools of psychotherapy from Freud through the present day, aptly references "a rather lumpy collection of what is passionately labeled humanistic psychology,"[4] a lumpiness that is due in part to the diverse backgrounds of its founders, leaders, proponents, and hangers-on through the years. As challenging as it might be to define humanistic psychology, so too has it been to identify its principal leaders, with different chroniclers of the movement highlighting other names as most representative of this upstart third force in psychology. Morgan lists Maslow, Rogers, and Fromm. Grogan focuses mainly on Maslow and Rogers while referencing May, Fromm, and personality psychologist Gordon Allport, author of *The Individual and His Religion: A Psychological Interpretation*. In *Shadow Culture: Psychology and Spirituality in America*, Eugene Taylor lists Maslow, Rogers, May, and Anthony Sutich, one of the founding editors of the *Journal of Humanistic*

2. Elkins, *Beyond Religion*, 32.
3. Elkins, *Beyond Religion*, 31.
4. Morgan, *Clinical Psychotherapy*, 17.

Psychology. I have settled on Maslow, Rogers, Fromm, and May, as these theorists appear to have been most actively and consciously engaged from the beginning in advocating what we typically refer to as humanistic psychology. And they were certainly the most read—their books reached a broad audience, with many taking residence on the bestseller lists. We will be taking a close look at several of their books throughout these pages.

THE FACE OF HUMANISTIC PSYCHOLOGY

Grogan focuses primarily on Maslow as the face of humanistic psychology, and he presented quite a face. With joie de vivre and an ever-present smile, he was "irrepressibly compelled . . . to view people as resplendent,"[5] a refreshing change from the often-dour faces of behaviorism and psychoanalysis. Early on, Maslow identified fourteen specific characteristics of self-actualizing people, highlighting a health and growth orientation and the challenge to reach beyond contemporary American society's adjustment and conformity mentality. To be health- and growth-oriented is to strive to transcend a culture that preaches mindless conformity and offers the psychology of adjustment (a low bar compared to personal fulfillment) as a national goal. Maslow appeared to understand intuitively that the person is called to more than the conventional; to him, persons are definable in terms of the degree to which they strive for self-actualization, signifying the process of becoming all of which one is capable.

Self-actualization was first introduced by the German neurologist and psychiatrist Kurt Goldstein, one of many refugees from Nazism who enriched the psychological and social sciences in America. He offered a broad description of the inherent growth potential of living organisms, and Maslow, seizing upon the concept, made it a foundational principle for his own psychological theorizing. One of the more helpful definitions of self-actualization in its psychological sense is from the German psychiatrist Frieda Fromm-Reichmann, also a European émigré, who describes it as the ability of persons "to recognize and use their talents, skills, and powers to their satisfaction, within the realm of their freely established, realistic set of values."[6] Some seventy years later, psychologist Scott Barry Kaufman, whose *Transcend: The New Science of Self-Actualization* introduces humanistic psychology's core principle to contemporary audiences, supplements Fromm-Reichmann's definition with a helpful list of the characteristics of self-actualization: acceptance, purpose, authenticity, truth-seeking,

5. Grogan, *Encountering America*, 9–10.

6. Fromm-Reichmann, *Principles of Intense Psychotherapy*, 191.

continued freshness of appreciation, peak-experiences, humanitarianism, good moral intuition, creative spirit, and equanimity.[7]

From the beginning, Maslow identified, as his personal and professional mission, the scientific verification of the characteristics of self-actualization, the essential values of which he would increasingly reference through words like *religious*, *mystical*, and *transpersonal*. And he wasn't shy about promoting these ideas and connecting with other like-minded souls; during the late 1950s, he compiled a mailing list of potentially sympathetic thinkers representing fields well beyond the boundaries of psychology, including social scientists, economists, theologians, academicians, artists, and others. Among the 175 persons on this 1950s version of LinkedIn were Carl Rogers and Erich Fromm. With Maslow's passionate call for self-actualization, the humanistic movement in psychology was off and running.

A MOVEMENT TAKES SHAPE

During the late 1940s and 1950s, humanistically oriented thinkers sought more hopeful and inspiring answers to the world's ills. World War II, the Holocaust, and the atom bomb were clear signals that older approaches weren't working, and the conformism and materialism settling over America during the '50s failed to offer an acceptable alternative.

Maslow had yet to publish *Toward a Psychology of Being*, but he had written several research articles and had advanced his thoughts on self-actualization since the early 1940s. Rogers had two books to his credit before his 1951 *Client-Centered Therapy*, the title of which signaled a marked transformation in the therapeutic relationship. The remarkably prolific Fromm, who had highlighted the importance of articulating a cogent response to the destructive individual and societal thought patterns of his day with his 1941 *Escape from Freedom*, had published several works—including *Man for Himself* and *Psychoanalysis and Religion*, both of which addressed questions of religion and values—before humanistic psychology succeeded in defining itself as a legitimate psychological orientation in 1962.

There were occasional interactions among these early pioneers: Maslow had his mailing list to share and promote his musings, and they read and supported each other's works. Maslow wrote an endorsement for May's *Love and Will*, and May, Maslow, and Rogers collaborated on *Existential Psychology*, which probed the intersection of existentialism and humanistic psychology. Erich Fromm served as Maslow's counseling supervisor, and Maslow, in turn, provided psychotherapeutic supervision for Rogers's

7. Kaufman, *Transcend*, 89.

daughter, Natalie. Referring to Fromm's 1947 *Man for Himself*, biographer Lawrence Friedman, in *The Lives of Erich Fromm: Love's Prophet*, observes that Maslow "made extended marginal comments in his copy . . . [and] used Fromm's volume to develop his own 'humanistic psychology.'"[8]

It is noteworthy here that Friedman refers to humanistic psychology as Maslow's "own"; if anyone could claim parentage of humanistic psychology, it would assuredly be Maslow. In 1962, the American Association of Humanistic Psychology was formed at Sonoma State College in California, with Abraham Maslow its most-recognized spokesperson.

What did this new organization propose in response to the conformist, materialist culture in which America found itself after the war? It promoted the belief that humans are innately driven toward growth, health, and wholeness, with pathology understood less as an innate characteristic of the person and more as a product of unfulfilled basic human needs and an unhealthy environment, whether that environment is familial, educational, religious, economic, or sociocultural.

The organization highlighted the importance of the person's subjective experience and the imperative of processing and learning from that experience. It recognized self-actualization as our natural goal, attainable through the process of meeting and transcending our basic needs. It gave prominence to human initiative, personal creativity, and—what attracted many in the religious communities to this new psychology—conscience and values. It focused on the person's distinctly human qualities, such as the propensity for creativity (rather than destruction), personal choice, dignity, self-worth, and meaningfulness. Significantly, its proponents insisted that these qualities could be studied scientifically; they could be identified, catalogued, and evaluated. The new humanistic psychology, this third force beyond behaviorism and Freudianism, had found its voice.

Or rather, its many voices, for it was a heterogeneous group formed from diverse backgrounds and perspectives. At the *New Knowledge in Human Values* conference that Maslow organized in 1957, presentations were offered by fifteen different speakers from the fields of psychology, physiology, art, zoology, sociology, philosophy, anthropology, physics, theology, economics, and Zen Buddhism. Thankfully, these presentations were preserved in book form under the same title and published in 1959. Something new was dawning—a different way of seeing the self, others, and the world—attracting thinkers across the academic, scientific, and religious spectrum.

8. L. Friedman, *Lives of Erich Fromm*, 150.

ON THE PERIPHERY: A WHO'S WHO OF HUMANISTIC PSYCHOLOGY'S "FRIENDS AND ACQUAINTANCES"

It was difficult to be active in the broad field of psychology during those years without being affected by the humanist movement. Nonetheless, there were many who, though clearly sympathetic towards humanist principles and practices, avoided embracing the specific label for one reason or another. Their contributions to the larger field of psychology were significant, and several became household names; reference to their lives and contributions will surface throughout these pages.

Viktor Frankl

Viktor Frankl, Holocaust survivor and author of the universally acclaimed *Man's Search for Meaning*, readily comes to mind, and one wonders whether he would have been more attracted to this new humanistic approach had he left Vienna for good and settled in America, as did so many of his background and generation. His emphasis on freedom and personal responsibility, meaning and purpose, and the essential dignity of the human person, as well as his focus on virtues, fit well within the humanistic psychology message. In Frankl's *Yes to Life: In Spite of Everything*, only recently translated into English and published, noted psychologist Daniel Goleman, who provides the introduction to the translation, refers to Frankl's work as "meaning-oriented humanistic psychotherapy."[9]

Was Frankl just an ocean away from warranting inclusion on the list of founding humanistic psychologists? Or would the occasional cultural excesses of the 1960s that were often, though unfairly, associated with humanistic psychology—for example, the encounter movement, a group experience in which free expression was encouraged in the pursuit of a nebulous goal that appeared to be no more than free expression itself—have given him pause? "True encounter is based on self-transcendence rather than mere self-expression,"[10] he so wisely observed.

Besides, through his contribution of logotherapy—which sought healing through the identification of personal meaning and was dubbed "the third Viennese school of psychotherapy" following Freud's psychoanalysis and Alfred Adler's individual psychology—Frankl was walking his own well-defined path. But he certainly had a role to play: Maslow's biographer Edward Hoffman notes that "particularly useful [to Maslow was] Frankl's

9. Frankl, *Yes to Life*, 122.

10. Frankl, *Unheard Cry for Meaning*, 72.

comment that we never self-actualize in a vacuum, but always in relation to people and circumstances around us."[11] Though walking different paths, Frankl and the humanistic psychologists recognized and respected the value of each other's work: the cover of my 1984 edition of *Man's Search for Meaning* bears a testimony by Carl Rogers, who honored the book as "one of the outstanding contributions to psychological thought in the last fifty years."

Frieda Fromm-Reichman

Frieda Fromm-Reichman's *Principles of Intensive Psychotherapy*, which bridged the world of psychoanalysis with that of humanistic psychology and stands alongside other classics in the field, including Rogers's *A Way of Being* and May's *The Art of Counseling*, also deserves mention here. Comfortable within the larger humanist movement and a lifelong friend and colleague of Erich Fromm, to whom she was married and later divorced, Fromm-Reichman directed her energies toward the humane treatment of those suffering from schizophrenia. Perhaps more than anyone else associated with humanistic psychology, she "walked the talk" through her lifework. More about Fromm-Reichmann's contributions to the development of humane approaches to psychotherapy will be offered in the chapter on Erich Fromm.

Erik Erikson

In 1964, the developmental pioneer Erik Erikson, who had left Europe over twenty years previously, published *Insight and Responsibility*, in which he demonstrated his humanistic approach to values in a closing chapter on the Golden Rule, which he refers to as his "baseline . . . [that] has marked a mysterious meeting ground between ancient peoples separated by oceans and eras."[12] In keeping with his life's work—the eight stages of human growth and development, from infancy through old age—he approached values developmentally and, echoing evolutionary biologist Julian Huxley, from a more evolutionary perspective, one that predicts "a new humanism, the acceptance by man . . . of the obligation to be guided in his planned actions and his chosen self-restraints by his knowledge and his insights."[13] In distinctly humanistic terms, he calls for an understanding of the Golden Rule that "would say that it is best to do to another what

11. Hoffman, *Right to Be Human*, 256.

12. Erikson, *Insight and Responsibility*, 220.

13. Erikson, *Insight and Responsibility*, 227.

will strengthen him—that is, what will develop his best potentials even as it develops your own."[14]

In one of the many listings of his eight stages of human development, Erikson added "virtues" to each, from hope at the trust-versus-mistrust stage to wisdom at the integrity-versus-despair, words reminiscent of Maslow's multiple listings of higher values. And when discussing his understanding of the "I," which Erikson described in distinctly spiritual and relational terms, he referenced qualities that identify the person with words such as *central*, *whole*, *indivisible*, and *coherent*, again suggestive of Maslow's frequent lists of values words. It could be said that Erikson, like Frieda Fromm-Reichmann, helped to bridge the world of psychoanalysis with that of humanistic psychology; he had been trained in classical psychoanalysis by Anna Freud, had applied that training to the larger world of parent-child and society-child interaction, and went on to describe an eight-stage life development process that points the way toward fidelity, love, caring, and wisdom.

Harry Stack Sullivan

Psychiatrist Harry Stack Sullivan, who understood mental illness as the result of failed social interaction skills during the early childhood years and who, in response, promoted an interpersonal approach to the psychotherapeutic relationship, likewise exhibited a predilection for humanistic thinking. Through his reference to mental illnesses as simply "problems in living," his emphasis on the humanity of the patient over his or her diagnosis, and his insistence that no matter what our condition in life might be, we are all "much more simply human than otherwise,"[15] Sullivan sought to humanize the practice of psychiatry. World War II, particularly the horrors of Hiroshima and Nagasaki, led Sullivan to realize that "drastic and very extensive change in the usual patterns of human thinking and behavior would have to be made, and quickly."[16] And like Maslow, Rogers, Fromm, May, and Huxley, he saw the new trends in psychology and the social sciences providing the leadership for this change.

Becoming convinced that not every generation has to experience war, Sullivan signed on to a 1948 UNESCO project in Paris that advocated for the application of the social sciences to global problems, the prevention of war, the advancement of social justice, the creation of a mutually interdependent

14. Erikson, *Insight and Responsibility*, 233.

15. Sullivan, *Conceptions of Modern Psychiatry*, 16.

16. Perry, *Psychiatrist of America*, 404.

world, the end of colonialism, and an internationalist approach to education. Julian Huxley, UNESCO's first director-general, was also instrumental in that project.

But it was Sullivan's basic humanity that most endears him to devotees of his life and works today. A story told by Robert C. Leslie in his small yet profound book, *Jesus as Counselor*, demonstrates Sullivan's fundamental respect for persons. At a state hospital, a noted psychiatrist presented a schizophrenic patient to an audience to demonstrate the futility of attempting communication with him. With a shrug, he turned to Sullivan, on the stage as a visiting doctor, and asked if he had any ideas to suggest. Leslie quotes an observer at the presentation:

> Sullivan's first move was to edge his chair just a little closer to that of the patient and to lean forward so that he could look directly at the patient in a very friendly, warm manner. To the amazement of all, the patient responded to every question and comment that was made by Dr. Sullivan. For half an hour or more they conversed together, seemingly oblivious to the fact that there was anyone else in the room.[17]

Sullivan, though little known outside academia, regularly receives plaudits from those within the psychological profession due to the profound humanity that imbues his work. In a recent conversation with a psychology professor at a Dallas university, I referenced my studies on the life and works of Sullivan, to which he immediately replied, "I *love* Harry Stack Sullivan!"

Gordon Allport

Gordon Allport, who is credited with introducing Viktor Frankl to American audiences and who wrote the preface to *Man's Search for Meaning*, had one foot in the humanistic psychology movement and the other in existentialism, while appearing to be resistant to both labels: he feared that the word *humanism* was unscientific and was repelled by the "turgid, verbalistic, and reckless"[18] writing and theorizing of the European existentialists. In *The Individual and His Religion*, his study of the intersection of psychology and spirituality, he presaged both James Fowler's classic *Stages of Faith* with his own stages of religious development and the humanistic work of Maslow and Fromm on the characteristics of healthy, authentic religion. Moving from childhood egocentricity and anthropomorphism to

17. Leslie, *Jesus as Counselor*, 104–5.

18. Allport, in May, *Existential Psychology*, 94.

mature adult religiosity, Allport capped his work with six attributes of the mature religious sentiment, stressing its rich complexity, dynamism, moral consistency, philosophical comprehensiveness, homogeneous pattern, and heuristic character.

Karen Horney

Psychologist Karen Horney, who befriended Fromm and Sullivan upon immigrating to America from Germany in 1932, demonstrated a consistent humanistic tendency in her writings, as well as a more female-friendly perspective on Freud's psychoanalysis. Confronting Freud's fixation on the Oedipus complex, she famously countered his accusation of "penis envy" in women with her charge of "womb envy" in men. John Morgan, who references Horney's attraction to the third force movement in *Clinical Psychotherapy*, describes her psychoanalytic goals in terms any humanistic psychologist would applaud: "to facilitate a systemic change in the individual's personal assessment of his life situation . . . by assisting the individual in reaching deep within his own sense of self-worth towards a looming potential found in self-realization and self-actualization."[19] Horney "emphasized the central role of parenting in the personality development of the child" and stressed the importance of a parental relationship based on nurturing, warmth, and expressive love.[20] And, like several of the theorists studied herein, Horney discovered the spiritual late in life, specifically through the teachings and practices of Zen Buddhism.

Alfred Adler

Alfred Adler, an Austrian psychologist who was one of Freud's earliest disciples and who greatly influenced the young Rollo May, might have been more attracted to the humanist movement in psychology had he lived a decade or two beyond 1937, the year of his death. His emphasis on the striving for personal superiority and mastery beyond our initial sense of inferiority—it was Adler who first enunciated the inferiority and superiority complexes—resonated well with the humanistic emphasis on self-actualization. Further, his passion for social justice would be recognized and honored—and occasionally equaled—by the humanistic psychologists. Adler is perhaps best remembered for his coining of the word *Gemeinschaftsgefühl*, which is often

19. Morgan, *Clinical Psychotherapy*, 197.
20. Morgan, *Damaged Self*, 116.

translated as "social interest" or "community feeling" and which signifies the importance of being aware of and sensitive to the needs of the larger community.

Adler was probably the most progressive of the men and women studied herein, both societally and politically. He was an early proponent of women's equality, railed against the social destructiveness of male dominance, promoted the active participation of fathers in the upbringing of their children, spoke out against corporal punishment, and argued against blind obedience to political leaders. We could readily imagine Adler and Erich Fromm—of the humanistic psychologists, the one who best articulated the importance of addressing societal concerns—deeply engaged in discussion about the broader social, historical, political, economic, and religious issues of the day—in their native German over drinks and cigars at a New York café, as those two famously social men were wont to do.

Anthony Sutich

Anthony Sutich, severely handicapped due to a childhood accident and representative of what a self-actualized person can accomplish despite disadvantageous personal circumstances, was a longtime associate of Maslow's. He was particularly instrumental in establishing, with Maslow and Stanislav Grof, a proposed "fourth force" in psychology, transpersonal psychology, which will be discussed in the chapter on Maslow. In addition, Anthony Sutich officially invited Rollo May to participate in the formation of the Association for Humanistic Psychology in 1961. Sutich was much enamored of May's existentialist writings and readily saw their philosophical value and relatedness to the humanistic psychology movement.

Virginia Satir

Finally, rarely mentioned in reference to the foundations of humanistic psychology is the pioneering family therapist Virginia Satir. Her absence may be attributed to the fact that she was less a theorist than a practitioner (although she had much to offer theoretically about family therapy) and less a psychologist than a family counselor. But if the heart of humanistic psychology could be personified, it would be in the person of Virginia Satir—anyone reading *The New Peoplemaking*, published in 1988, cannot help but be awed by her fundamental humanity. Honored as "America's premier family therapist,"[21] she could channel the most basic principles formulated by Maslow and Rogers into heartfelt portraiture, as in the following sample from *The New Peoplemaking*:

> Very early, I understood that growth was life force revealing itself, a manifestation of spirit. I looked at the tiny seeds I planted and watched them grow into big plants. My reverence for life was set early in life. . . . No plants ever grew because I demanded that they do so or because I threatened them. Plants grew only when they had the right conditions and were given proper care, which, for me, includes loving them and sometimes talking to them. Finding the right place and the proper nourishment for plants—and people as well—is a matter of continual investigation and vigilance.[22]

The overarching theme of this book is the discovery and redefinition of the spiritual within the humanist movement in psychology. Our principal focus is on the work of the humanistic psychologists Maslow, Rogers, Fromm, and May. Each lived a multifaceted life as a teacher, writer, therapist, and social commentator. Each was born in the decade 1900–1910, and their lives spanned the twentieth century, the first to be born (Fromm) entering this world in 1900, and the last to pass on (May) exiting in 1994. Each set aside the practice of the religion of his birth (with varying degrees of intensity and finality), each moved more and more toward spiritual matters as he aged (in the case of both Maslow and Rogers, much to their surprise), and each became a household name in an America fascinated with positively oriented psychology. After reviewing their contributions, we will look at the Englishman Julian Huxley, whose life and works in many ways paralleled the four American (or *Americanized*, in Fromm's case) humanistic psychologists and added a unique evolutionary perspective growing out of his profession as a biologist. Before engaging their contributions, however, we must first pay homage to the man whose epochal discoveries about the psyche and challenges to God, religion, and the spiritual domain dominated the psychological world that Maslow, Rogers, Fromm, May, and Huxley were born into. That man is, of course, Sigmund Freud.

21. Westley, *Theology of Presence*, 26.

22. Satir, *New Peoplemaking*, 334–35.

Chapter 2

Giving the Devil His Due

The Legacy of Sigmund Freud

You are not so godless, since whoever lives for the truth lives in God, and whoever strives for the freeing of love "dwelleth in God." If you would fuse your own contribution with the great world harmony, like the synthesis of notes in a Beethoven symphony into a musical whole, I could say of you, "There never was a greater Christian."

—Lutheran pastor Oskar Pfister, in response to Freud's self-description as a "godless Jew," quoted in Lucy Freeman, *Freud Rediscovered*

In *The Handbook of Humanistic Psychology*, published in 2001, contributor Donald Moss, dean of the College of Integrative Medicine and Health Sciences at Saybrook University, notes that Sigmund Freud "laid down many of the foundations taken for granted by humanistic psychologists."[1] He references several of Freud's most noteworthy insights, for example:

- There is a causal relationship between early childhood experiences and later physical and psychological symptoms.
- All human activities, including such experiences as dreams and slips of the tongue, can reveal parts of our stories not yet accessible to consciousness.

1. Moss, "Roots and Genealogy," 13.

- The human personality can be understood developmentally and can be affected by our early relationships and trauma throughout life.
- Healing can arise from the "talking cure," as a patient of Freud's mentor, Josef Breuer, once described this revolutionary and now time-honored approach to the counseling craft. Although "invented" by Breuer, it was Freud whose revolutionary theories and subsequent fame ensured its permanence.

It would be hard to make a case for Freud as a humanistic psychologist, but it would likewise be difficult to make a case for humanistic psychology without Freud's discoveries. As John Morgan observes, "Every professional today practicing in the cognate fields of counseling is beholden to Freud and his system of theory and analysis whether they will admit it or not."[2]

In response to the two dominant psychologies of the day—Skinner's behaviorism and Freud's psychoanalysis—Abraham Maslow, as noted, proposed his own third way, which would come to be called humanistic psychology. Behaviorism was largely ignored as this new approach was emerging; little effort was expended in responding to it, and it was more often than not treated as if it were something one outgrew. But Freud had to be answered. He was the master, the eminent doctor of Vienna, whose teachings dominated the intellectual landscape of the day and whose presence was felt throughout Europe and, increasingly, in America. He lectured Saturday evenings at the University of Vienna, led the Wednesday Psychological Society meetings (formed of his own chosen acolytes), and presented his theories at B'nai B'rith, the Jewish social, civic, and humanitarian organization to which he belonged, despite his persistent attacks on all things religious.

Freud could not be ignored, nor should he have been. And it was largely in response to his characteristic pessimism about the human condition, as well as his rejection of the spiritual domain, that humanistic psychology would confront the master. It all starts with Freud, and so must our study of humanistic psychology and spirituality, the latter a world Freud had difficulty abiding.

WHO WAS THIS FELLOW FREUD?

Sigmund Freud, the firstborn son of Jacob and Amalia Freud, was born in 1856 in Freiberg, Moravia, a land with a long history of Jewish presence. Today part of the Czech Republic, Moravia was then within the Austrian Empire. When Sigmund was four, his family moved to Vienna; that historic

2. Morgan, *Clinical Psychotherapy*, 23.

city, for centuries the epicenter of European culture and history, together with Judaism, a faith whose origins extend at least two millennia before the founding of Vienna, would serve as a supportive infrastructure for his life. Vienna offered a bourgeois, liberal climate within which his family and civic values might develop, while Judaism in large part defined the cultural and religious worldview that he would both reject (forbidding it in his home, for example) and embrace (through his personal and professional associations and membership in B'nai B'rith).

Although not sharing his son's intellectual inclinations, Jacob, a wool merchant, fully supported his educational efforts. But young Sigmund, described by biographer Peter Gay as "an apprentice explorer, rooting about,"[3] needed more than educational support; he needed intellectual mentors, scholars who would guide him in a direction that would suit his interests and his potential. When the student is ready, the teachers will appear, as the ancient proverb promises, and Sigmund found them, most notably Josef Breuer, with whom, in 1895, he wrote *Studies in Hysteria.* We will see this hunger for mentors in other luminaries studied, particularly Abraham Maslow.

Freud entered medical school at the University of Vienna in 1873, graduating eight years later with specialties in neurology and psychiatry. In 1888, he married Martha Bernays, with whom he had six children. At home, Freud lived the life of a stereotypical bourgeois family man, with Martha, in turn, the ideal Viennese bourgeois wife, taking care of the domestic duties so her husband could attend to his work. *Herr Doktor Freud* ate his midday meal at the regularly appointed time each day, surrounded by Martha and the children. As John Morgan observes in a fascinating commentary on Freud and Charles Darwin, they "were both, according to the 'domestic records' of personal letters and recollections of their family, children, and friends, loving, caring, attentive and doting fathers and husbands."[4]

Freud's relationships with friends, colleagues, and disciples were more complicated than those he had with mentors and family members. Peter Gay, perhaps the most respected and quoted biographer of Freud, cites Freud's comment in *The Interpretation of Dreams* that "an intimate friend and a hated enemy have always been necessary requirements of my emotional life."[5] Alfred Adler, who embraced Freud's psychoanalytic method but rejected the emphasis on early childhood sexuality, and Carl Jung, "the Swiss doctor of the soul" whose developing insights on the unconscious veered too sharply from those of Freud, were two of many early disciples

3. Gay, *Freud*, 29.
4. Morgan, email to author, Aug. 19, 2014.
5. Gay, *Freud*, 55.

who found themselves on the receiving end of both Freud's intimate friendship and deep rancor. Jung assumed the nobler position in his break from Freud, however, by reminding him, in words that might serve well as the learner's credo, that "one treats a teacher badly if one remains a pupil."[6]

A widespread ailment of the times was hysteria, manifested typically by fainting, temporary paralysis, or hallucinations, and applied almost exclusively to women (*hysteria* derives from the Greek word for womb). Today, hysteria is an antiquated and pejorative term, replaced over the years by neurosis, which describes any physical ailments that attend to psychological issues. Neurosis itself is rarely used today, replaced largely by the two diagnoses that have come to define our age, depression and anxiety.

As Freud progressed in his medical practice, he noticed that certain ailments, like hysteria, were proving resistant to the treatment modalities common in the day; consequently, his interests moved away from identifying physical causes for neurosis and toward psychological causes. The discovery of those psychological causes called for a new approach to working with patients, one that placed far more emphasis on listening attentively to the client's words—the "talking cure," the staple of all psychotherapy today. As Gay observes, "listening became, for Freud, more than an art; it became a method, a privileged road to knowledge that his patients mapped out for him."[7] In highlighting the importance of listening, Freud set the stage for the later development of the art of counseling, which the humanistic psychologists would perfect.

Freud shared his discoveries with the world through his writings, which he seemed to be continually revising, as well as his presentations at B'nai B'rith and the University of Vienna. In *The Interpretation of Dreams*, he argued that the "dream is the (disguised) fulfillment of a (suppressed, repressed) wish."[8] In *The Psychopathology of Everyday Life*, he normalized neurosis by demonstrating that the line between normal folks and neurotics is more permeable than we might think. This normalization of ailments like depression and anxiety, which we might refer to as part of an ongoing humanization process of mental illness, is today taken for granted. And in *Three Essays on the Theory of Sexuality*, his "sex book," Freud worked through his theories of neurosis as the result of unaddressed and unmastered sexual conflicts from childhood.

Beginning in 1902, several physicians and academics gathered around Freud for weekly discussions, the most notable of whom was Alfred Adler.

6. Bair, *Jung*, 223.
7. Gay, *Freud*, 70.
8. Gay, *Freud*, 109.

By 1908, this gathering would become the Vienna Psychoanalytic Society, and, thanks to psychologist Otto Rank, secretary, we are given a glimpse of the energy, diversity of positions, and contentiousness of those meetings —and the break in relationships: Adler split from Freud in 1911, and by 1913 Jung had separated as well. By then, the small group had become the International Psychoanalytic Association.

During these years, Freud would experience much physical and emotional pain, most acutely through the death of his daughter Sophie, married with two children, who succumbed to the influenza outbreak that followed the First World War; that pandemic has received increasing attention in our own time due to the devastation of the coronavirus. In 1923, Freud contracted cancer of the palate and had his first of numerous surgeries, resulting in the insertion of a prothesis that caused continuing discomfort and pain. And in 1925, one of his closest associates, psychoanalyst Karl Abraham, died at age forty-eight of suspected lung cancer; many more friends (and ex-friends) would soon follow.

Yet there was joy, too, during those years, and much was accomplished. During the war, Freud continued to publish, see clients, and lecture on Saturday evenings at the University of Vienna. Between 1920 and 1923, he completed *Beyond the Pleasure Principle* (in which he introduced the death drive), *Group Psychology and the Analysis of the Ego* (through which he expanded his thoughts beyond the inner drives to outer societal pressures), and *The Ego and the Id* (in which he broadened his theory of the unconscious to include not only the id but aspects of the ego and the superego as well). He also expanded his understanding of the sexual development of the child through the oral, anal, and phallic stages.

Perhaps the source of Freud's greatest joy during these years was the presence of his youngest daughter, Anna, who frequently eavesdropped on her father's conversations, studied his books, and attended his lectures. She became a psychoanalyst and published and presented her own psychoanalytic work, among which was *The Ego and the Mechanisms of Defense*. She would become her father's closest confidant, representative, and, ultimately, nurse—"By the early 1920s, the two had become, and they were to remain, intellectually and emotionally inseparable."[9]

Biographer Peter Gay paints a picture of Freud as being somewhat more progressive in his attitudes toward women than was common in the Vienna of his day. He is described as a conservative, "unreconstructed nineteenth-century gentleman in his social, ethical, and sartorial style . . . [with]

9. Gay, *Freud*, 442.

old-fashioned manners . . . [and] ideals,"[10] and although he "might hold to the sweet, competent housewife as his ideal . . . he never obstructed—on the contrary, he fostered—aspiring female psychoanalysts, and took their views seriously."[11] Freud had valued female associates throughout his life, including the psychoanalyst Marie Bonaparte, whose influence and wealth made possible his escape to London in 1939 as the Nazi reach extended into Austria.

During the closing years of the 1920s, Freud wrote two books that explicated his constantly developing thoughts on religion and culture. In *The Future of an Illusion*, he argued that science and religion are incompatible. In *Civilization and Its Discontents*, he applied his expanding understanding of id and ego to civilization itself, concluding that we are destined to struggle culturally just as we are intrapsychically. We will look closely at *The Future of an Illusion*, which directly addresses the place of religion in society, later in this chapter.

Though "a consistent militant atheist since his school days,"[12] Freud never lost his identification as a Jew; in fact, it strengthened during the 1930s as fascism gained a firmer hold in both Austria and Germany. Throughout those dark times, he proudly and defiantly proclaimed his Jewish heritage and resisted leaving his homeland. However, as restrictions against the Jews worsened and life in Austria became increasingly perilous (and personal—two of his children were interrogated by the Gestapo), Freud and his family emigrated to England, where he would live the final year of his life. Four of Freud's sisters were among the millions who perished in the concentration camps.

As Freud's cancer worsened and further surgery was no longer tenable, his personal physician, Max Schur, honored a contract he and Freud had made not to prolong unnecessary suffering. The doctor administered several injections of morphine—but not after talking it over with the ever-present Anna. Her father died in London on September 23, 1939.

A FREUDIAN SYNOPSIS

As noted, Sigmund Freud had a profound and lasting impact on all psychologies that followed in his wake, certainly including humanistic psychology. Maslow, Rogers, Fromm, and May frequently referenced the legacy of Freud, and they assumed a familiarity with his terminology and a general

10. Gay, *Freud*, 507.
11. Gay, *Freud*, 508.
12. Gay, *Freud*, 525.

understanding of his writings in the audiences to whom they spoke, wrote, and taught. They could not have done otherwise, given Freud's dominance in the field. To better understand the legacy he left, the psychological world the humanistically oriented thinkers inherited, and the challenges he presented to them, we will review Freud's core teachings regarding the levels of consciousness, the structure of personality, the stages of psychosexual development, dream theory, and psychoanalytic therapy.

1. The Levels of Consciousness

In psychological terminology, consciousness refers to mental activities such as perceptions, thoughts, feelings, and intentions—everything we are aware of in the moment. Freud observed that psychoanalysis, the name he gave to both his psychological theory and his approach to therapy, has nothing to add to our understanding of the conscious; instead, psychoanalysis is about the unconscious—or better, it is about making the unconscious conscious.

In mapping the human psyche, Freud extended the understanding of consciousness to include a preconscious and, more significantly, an unconscious. The preconscious refers to that which one is not at present conscious of but can readily bring to consciousness by simple recall, and the conscious and the preconscious enjoy a seamless back-and-forth flow of information. No defenses are getting in the way, and no source of neurosis is to be discovered in the interaction between conscious and preconscious, and Freud had little interest in those domains.

What drew Freud's attention was the unconscious, which consists of that psychic material that "must be inferred, recognized, and translated into conscious form."[13] As its content—sexual fantasies, perhaps—can be disorienting and challenging to our sense of self, it is typically met with resistance from the patient. Yet much truth resides in the unconscious, and discovering what it has to reveal is the goal—the "holy grail"—of Freud's psychology, as it identifies the true source of what ails us and indicates the path toward healing.

Humanistic psychologists were also interested in helping their clients access the unconscious—Fromm, for example, wrote a book on dream interpretation titled *The Forgotten Language*—but it was not their primary concern. As we shall see, what mattered to them was more the attending to and processing of one's present experiences; for those within the humanistic circle, the starting point of knowledge is less the unconscious than one's conscious, subjective experience.

13. Freud, *Outline of Psychoanalysis*, 32.

2. The Structure of Personality

In the beginning was the id. Freud's theories on the structure of personality begin with our organic instincts and inherited past, the components of the id, the oldest region of the psyche, "the matrix of animal instinct."[14] There is an evolutionary feel to Freud's discussion of the id—unsurprising, as he was a devotee of Darwin.

The id is the dimension of personality focused on immediate gratification. But the world, with its persistently nettlesome natural consequences, presents challenges to that gratification: "Immediate and unheeded satisfaction of the instincts, such as the id demands, would often lead to perilous conflicts with the external world and to extinction."[15]

As the id, the locus of the pursuit of pleasure, confronts the world and its unforgiving demands, the ego emerges as a cautionary intermediary between the two. Representing the reality principle, the ego is about self-preservation; it asks, *Is it safe?* In common parlance today, the ego is often referenced as "the executive function." It can refer to this one dimension of personality or its composite. Its job is to help us navigate the sociocultural matrix, meeting our own needs while heeding the world's demands and avoiding its distractions.

The id, uninhibited and instinctually driven, asks, *Is it pleasurable?* The forces that drive the id are the instincts, which Freud, somewhat tentatively, reduced to two, Eros or libido (the life principle) and Thanatos or aggression (the death drive). The libido's goal, made known to us mainly through the sexual function, is unitive and connective; that of the death instinct is destructive. As the ego is struggling to tame the id (and being influenced by it in return), it is also storing information about the world, both learning from it and adapting to it. The ego is doing its job well if it simultaneously meets the needs of the id and the outside world, no small task.

None of this taming, adapting, and learning takes place in a void. Our developing ego has parents and a childhood extended well beyond the rest of the animal kingdom. Through all those years of parent/child interaction, all those years of listening to parental voices (and all the complementary voices of other adults and the larger culture), a third psychic element develops, the superego, the seat of "ought-tos" and "supposed-tos" and "shoulds." The superego's main function is to proscribe; it asks, *Is it right and proper?* It is the realm of "values, norms, and attitudes . . . introduced in the maturation

14. Freeman, *Freud Rediscovered*, 251.

15. Freud, *Outline of Psychoanalysis*, 84.

process of the human individual."[16] Internalizing the superego by identifying universally accepted values would become a primary goal of humanistically oriented thinkers in multiple fields, including psychology, philosophy, biology, and religion.

3. Psychosexual Development

Freud struggled with his own resistance as he worked through his controversial sexual theories—appropriately, as he soon faced opposition from a wary Victorian public in late nineteenth- and early twentieth-century Vienna and beyond. Developed through his fine-tuned observation of his patients' symptoms, his theories on psychosexual development would soon take center stage in his work. Freud identified three principles governing sexual function: sexuality begins shortly after birth, not in adolescence; it is not reducible to the reproductive; and it includes obtaining pleasure throughout the body, not just through the sex organs.

The first organ of the body to emerge as an erogenous zone is the mouth. Freud observed that "physiology should not be confused with psychology":[17] although the child nursing at the mother's breast initially seeks nourishment, the pleasure continues beyond that need to the sexual. "Sucking for nourishment is the starting point of our whole sexual life . . . the unattainable prototype of even later sexual satisfaction,"[18] adds biographer Lucy Freeman. This is the first stage of psychosexual development, the oral, which lasts about a year.

During the second stage, the anal, which begins with toilet training at around age two, the child shifts attention to the anal region and focuses on replacing expulsion with retention. Two of Freud's classic defense mechanisms, introjection (the internalizing of others' attitudes and behaviors, most notably the parents') and projection (the attribution of unwanted thoughts and feelings to others), find their origin in the oral and anal stages of development.

During the third stage, the phallic, the Oedipus complex emerges, beginning around age three and lasting until five or six. Fully embracing the Oedipus myth (eternalized by Sophocles's fifth century BCE tragedy *Oedipus Rex*) as integral to the story of the human race, Freud wrote of the male child experiencing his mother as the initial love interest and his father as a rival hated to the point of desiring his death. Freud came to understand

16. Morgan, *Damaged Self*, 19.
17. Freud, *Outline of Psychoanalysis*, 84.
18. Freeman, *Freud Rediscovered*, 99.

the mother-child relationship as the prototype of all future relationships, as well as his greatest discovery: "I venture to say," he wrote near the end of his life, "that if psychoanalysis could boast of no other achievement than the discovery of the repressed Oedipus complex, that alone would give it a claim to be included among the precious new acquisitions of mankind."[19]

Much of the future of post-Freudian psychology would involve revisions of Freud's interpretation of the Oedipus myth that would present it more as a metaphor for the influence of parent/child interaction on the evolving personality of the child and of the child's need to detach and differentiate from the parents. It is in this context that Freud spoke of the child as psychologically father to the man: what happens in early childhood and how the child interprets it and responds to it will greatly influence the person he or she will become.

The phallic stage of early childhood sexuality is followed by a lengthy latency period, after which the child, now an adolescent, enters the genital stage. The genital stage is the turning point in the developmental sequence, the point at which the sexual drive reoccurs but is now directed outside the family. This is the ultimate goal of psychosexual development: the release of the parent of the opposite sex as the primary libido object and its redirection to another.

Often overlooked in commentaries on Freud's stages of psychosexual development is the fact that Freud was the first to approach personality development in terms of stages. He opened the door for later psychological thinkers such as the Swiss psychologist Jean Piaget, "the greatest developmental psychologist of all time,"[20] according to social psychologist and author Jonathan Haidt, and Erik Erikson, who would famously build upon Freud's work, extending it throughout the life cycle and on to old age. But it was Freud who first proposed the idea of developmental stages. In this, as in so many other areas, Freud led the way.

Freud's theories of psychosexual development would receive criticism from many of the founders, contributors, and commentators of the classical schools of psychotherapy that developed out of his original insights. John Morgan, for example, refers to the centrality of sexuality in child development as "Freud's fundamentally erroneous mistake"[21] and criticizes the "monotonous pansexuality of the psychoanalysts in the Freudian camp."[22]

19. Freud, *Outline of Psychoanalysis*, 75–76.

20. Haidt, *Righteous Mind*, 6.

21. Morgan, *Damaged Self*, 83.

22. Morgan, *Damaged Self*, 87.

Abraham Maslow saw Freud's work as woefully incomplete as it focused solely on the negative side of the species, on the intrapsychic struggle among the id, ego, and superego, and he set as his own task the completion of what Freud neglected. Erich Fromm, in *The Art of Loving*, spoke for many in the humanist camp when he criticized Freud for reducing the sexual instinct to little more than the result "of a chemically produced tension in the body which is painful and seeks relief [and love itself as] exclusively the expression—or a sublimation—of the sexual instinct, rather than recognizing that sexual desire is one manifestation of the need for love and union."[23]

For the humanists, love would be a peak-experience, a paramount human value, a source for personal and worldwide healing, an encounter with the sublime. It was no mere biological experience. Nonetheless, these theorists, and numerous others who could be included here, never wavered in their recognition of Freud's genius, and it is the rare psychiatrist, psychologist, or psychotherapist today who would not point to Freud's psychosexual theories as groundbreaking and foundational to the further development of psychological thought.

4. Theory of Dreams

In the popular imagination, Freud is best known for his theories about dreams, initially set forth in his classic 1899 work *The Interpretation of Dreams*. As in many other areas, Freud set the standard for therapeutic dream work, which remains popular with many practitioners of talk therapy today. Rivaled only by the work of his one-time protégé Carl Jung, Freud's insights on the unconscious and the occasional treasures revealed therein have resulted in no shortage of counseling clients probing the symbolic meanings of their dreams for clues into the source of their struggles or of spiritual travelers seeking guidance for the soul.

As noted, psychoanalysis focuses on the unconscious, and the dream is the primary means, the "royal road" in Freud's often-quoted words, through which we learn about that hidden dimension of the psyche. Freud opened his discussion on dreams, which he understood as messages from the unconscious to the conscious, with the assertion that the dream we awaken to, which he called the manifest dream, is not the true dream but only a distortion. The true dream is called the latent dream, and the process that produces the manifest dream from the latent dream—the process responsible for the distortion—is the dream-work.

23. Fromm, *Art of Loving*, 33.

Freud saw the dream-work as fulfilling the role of guardian of our sleep by disguising or censoring any disturbance that the latent dream might cause. Some repressed desire from our childhood, typically related to and instigated by an unresolved problem, unfulfilled wish, or experience from the previous day, is seeking expression. The ego resists, and the ensuing conflict creates the distorted compromise of the manifest dream. What we recall upon awakening is, therefore, a sanitized version of a repressed desire deep in the unconscious. Freudian dream therapy strives to interpret, encode, and reveal that unacceptable content—within the safe and confidential environment of the psychoanalyst's office.

Interpretation of the manifest dream is complicated by our understandable resistance to the unacceptable content in the unconscious and by the dual dream processes of condensation (wherein multiple images are combined into one) and displacement (wherein characteristics of one figure are portrayed in another). But, Freud advised, the effort is worthwhile, for what we may discover in the true, latent dream are rich linguistic symbols, repressed early childhood memories, and material from our "archaic heritage . . . phylogenetic material in the earliest human legends and in surviving customs . . . human prehistory."[24] This reference to our "archaic heritage" emerging from the unconscious became a signature feature of the dream psychology of Carl Jung, one of the many thinkers who flocked to Vienna to learn from the master, only to abandon him and strike out on their own.

This dream interpretation (deciphering the latent content from the manifest dream, essentially the opposite of the dream-work) is accomplished through the associations provided by the patient and the explanations of the symbolic content suggested by the psychoanalyst. Freud emphasized that this is not a perfect process, and that although it more often than not provides a satisfactory explanation, the message of the latent dream occasionally remains unresolved. The resistant unconscious is not as decipherable as we might wish.

5. Putting It All Together: Psychoanalytic Therapy

What occasionally gets lost in discussions about Freud's theories is their point of origin, their source, and how that led to the development of the "talking cure" as the favored response to neurosis. Freud was no philosophical dreamer; he was a medical doctor, a neurologist, and a psychiatrist, and his theories developed directly from his efforts to heal his patients. The "talking cure" was not intuited. It arose in response to Freud's discoveries

24. Freud, *Outline of Psychoanalysis*, 40.

that physical ailments derived from psychological struggles and that allowing the patient to talk it out appeared to produce a gold mine of information from the unconscious that could be directed toward both psychological and physical healing. Further, Freud famously tested out what he was learning on himself through years of "self-analysis" of his own dreams.

Neurosis signifies chronic distress as symptomized by common ailments—depression, anxiety, obsessive compulsive disorder, phobia, negative thought patterns, for example—and that causes difficulties adapting to the environment and living a life of personal fulfillment. An underlying assumption of the use of the word *neurosis* by Freud is that its many manifestations stem from a common cause (even if broadly described) and can be addressed through a singular psychotherapeutic response (Freud's own psychoanalysis).

Further assumed is an acceptance of the ubiquity of neurosis throughout the population, of the universality of suffering within Homo sapiens. M. Scott Peck's sentiment with which he opens his 1978 classic, *The Road Less Traveled*, that "life is difficult," serves as an apt summation of the universality of neurosis. Harry Stack Sullivan's "one genus hypothesis"—the humble recognition that we are all more simply human than otherwise, and our shared humanity, including the universality of suffering, is what is most distinguishing about each of us—suggests a similar universal experience. Rollo May referred to neurosis simply as "the general classification of personality difficulties when they become severe."[25] The humanistic psychologists readily accepted the universality of neurosis, and they would differentiate themselves from Freud in their broadening of both the causes and the responses.

Freud posited the cause of neurosis within the sexual domain, with psychoanalysis the prescribed cure. Specifically, Freud believed that neurosis results from a weakening of the ego. The demands placed upon the ego by repressed material from the id, expectations and admonitions from the superego, and struggles from the outside world all conspire to produce a psyche in conflict, invariably about the sexual instinct: "The symptoms of neuroses are . . . without exception either a substitutive satisfaction of some sexual urge or measures to prevent such a satisfaction."[26]

The goal of the therapist, then, is to join with the patient's ego to help strengthen it. Freud was fond of military analogies, and he explained the therapist's role as akin to an outside ally going to the aid of one side in a civil war. There's a war going on in there, and we must join with the ego, the voice of reason, and help it keep the id and the superego in their proper

25. May, *Art of Counseling*, 51.

26. Freud, *Outline of Psychoanalysis*, 67.

places—"to give [the patient] ego mastery over lost provinces of his mental life."[27] Therapists make a pact with their patients, Freud suggested, offering their strict discretion and openness (confidentiality and willingness to accept what is heard) in return for the complete candor of the patient. He likened the therapist's role to that of a confessor but more so: penitents tell their confessors what they know, whereas patients, through dreams, slips of the tongue, free associations, and other stirrings from the unconscious, tell what they don't know.

Further, as David Bakan observes in *Sigmund Freud and the Jewish Mystical Tradition*, the psychoanalytic confessor "listens to the patient's discussion of his deepest 'sins' and does not blame . . . if there is any blame which is implicitly or explicitly contained within the psychoanalytic mood, it is directed against the parents of the patient in their treatment of him when he was an infant and a child."[28] Freud proclaimed that the "fundamental rule of analysis [is] the patient must tell all, even if disagreeable, unimportant, nonsensical."[29] The patient must be confident that the analyst, the Freudian term for what today we typically refer to as a therapist, will serve, in the eyes of the patient, as "a more indulgent and more forgiving parent,"[30] one who can accept the patient's shortcomings with equanimity.

Nonetheless, the patient has a way of frustrating this intruder in that civil war between id and ego. Over time, he or she begins to see the analyst in terms of a past relationship, typically the parent figure, and proceeds to transfer to the analyst feelings and images that apply to that other. As suggested above, this transference, a key concept in Freudian therapy, may initially proceed in a positive direction. The patient may see the analyst as savior, healer, wisdom teacher, lover, and, most often, the "good parent," thereby allowing the analyst access to the patient's superego. This, in turn, offers the analyst an opportunity to replace the unhealthy demands of the superego with more realistic expectations.

However, this positive transference creates a challenge of its own, that of replacing one dependency with another, a temptation Freud enjoined practitioners to avoid. Further, just as transference recreates a past relationship's positive dimension, so does it recreate the negative. The key is to remember, and to help the patient understand, that what is being experienced in the present is not about the analyst; it is about someone from the patient's past. All of this, the positive and the negative, provides information for the

27. Freud, *Outline of Psychoanalysis*, 50.

28. Bakan, *Sigmund Freud*, 59.

29. Freud, *Outline of Psychoanalysis*, 52.

30. Bakan, *Sigmund Freud*, 59.

analyst as the patient acts out parts of his or her life story that would not otherwise be encountered. And, noted Freud, "a patient never forgets again what he has experienced in the form of transference; it carries a greater force of conviction than anything he can acquire in other ways."[31]

Through the patient's free associations, repressed material, resistances, transferences, dreams, slips of the tongue—indeed, everything that is said and not said—the analyst seeks to uncover the neurosis represented by the symptoms. Freud observed that overcoming the patient's resistance is the most difficult part of the work, adding that even the superego offers resistance—in the form of guilt, a voice telling the overly scrupulous patient that he or she deserves to suffer and struggle. When interpreted in the light of basic psychoanalytic formulations such as the role of the unconscious, the interplay of id, ego, and superego, and the relationship of sexual and aggressive drives to the patient's current life situation, those struggles are made more understandable and manageable.

FREUD AND THE PLACE OF RELIGION IN SOCIETY: THE FUTURE OF AN ILLUSION

With this review of Freud's theories as background, we can now consider his specific insights on religion and spirituality, which he developed within the context of his more global thoughts on society and culture. Freud biographer Peter Gay, in his introductory comments to *The Future of an Illusion*, Freud's major religious work (or, more accurately, *anti*religious work), writes that "Freud was a convinced, consistent, aggressive atheist . . . a 'godless Jew,'"[32] those last words being Freud's own. Freud saw religion and science as oppositional, and later in life he addressed that opposition by applying his psychoanalytic insights to the religious dimension—with all the energy that Gay's description suggests.

Written in 1927, when Freud was seventy-one years old, *The Future of an Illusion* opens with the observation that "every individual is virtually an enemy of civilization":[33] given the need to fulfill our instinctual satisfactions, we are consistently frustrated by civilization's relentless restrictions. Freud wonders if there is a way to reduce the burden of the sacrifices we must make to reign in our instincts and concludes that only societal coercion will serve that purpose: our passions and disinclination to make the required changes stand in the way of our accomplishing that task on our own. Although he

31. Freud, *Outline of Psychoanalysis*, 55.

32. Freud, *Future of an Illusion*, xxiii.

33. Freud, *Future of an Illusion*, 6.

uncharacteristically suggests a possible, more hopeful future—"New generations, who have been brought up in kindness and taught to have a high opinion of reason, and who have experienced the benefits of civilization at an early age, will have a different attitude"[34]—his orientation remains pessimistic. We can imagine the incurably optimistic Maslow speaking those words—and believing that imagined future to be imminent. We can also hear those sentiments in the evolutionary hopefulness of Julian Huxley.

Freud credits societal coercion throughout the ages for eliminating much of the worst of what Homo sapiens has wrought, such as incest, cannibalism, and the lust for killing. The result of that coercion has been the internalization of these prohibitions through the superego and, as a result, the possibility of our development as moral beings and the reduction of the need for further societal coercion. He sees this internalization of our moral values as leading to our eventual outgrowing of religion, suggesting it will take many generations to accomplish.

Freud observes that we have much left to do regarding contemporary vices such as avarice, aggression, and fraud, as well as toward addressing the plight of the marginalized in a culture that "has not got beyond a point at which the satisfaction of one portion of its participants depends upon the suppression of another, and perhaps larger, portion—and this is the case in all present-day cultures."[35] Freud is not optimistic about society's readiness to prohibit oppression in the short term, and he castigates as undeserving of a successful life-term any civilization that would propagate it. Like Maslow and Fromm, Freud had internalized the prophetic Old Testament cry for justice, his antireligious fulminations notwithstanding.

Freud discusses the cultural ideals and societal mythologies that serve to unite a populace by distracting them from their internal class hostilities and refocusing their animosities on some identified foreign enemy. The result of this is the identification, both politically and emotionally, with a leader, a projected father figure, who will save the people from their sense of helplessness in the face of life's threats and challenges and whom the people will eventually come to see as embodying their ideals. Freud wrote this in 1927, as fascism began showing its ugly face in Germany and Italy. His remarks on cultural and societal identification with a savior leader resonate in the present day, as Madeleine Albright, former United States secretary of state who passed away in 2022, wisely observes in her 2018 bestseller *Fascism: A Warning*. Of the various humanistic psychologists, Erich Fromm was the most attuned to these topics, notably in *Escape from Freedom*.

34. Freud, *Future of an Illusion*, 9.

35. Freud, *Future of an Illusion*, 15.

Segueing from societal threats to more significant, more cosmic insecurities, Freud discusses the evolution of religion, beginning with reference to our helplessness against the superior powers of nature and fate. This helplessness results in our turning toward our parents for protection against the unknown and the feared. With the parent (particularly the father) as the image of strength and protection firmly in place, our primitive ancestors then projected those characteristics onto the forces of nature, making gods of them in the process. Freud assigns to these man-made gods three tasks: "[to] exorcise the terrors of nature . . . [to] reconcile men to the cruelty of Fate . . . [and to] compensate them for the sufferings and privations which a civilized life in common has imposed on them."[36]

But rather than serving as bulwarks against nature's vicissitudes and the cruelty of fate, the gods have demonstrated little but disinterest toward their effects on our lives, and nature itself has demonstrated no inclination to bend to our will. We are left at the mercy of both nature and fate. What, then, of the third task of the gods, to compensate us for civilization's restrictions and privations? In response to this task, the gods provided us with a set of beliefs, including that of a providential pantheon and a moral code, "born from man's need to make his helplessness tolerable and built up from the material of memories of the helplessness of his own childhood and the childhood of the human race."[37] With the gods in their heaven and the moral code in place on earth, humanity is offered some measure of protection and consolation.

Over time, Freud adds, a specific population group, the Jews, succeeded in concentrating the attributes of the divine within the image of fatherhood, thereby recovering the lost intimacy of childhood. The reward for the Jewish people was the gift of "chosen-ness"—or, in America, notes Freud, the sense of being God's own country. (In another context, Freud critically references the Dayton, Tennessee, "monkey trial," taking place as he wrote those words. Freud never let an opportunity pass to proclaim his distaste for what he saw as America's religious and cultural primitiveness.)

Freud addresses the counterargument that religion is of divine, not human, origin by observing that an objective study of history demonstrates religion's evolution out of the father-son relationship and humanity's need for cosmic protection, just as the infant needs parental protection. The outcome of this, he repeats, is that the child, who both loves and fears the father, projects the father's strengths and protectiveness onto a God or gods. God

36. Freud, *Future of an Illusion*, 22.

37. Freud, *Future of an Illusion*, 23.

is no more than a magnified father, a projection of humanity's experiences as powerless children turning to a protective parent in a threatening world.

Having dispensed with the idea of the need for a God, Freud turns his attention to the body of religious ideas transmitted through the years and believed largely on the strength of their antiquity and connection to our ancestors. Freud observes that much of what our ancestors believed has been proven false by science, with the so-called proofs of the truth of religious teachings shown to be rife with contradictions, a multiplicity of revisions over time, and falsifications. He mocks the *credo quia absurdum* of the "church fathers," the argument that religious teachings and doctrines somehow stand outside the jurisdiction of reason and that the very absurdity of a doctrine is justification for one's belief. He notes that this may work as a personal confession of faith but not as one that can be universalized. Humanistic psychology's emphasis on the need for a scientifically demonstrated and universally validated ethics stems from these concerns expressed by Freud and others.

Having confronted the arguments supporting religion, Freud advances his central thesis that religious doctrines "are not precipitates of experience or end-results of thinking: They are illusions, fulfillments of the oldest, strongest, and most urgent wishes of mankind. The secret of their strength lies in the strength of those wishes."[38] The terrifying helplessness we experienced as children aroused a need for protection, which would be fulfilled by the love and care provided by the father.

Upon recognizing that this helplessness lasts throughout life, we created the need for a more powerful father, and forthwith our fear of danger was allayed through the benevolent role of a loving God. To complete the picture, our demand for justice is addressed by establishing a moral world order and our wish fulfillments through prolonging an earthly life in heaven. Given these underlying assumptions, answers readily flow for the great questions of life—where we come from, how we are to live, what happens after death—providing a blessed relief for the psyche and a salve for a restive populace. Thus, religious doctrines are illusions, emerging from a wish fulfillment that can neither be proven nor refuted. And, Freud continues, adding insult to injury, "[where] questions of religion are concerned, people are guilty of every possible sort of dishonesty and intellectual misdemeanor."[39]

Freud addresses the argument that it is belief in God and a moral order, and that alone, that restrains humankind from exempting itself from the laws of society and descending into chaos. Therefore, so goes the argument,

38. Freud, *Future of an Illusion*, 38.

39. Freud, *Future of an Illusion*, 41.

we must act "as if" there were a God. In addition, to set aside belief in God would deprive millions of their main consolation in life. But Freud has little sympathy for a consolation that comes at the price of living an illusion, and he counters that it would be better for civilization's sake to dispose of it, noting that it is no more healthy for a society to live an illusion than it is for an individual to do so.

Religion has clearly failed to address all of humanity's needs, Freud argues, and there is little evidence that people were more moral when religious doctrines ruled. We have always been good at externalizing "the precepts of religion and thus to nullify their intentions,"[40] he adds, echoing a universal complaint against the failures of established religions throughout the ages. One of the major themes of the humanistic psychologists, most notably Erich Fromm, was to identify the universal truths within those "precepts of religion" and to live them out, individually and societally.

In support of his argument that moral chaos will not ensue when religious beliefs are set aside, Freud responds that there is a purely rational explanation for the prohibition against murder, namely, the need for an ordered society. Suppose we could learn to be content with the social reasons for prohibiting murder and other crimes. In that case, Freud argues, we could progress from formulating laws designed to exert control to establishing laws intended to serve others' interests—and laws that would change over time as needed, improving in the process. Likewise, just as childhood neuroses are eventually overcome through maturation, so too will humanity's neurotic belief in God be replaced. Freud sees religions as "neurotic relics [for which] the time has probably come, as it does in an analytic treatment, for replacing the effects of repression by the results of rational operation of the intellect."[41] To Freud, religion is fundamentally a psychological problem to be treated by psychoanalysis.

Freud dismisses the argument that attacks on religion threaten the foundation of education and civil life, countering that humanity will one day reach a place at which it will outgrow the need for a religious protector of those institutions. No utopian, he does not believe that this maturation will arrive soon, yet he expresses confidence that when it does, it will likely result in the same altruistic goals the Judeo-Christian world advances. He adds that although religionists must continually defend their doctrine or their world collapses, men and women of science can readily abandon their views as new evidence emerges, an argument that Carl Rogers, who learned science firsthand on his parents' farm, and Julian Huxley, evolutionary

40. Freud, *Future of an Illusion*, 48.

41. Freud, *Future of an Illusion*, 56.

biologist, would much appreciate. Science advances, and "a rough approximation to the truth is replaced by a more carefully adapted one, which in turn awaits further perfectioning."[42] Freud concludes with words that challenge the believer and inspire the nonbeliever: "No, our science is no illusion. But an illusion it would be to suppose that what science cannot give us we can get elsewhere."[43]

Freud was no friend of religion; further, he was suspicious, even dismissive, of what today we would call the spiritual. Three years after the publication of *The Future of an Illusion*, he wrote *Civilization and Its Discontents*, in which he discusses a friend's reference to an "oceanic feeling," described as a "sensation of eternity, a feeling of something limitless, unbounded and—as it were, 'oceanic.'"[44] This oceanic feeling is posited as the source of our religious energy, a sense of being one with the universe, somewhat akin to what Maslow would call the peak-experience, or the awe, wonder, and reverence that many encounter when confronted with the sublime. In *The Art of Loving*, Erich Fromm describes the oceanic feeling as "the essence of mystical experience and the root of the most intense sense of union with one other person or with one's fellow men."[45]

Freud asserts that he has not experienced that feeling himself, adding that "it is very difficult for me to work with these almost intangible quantities."[46] Yet, it intrigues him enough that he is drawn to take it seriously. He offers a "psycho-analytic—that is, a genetic—explanation of such a feeling,"[47] an explanation in terms of the structure of the personality, specifically, the ego's original oneness with the world before the world began to be recognized as separate. From Freud's perspective, rather than being of spiritual origin, the oceanic feeling can be traced back to our infantile helplessness, an indication of nothing more than an early attempt to protect the fragile ego from the threats posed by the external world.

A SPIRITUAL, HUMANISTIC OPENING IN THE FREUDIAN MIND?

Many of Freud's perspectives on religion shared in both *The Future of an Illusion* and *Civilization and Its Discontents* would be met with approval by

42. Freud, *Future of an Illusion*, 71.
43. Freud, *Future of an Illusion*, 71.
44. Freud, *Civilization and Its Discontents*, 11.
45. Fromm, *Art of Loving*, 83.
46. Freud, *Civilization and Its Discontents*, 21.
47. Freud, *Civilization and Its Discontents*, 12.

the leading lights in the humanistic psychology movement. But there would also be frustration: Where is the spiritual element? How can the person become all that he or she is meant to be without the oceanic feeling, the peak-experience, a sense of the sacred, which many would recognize as essential traits of the fully self-actualized person? Humanistic psychology had a number of tasks in responding to Freud, the reassertion of the spiritual dimension of the person being a foundational one.

Reference was made earlier to Freud's self-description as a "godless Jew." Yet his efforts to explain the oceanic feeling within the context of personality development suggest perhaps a modicum of respect for religious or spiritual feelings—as well, of course, as a desire to locate all phenomena within his theory of personality. Although Freud famously describes religion as an infantile illusion, he appears drawn to address it, if begrudgingly. In a conversation between Freud and Oskar Pfister, a Swiss pastor and friend, during which Freud refers to himself as godless, Pfister replies,

> You are not so godless, since whoever lives for the truth lives in God and whoever strives for the freeing of love "dwelleth in God." If you would fuse your own contribution with the great world harmony, like the synthesis of notes in a Beethoven symphony into a musical whole, I could say of you, "There never was a greater Christian."[48]

For his efforts to find common ground between religion and psychiatry, Oskar Pfister was honored by the American Psychiatric Association and the Association of American Chaplains with an annual award in his name bestowed upon a person who has made a significant contribution in that area. Past recipients referenced in these pages include Viktor Frankl, James Fowler, and Irvin Yalom.

Does the attention Freud gives to addressing the oceanic feeling attest to some lingering religious feeling, just as an early sense of oneness with the universe remains in the ego after it has successfully identified itself as separate from the world? Indeed, in *Civilization and Its Discontents*, Freud references St. Francis and Jesus approvingly, in addition to paying homage to his own Jewish heritage.

According to David Bakan, psychology professor at the University of Chicago, Harvard, and NYU who passed away in 2004, Freud paid more than homage to his Jewish heritage, and his relationship to the religion of his ancestors was far deeper than the words "committed atheist" might suggest. In *Sigmund Freud and the Jewish Mystical Tradition*, Bakan builds a solid, though controversial, case for Freud's self-identification as a Jew and

48. Freeman, *Freud Rediscovered*, 209.

references his frequently quoted biographical statement that "my parents were Jews, and I have remained a Jew myself."[49] He makes note of Freud's refusal to accept royalties on Hebrew and Yiddish translations of his works,[50] his membership in the Yiddish Scientific Institute, and—what serves as his book's hypothesis—that "the development of psychoanalysis is essentially incomplete unless it be viewed against the history of Judaism."[51] Bakan concludes a chapter titled "Freud's Positive Identification as a Jew" by observing that it is important

> to distinguish between Freud's sense of identity as a Jew and his acceptance of Jewish religious doctrines. The intensity of his feelings on his Jewish identity was matched by the rejection of religious doctrine and practice. His works on religion are *against* the classical Judaeo-Christian religious doctrines. Yet his sense of Jewish identity was so strong that we might consider his *genetic* conception of the Jew . . . as the theoretical counterpart of his deep feeling of Jewish identity.[52]

Although Freud remained throughout his life a "convinced, consistent, aggressive atheist," in Peter Gay's words, he would not forego his self-identification as a Jew. Furthermore, as we have seen, he allows at least a hint of openness to a place for the spiritual in the lives of men and women, a small space for that which he admittedly had not experienced himself and was as much puzzled by as antagonistic to. Widening that space would be among the many challenges of humanistic psychology.

49. Bakan, *Sigmund Freud*, 46.
50. Bakan, *Sigmund Freud*, 53.
51. Bakan, *Sigmund Freud*, ix.
52. Bakan, *Sigmund Freud*, 52–53 (emphasis in original)

Chapter 3

Prophetic Thundering

The Messianic Fervor of Abraham Maslow

Heaven exists all the time all around us, always available to step into for a little while at least. And a single glimpse of heaven is enough to confirm its existence, even if it is never experienced again.

—Abraham Maslow, *Religions, Values, and Peak-Experiences*

As noted in the first chapter, Abraham Maslow was "the face of humanistic psychology." No others associated with that movement, their immense talents and contributions notwithstanding, could have served that role better. Maslow's mix of intellectual curiosity, messianic fervor, boundless energy, passionate dedication to the cause, and genuine and infectious joie de vivre served the job description to a T.

In addition, Maslow wrote the book that introduced humanistic psychology to the world, *Toward a Psychology of Being*, in which he outlined what would become the core values of the movement most associated with his name. Further, he set a pattern to be followed by each of the humanistic psychologists studied in these pages—paying homage to, while at the same time distancing from, the esteemed doctor of Vienna, Sigmund Freud. Maslow invariably insisted that what he advocated in no way invalidated the Freudian corpus; on the contrary, what Freud left behind stands as the point of departure for his own thinking. At the same time, he hastened to define how distinct that departure would be, noting that his approach adds to—even *completes*—what Freud taught by focusing not on the neurotic struggle within the human psyche but on the human potential for health and self-actualization, and "humanity's immense potential for creativity, spirituality, and humanitarianism."[1] As Maslow explains in *Toward a Psychology of Being*, what he is teaching "in no way denies the usual Freudian picture. But it does add to it . . . it is as if Freud supplied us the sick half of psychology, and we must now fill it out with the healthy half."[2] For Maslow, Freud was to be both liberally *complimented* and diligently *complemented*.

As a "lifelong atheist who had always associated religion with dogma and superstition,"[3] Maslow surely had no idea when he wrote those words in 1962 that by the end of that decade his probing of human health and potential would lead him beyond humanistic psychology—beyond the third force movement with which his name is most associated—to a deeper, mystical worldview, which he would call transpersonal psychology. Such was the passionate vision of Abraham Maslow, which was, given his ebullient personality, irresistibly contagious.

RELIGIOUS BEGINNINGS—RESISTANCE AND PREJUDICE

Maslow lived during one of the most turbulent periods in modern history. Born in Brooklyn in 1908, he witnessed the return of soldiers from the First World War and the carnage of the Second, including the Holocaust and the atomic bomb. In the latter half of the century, he experienced the civil unrest of the 1960s, occasioned largely by another war for another generation and the struggle to end racial segregation in the American South. Further, he witnessed the assassinations of a president, a presidential candidate, and several prominent civil rights workers, including a winner of the Nobel Peace Prize.

An indication of the strangeness of the times is found in the acknowledgments section of Edward Hoffman's 1988 biography of Maslow, *The Right to Be Human*, in which he recognizes the contributions of countercultural figures like Dr. Timothy Leary, of "turn on, tune in, and drop out" fame, and revolutionary anarchist Abbie Hoffman, as well as distinguished founders of schools of psychology, such as Carl Rogers, Viktor Frankl, and B. F. Skinner. They were strange and turbulent times indeed, and through

1. Kaufman, *Transcend*, xxiv.
2. Maslow, *Toward Psychology of Being*, 15.
3. Hoffman, *Right to Be Human*, 256.

it all, Abraham Maslow maintained a steely focus and a frantic pace as he responded to a generation's hunger for something beyond orthodox Freudianism and behaviorism.

Maslow's parents were Russian Jewish émigrés, part of that ongoing exodus from the Old World to the New that is central to the larger American story. At age fourteen, his father, Samuel, left Kiev (the capital of Ukraine), a city scarred by the frequent occurrence of anti-Jewish pogroms. Arriving in America with no knowledge of English, speaking only Russian and Yiddish, he traveled first to Philadelphia and then to New York, where he entered the cooperage business and met and married a first cousin. Abraham was their first child; seven more followed.

Abraham's mother, though not particularly observant in her Jewish faith, was intensely superstitious and used the threat of God's punishment for the slightest misbehavior. Abraham's early religious cynicism began with testing his mother's admonitions and discovering that God was not, indeed, standing in wait for the least provocation to mete out punishment against him. He learned from his mother's religiosity to despise religion—or to run away from it, as he did at his bar mitzvah, literally bursting into tears and fleeing the synagogue. Later in life, however, his cynicism subsided, and he came to embrace his Jewish heritage as contributory to his developing psychology and spirituality. In addition to harboring religious superstitions, his mother was reportedly cruel in her treatment of young Abraham, so much so that he refused to visit her in his adulthood, even declining attendance at her funeral. One wonders what effect this had on his developing spirituality—might he have embraced his Jewish heritage more deeply and earlier on, as did Erich Fromm, had it not been so closely associated with memories of his mother?

Raised in an ethnic but non-Jewish Brooklyn neighborhood, Abraham was frequently accosted by anti-Semitic street gangs. He was more bewildered than hurt by the ethnoreligious antagonism, exhibiting an attitude characteristic of one with a developing intellectualism and the sense of being an outsider who was not fitting in well with the larger culture. Both his sense of isolation at home and the street variety of prejudice he frequently encountered in the neighborhood caused Abraham to retreat to the public library, his haven in more ways than one. He also took refuge in his schooling, where he was awed by his teachers; enchanted by the books of Upton Sinclair, Charles Dickens, and other social reformers; and inspired by the many left-wing political commentators who found a welcoming home in early twentieth-century Brooklyn. Later in life, he would appreciate these early progressive writers and teachers as secular counterparts of the Jewish prophetic tradition.

As the word *prophetic* will surface throughout these pages, a few words are in order about its meaning in the context of the intersection of humanistic psychology and secular Judaism, and, by extension, its impact on the larger world of both Judaism and Christianity today. Steven Nadler, in *A Book Forged in Hell*, a fascinating study of the seventeenth-century Portuguese/Dutch humanist Baruch Spinoza, provides essential context for our understanding of the word *prophetic*. Prophecy, according to both Spinoza and Nadler, refers to the "intuitive grasp of the essences of things, a deep causal understanding that situates them in their necessary relationships to each other and, more importantly, to higher, universal principles."[4] This "deep causal understanding" does not spring from the biblical prophets' supposed erudition—these were simple men, lacking "philosophical wisdom, theological training, or scientific knowledge"[5]—but from a superior ethical sensitivity and vivid imagination that allowed them to readily perceive God's revelations and translate them into corrective action toward the world's problems.

Father Richard Rohr, founder of the Center for Action and Contemplation in Albuquerque, New Mexico, seconds Nadler's words in his discussion of the "prophetic path," observing that prophets "do not have to be highly educated, powerful, or well-known; they are everyday people perched at the edge of the inside of our institutions, distant enough to critique injustice, but close enough to be heard."[6] Rohr goes on to quote Rabbi Nahum Ward-Lev, spiritual director and scholar-in-residence at Temple Beth Shalom in Santa Fe, New Mexico, who describes the prophetic vison as one that "supports the evolution of life toward greater consciousness, and every movement toward justice and communal well-being," a reminder of the ongoing commitment of Judaism to social justice. In the spirit of Rohr's and Ward-Lev's words, to be called prophetic in the context of humanistic psychology in the twentieth and twenty-first centuries primarily suggests a deeper sense of ethical responsibility toward the world, a social justice orientation with or without possessing philosophical wisdom, theological training, and/or scientific knowledge.

Like many New York City youth on the lower end of the economic spectrum, Abraham was attracted to the free tuition and academic scholarship of the City College of New York and readily signed on. However, he soon transferred to Cornell, mainly because a cousin with whom he was close had chosen to matriculate there. At Cornell, he again encountered

4. Nadler, *Book Forged in Hell*, 67.
5. Nadler, *Book Forged in Hell*, 69.
6. Rohr, "A Liberating Path."

anti-Semitism, but more of the elitist, Ivy League sort than of the street gang variety of his Brooklyn youth. Ever restless, Abraham transferred again, this time to the University of Wisconsin at Madison, a campus long recognized for its progressive faculty and vaunted psychology department; Maslow would receive his BA, MA, and PhD at Madison. In addition, he discovered the social sciences, which would feed his innate passion for personal, societal, and global transformation. In 1928, at age twenty, Abraham married his first cousin Bertha; his life with her and their two children would be a source of much peace and contentment for him. In later years, he described his first kiss with Bertha—the only woman he would ever kiss—as his first peak-experience.

At Madison, Maslow studied under the direction of Harry Harlow, famous for his attachment studies with monkeys that demonstrated the primal need for belonging; years later, Maslow incorporated this need for belonging into his integrated, hierarchical approach to human needs. Thanks to a sympathetic professor who lobbied for the hiring of a Jew on the faculty, Maslow obtained a postdoctoral appointment at Columbia, where he worked under the humane and celebrated Edward Thorndike on the research of sexual dominance in monkeys. This experience established his lifelong respect, if not always enthusiasm, for the value of research. Yet true to the times, Columbia, far from being admirably inclusive, "routinely banned all but a handful of 'showcase' Jewish professors from tenured faculty positions."[7] Upon completion of that project, Thorndike recommended Maslow for an appointment at another college, to which he was denied entry, again due to his Judaism.[8]

Having experienced prejudice throughout his life, Maslow often reflected upon his professional future and the difficulties his being Jewish might cause him going forward. Anti-Semitism was much in the air, and not only in Europe. But when it was suggested that he change his first name, his ethnic pride rose to the surface, and he refused. In fine Brooklyn form, he asserted, "If I'm a Jew, I'm a Jew, and I'll stuff it down your throat if you don't like it."[9] Anti-Semitism became a running theme in his life, serving, among other things, to keep him connected to his Jewish ancestry and the prophetic spirituality central to that tradition. Much later in life, Maslow

7. Hoffman, *Right to Be Human*, 84–85.

8. An Oct. 13, 2022, article in *The New York Times*, written by Amanda Holpuch and titled "Stanford Apologizes for Limiting Jewish Admissions in the 1950s," reported that the Palo Alto, California, university both suppressed Jewish admissions throughout the 1950s and, in subsequent years, denied that it had done so. Apparently, antisemitism was the norm in the upper echelons of academia on both coasts during those years.

9. Hoffman, *Right to Be Human*, 48.

would recognize his awareness of anti-Semitism, and his response to it, as formational in his thinking.

But there is more than his religious inheritance and his experience of prejudice that accounts for Maslow's natural attraction to the spiritual. As a brief stint in medical school demonstrates, he was characterologically more attuned to the inner world and more sensitive to the emotional dimension of life. Although trained as a dispassionate scientist, he was by nature anything but dispassionate, and he became easily disheartened by the cold approach to the sanctity of the human person he repeatedly discovered in his classes. In a 1965 lecture appropriately titled "The Taboo of Tenderness: The Disease of Valuelessness," presented thirty years after his medical school experience, Maslow referenced an operation involving the removal of a woman's cancerous breast. He described the procedure as

> almost paradigmatic in its efforts to desacralize: that is, to remove the sense of awe, privacy, fear, and shyness before the sacred and the forbidden, and of humility before the tremendous . . . [there] were, of course, no prayers, no rituals or ceremonies of any kind, as there most certainly would be in most preliterate societies.[10]

Though absent in that operating room, a sense of the sacred—of awe, wonder, poignancy, and reverence—came readily to Maslow.

With medical school clearly not to his liking and various university appointments blocked because of his religion—a religion, paradoxically, that he did not practice—Maslow returned home to Brooklyn, taking a position at Brooklyn College. Abuzz with immigrants and a hotbed of radical thought and action, Brooklyn often served as home base for Maslow, a place to return to when a return to the familiar was needed.

EARLY INFLUENCES—RELATIVISM, BEHAVIORISM, AND UNIVERSAL HUMAN VALUES

One effect of Hitler's rise to power in Germany was the exodus of scholars from Central Europe to the United States, particularly New York, a city that Maslow described as the center of the psychological universe, even comparing it to Athens.[11] Contemporary humanistic psychologist Scott Barry Kaufman describes the exodus of psychoanalysts to New York City at the time as "a truly unprecedented cultural renaissance,"[12] and Maslow took full

10. Hoffman, *Right to Be Human*, 66–67.

11. Kaufman, *Transcend*, 83.

12. Kaufman, *Transcend*, 83.

advantage of it. He readily gravitated toward immigrant scholars such as the biologist Kurt Goldstein, from whom he borrowed the term *self-actualization*, and Erich Fromm, whose views on world betterment and social justice he found particularly attractive. Likewise, he was drawn to Alfred Adler, whose invented word *Gemeinschaftsgefühl*, signifying a passionate feeling for community, was praised by Maslow as "the only one available that describes well the flavor of the feelings for mankind expressed by self-actualizing subjects . . . a deep identification, sympathy, and affection."[13]

This "university in exile," which found expression through institutions such as the New School for Social Research, the City College of New York, Brooklyn College, and Columbia, much affected Maslow's sense of Jewishness, keeping the spark of religion alive, even as it carried a secular, nontheistic undertone. That spark would never die. And it would serve, perhaps more often unconsciously than otherwise, as a pervasive influence on the ongoing development of humanistic psychology itself, as numerous commentators have suggested.[14]

Another prominent Jewish immigrant who influenced Maslow during the years he struggled to define his own thinking was Max Wertheimer, who fled Germany in 1933. Wertheimer's gestalt theories, which emphasized the intuitive approach to learning—the *aha!* moment—foreshadowed Maslow's later formulation of the peak-experience. In addition, Wertheimer, whose thinking in these areas was pioneering, argued against both ethnocentric bias and cultural relativism in psychological theory and, significantly, toward the recognition that science can identify a universal set of values conducive to health that might serve as a yardstick against which to measure a culture's well-being.

Much influenced by the cultural relativism of the social sciences he was studying, Maslow was understandably critical of both ethnocentrism

13. Maslow, *Motivation and Personality*, 165.

14. Houston rabbi Ann Elizabeth Belford, for example, in a fascinating 2016 article in *Foundation Theology* journal titled "'Third-Force' Psychologists and Judaism's Shared Positive View of Humanity," which links humanistic psychology and Judaism, argues that "the peak-experiences Maslow describes in *Toward a Psychology of Being* . . . sound remarkably similar to religious, mystical experiences, what Jewish mystics called *devekut*, or cleaving to God" (13). More importantly, Belford argues, the influence of Judaism is evident in humanistic psychology's premise that the person is essentially good and should be treated as such, and she notes Carl Rogers's emphasis on warmth, caring, and positive regard in the therapeutic relationship as representative of that assumption of goodness (13). Belford summarizes by observing that at its heart, "Judaism views humans as being created with a spark of divinity, in God's own image. . . . Rogers and Maslow shared this understanding of human nature" (12). The influence of the vast body of Hebrew Scripture and Jewish scholarship on humanistic psychology is evident in writings and statements by many of the movement's proponents then and now.

and the American Freudian emphasis on adjustment to social norms. Yet as Wertheimer's thoughts on the need for a system of universal values to address the world's ills began to formulate in his own thinking, Maslow's attachment to a relativist worldview began to unravel.

The left-wing radicalism he continually encountered in academia—a cluster of ideologies that suggested no uncertainty about what society needed or the values that defined it—further solidified his growing antipathy toward relativism, which many on the left of the political spectrum discarded in favor of the identification of universal, prosocial values. A prime example of this was Erich Fromm, who consistently advocated for identifying and promulgating humanistic values as the cure for the world's afflictions. As early as 1941, Maslow wrote about the need for a scientific, reason-based approach to identifying those values.[15]

Maslow's continuing progression away from a relativist worldview was further incentivized by an opportunity to engage in sociological fieldwork among the Blackfoot Indians in Canada during the 1930s, a project urged upon him by the anthropologist Ruth Benedict, an associate of Margaret Mead's. Upon experiencing their customs, rituals, and traditions, Maslow noticed that despite a lifestyle distinctly different from his own, the Blackfoot appeared to honor many of the same values that he was beginning to identify and catalogue—as well as some that clearly transcended American values, for example, their perspective on property and possessions. What was important to the Blackfoot was not the accumulation of possessions but the sharing of them with the community: "The wealthiest individual in Blackfoot eyes was the one who had given away the most to others,"[16] suggesting to Maslow a more highly evolved attitude toward material possessions than that experienced within the Anglo-American values system of the day. Further, Maslow observed the same range of personalities among the Blackfoot that one might find anywhere, leading to his conclusion that they are "first human beings and *secondarily* Blackfoot Indians."[17]

These experiences—the social justice radicalism encountered in academia, the influence of Max Wertheimer and others regarding ethnocentrism and cultural relativism, and the sojourn among the Blackfoot—would, over time, define a new life path for Maslow: the formulation of a universal values system, a new code of ethics through which a fractured world might rediscover meaning, purpose, and connection. As author Frank Goble observed in *The Third Force*, "The belief that there are values or moral

15. Kaufman, *Transcend*, 85.

16. Hoffman, *Right to Be Human*, 121.

17. Hoffman, *Right to Be Human*, 121 (emphasis in original).

principles common to the entire human species, which can be scientifically confirmed [is perhaps] . . . the most unique aspect of Maslow's Third Force theory."[18] Out of this search for universal human values would emerge a sense of the human ideal, identifiable in all cultures and at all times, and approachable, if not attainable, by all.

Just as the cultural relativism of Maslow's early years was being set aside, so too was his early interest in behaviorism, which favored learning and conditioning over genetics in forming the personality. Although acknowledging that environment influences the development of personality, Maslow emphasized that it is not reducible to it, a position strengthened upon the births of his two daughters in 1938 and 1940. Awed by the sight of his first child, a peak-experience that could not be reduced to behavioral stimulus and response explanations, and equally moved by the birth of his second, whose distinctly different personality was apparent from the beginning, Maslow could no longer entertain a narrow behaviorist perspective on human development.

Professional experiences at Brooklyn College further distanced Maslow from a behaviorist worldview. In addition to teaching psychology courses, he was being sought out by students for counseling sessions, an experience wherein behaviorism has little to offer, particularly to adolescents seeking meaning, purpose, and connection in their lives. For Maslow, counseling was about growth toward personal meaning, not the cure of illness.

Nonetheless, it must be added that Maslow always valued his training during those early behaviorist years, and he maintained a lifelong friendship with behavioral psychologist B. F. Skinner. In a letter to Skinner in 1965, he affirmed their different approaches and perspectives and suggested they were primarily related to their contrasting personalities: "What you choose to specialize in is a matter of characterological taste. I like playing around with the beginnings of knowledge, raising new questions, and so on. Other people like to work on more solid ground. Both approaches are okay."[19] Characteristically, Maslow did not dismiss behaviorism as incorrect; instead, he saw it as incomplete—"too narrow and limited to serve as a *general* or comprehensive philosophy"[20] that could address the needs, joys, hopes, passions, and aspirations of those on the path to self-actualization.

Shortly after the United States entered World War II, Maslow had an experience that moved him closer to his own sense of meaning, purpose, and mission. Observing a military parade with its cheering crowds and

18. Goble, *Third Force*, 87.

19. Maslow, "Letter to B. F. Skinner," 198.

20. Maslow, *Psychology of Science*, 5.

chauvinistic undertones, he was struck by the need to propose an alternative to the frightful enthusiasm for war he had witnessed. Overcome with a transformative sense of personal mission, he imagined a peace table around which were seated world leaders discussing how to live in harmony. He became determined to create a psychology to help make that vision a reality. Furthermore, he saw his developing theory of motivation—the focus on what people need to live fulfilled lives and the values that govern that process—as the pathway to this new psychological approach. Believing that people were more alike than different, he was confident that the effective use of science could lead to the identification of values universal to all humanity. Furthermore, he believed that championing those values could effectively address the folly of war and other societal ills.

Maslow launched these efforts by sharpening his focus on the qualities found in people who appeared to be living healthy, contributing, prosocial lives. Drawing upon the characteristics he observed in the personalities of people like Max Wertheimer and Ruth Benedict, he presented his first of many lists of healthy character traits, qualities such as self-esteem, self-knowledge, the ability to give and receive love, and the willingness to question social conventions.

FROM BASIC HUMAN NEEDS TO SELF-ACTUALIZATION AND UNIVERSAL VALUES

In a 1943 paper titled "A Theory of Motivation," Maslow first outlined his classic approach to human needs—his celebrated hierarchy of needs—in which he demonstrated that in addition to the basic physiological and safety needs common to all humanity, there are also higher needs, such as love, belonging, esteem, and self-actualization. And the more Maslow studied this, the more he understood self-actualization, the highest human need, as a universal possibility, not the sole property of the Wertheimers and Benedicts of the world. Two years later, he started a "Good Human Being Notebook" to organize all his listings in a single place, just as today we might create a computer file to hold and preserve the findings of our own research projects.

Out of this focus on human motivation would emerge Maslow's recognition that our basic needs are better understood as *values* that are common to the species—love, belonging, self-esteem, the actualization of our potentialities, all that we strive for as human beings. And just as it is possible to differentiate between that which supports our physiological health and that which is detrimental to it, so too we can identify that which supports our ability to develop to our fullest human potential and that which detracts from it. We can readily identify what foods are more valuable for our physical health; likewise, we can determine what qualities are more valuable for our spiritual health, that is, what makes us contributing, connective, compassionate people.

It is interesting to note that the pyramidal structure of human needs frequently presented in introductory psychology textbooks was created not by Maslow but by a management consultant during the 1960s who recognized its potential application to business management principles.[21] The result of the creation of this now ubiquitous visual was, on the one hand, the popularization of Maslow's name beyond the world of psychology, while, on the other hand, having the effect, according to contemporary humanistic psychologist Scott Barry Kaufman, of "reducing Maslow's rich and nuanced intellectual contributions to a parody [that] has betrayed the actual spirit of [his] notion of self-actualization as realizing one's creative potential for humanitarian ends."[22] Thankfully, that parody crumbles with even a cursory review of Maslow's works—for example, *Toward a Psychology of Being*; *Religions, Values, and Peak-Experiences;* or *The Farther Reaches of Human Nature*—which are encouraging in their descriptions of human possibilities and profound in their implications for the future of humankind.

As Maslow came to see his discoveries as having a potentially revolutionary impact on human development, his need to propagate his message intensified—whether or not he had conducted the level of research he believed it warranted. Preach the message and do the research, in that order, became his methodology. He never lacked confidence in the potency of his insights, but as the years went on, he tired of doing the research and increasingly encouraged others to step up to the task: "The grander Maslow's vision became, the harder he found it to concern himself with the details."[23] Over time, he became less the scientist and more the philosopher.

Maslow was flying in the face of traditional psychology with his emphasis on identifying higher values—the proper object of science is verifiable, testable hypotheses, not value judgments about good and bad, right and wrong. Yet the more he encountered self-actualizing people—men and women who lived productive, contributing lives of personal fulfillment—the more he noticed a correlation between what is psychologically healthy and what is ethical: "The healthy person finds happiness in helping others . . .

21. Kaufman, *Transcend*, xxix.

22. Kaufman, *Transcend*, xxix.

23. Grogan, *Encountering America*, 85.

his vocation and avocation become the same."[24] Where others saw facts and values in terms of polarity, he envisioned a transcending, synergistic relationship, a principle he learned from Ruth Benedict. These early stirrings toward ethical humanism, one that describes ethics as "coming from within the human experience, an 'internal' code of behavior,"[25] would more and more define his life path.

The word *Being* takes center stage when Maslow talks about self-actualization and values. As we progress through and meet the basic needs of life, we are in the process of Becoming; upon reaching self-actualization, we experience Being, which signifies the fullness of what we are capable of experiencing in life, the fullness of what it means to be a person—the best version of ourselves, as we might say today. When we discuss self-actualization, we are in the realm of Being-psychology (shorthanded to B-psychology), the study of the person at his or her fullest potential. Maslow refers to the quality of knowing and understanding at that stage as B-cognition and the values therein encountered as B-values, the values found within those living authentic, contributing lives. For Maslow, B-values are central to what it means to be human and essential to the full flowering of the human.

Although Being signifies the fullness of what can be attained in life, it should not be understood as stagnant. In his final work, *The Farther Reaches of Human Nature*, published posthumously, Maslow refers to *metamotivation*, growth at the level of the B-values. The deprivation of metamotivation results in metapathology, for which "we may need *metacounselors* to help with the soul-sicknesses that grow from the unfulfilled metaneeds."[26] With perhaps a touch of self-deprecating humor, Maslow even referenced incidences of *metagrumbling* resulting from the frustrated idealism supposedly common among the self-actualized.[27] Maslow's thinking was nothing if not expansive.

As Maslow turned his attention increasingly toward identifying fundamental human values and celebrating the self-actualized person, he found himself more and more drawn toward the spiritual. To learn more about the qualities of self-actualized persons, the exemplars of humanity, he read prolifically of the lives of great men and women, the saints and sages of history whom he believed were ideal models for what might become less the exception and more the norm. As he observed in *The Farther Reaches of Human Nature*, if we want to know how fast a person can run, we don't collect

24. Goble, *Third Force*, 28.

25. Morgan, *Beyond Divine Intervention*, 36.

26. Maslow, *Farther Reaches*, 44 (emphasis in original).

27. Kaufman, *Transcend*, 221.

an average human population sample; we look to the Olympic gold medal winners. And "if we want to know the possibilities for spiritual growth, value growth, or moral development in human being, then I maintain that we can learn most by studying our most moral, ethical, or saintly people."[28] In addition, Maslow began to make note of mystical episodes common in the lives of self-actualized persons, episodes of awe, of wonder, of marveling at life itself, a natural mysticism that he insisted was intrinsic to the person and available to all.

Understanding that the word *value* is itself value-free—there are both healthy and unhealthy values—Maslow called for resisting societal values that might be counterproductive to the person's total development. He did not hesitate to note harmful values, such as authoritarianism (which he saw as the worst sociopolitical disease of the times, an insight likely influenced by Fromm, who wrote extensively of the dangers of authoritarianism in books like *Escape from Freedom* and *The Sane Society*) and prejudice (which, having experienced it directly throughout his life, needed no external influence). His efforts were directed toward identifying and elevating to universal acceptance those values that contribute to humanity, and he saw Carl Rogers, Erich Fromm, Rollo May, and others as key allies in this work.

Maslow's increasing interest in spirituality and connectedness to the religion of his ancestry, the possibility of which he no doubt would have adamantly denied on the day of his bar mitzvah, was strengthened by his appointment as head of the psychology department at Brandeis University in its opening year of 1949. Brandeis was explicitly established to advance the Jewish ideal of excellence in learning, and nearly all of the friends he developed there were secular Jews. Interestingly, he found his Brandeis students lacking in passion compared to his poorer and more radicalized Brooklyn College students. He endeavored to "uplift them morally as well as intellectually, to see them visibly mature on the path to self-actualization."[29] It was said of Maslow at that time that he had "a Messiah complex, but he never sought to impose it on others"[30]—except, perhaps, on his students.

Ten years after the publication of *Motivation and Personality*, Maslow published *Religions, Values, and Peak-Experiences*, in which he discussed peak-experiences as moments of awe, wonder, and emotional intensity that open to the mystical realm. Biographer Hoffman notes that "he amassed perhaps more up-to-date material on mysticism than any major American psychologist in more than fifty years, since William James's *Varieties of*

28. Maslow, *Farther Reaches*, 7.

29. Hoffman, *Right to Be Human*, 211.

30. Hoffman, *Right to Be Human*, 211.

Religious Experience."[31] This mystical world was new territory for Maslow, although he had been clearly moving in that direction for some time. It was certainly new territory for conventional psychology, which paid it little heed: Maslow's initial work on mystical experiences was repeatedly rejected for journal publication.

In *Beyond Religion*, Pepperdine University psychology professor David Elkins differentiates between spirit, which is about height, and soul, which is about depth. The former is "about climbing, striving for success, achieving. [But midlife] is a time of the soul; it is about descending into our depths to forge new value for the second half of life."[32] Maslow, almost fifty, was entering "a time of the soul."

SEEKING NEW KNOWLEDGE IN HUMAN VALUES

A critical moment in Maslow's work with values occurred in October 1957 with the convening, at the Massachusetts Institute of Technology, of the First Scientific Conference on New Knowledge in Human Values, organized to promote the cause that was increasingly defining his life mission. The addresses were published two years later, edited by Maslow, who also contributed a preface and a key article. In his theme-setting preface, Maslow presents the raison d'être for the conference and the book, opening with the challenge that although "the ultimate disease of our time is valuelessness . . . [and] this state is more crucially dangerous than ever before in history . . . something can be done about it by man's own rational efforts."[33]

After describing this state of valuelessness in terms of emptiness and rootlessness, an absence of something to believe in, Maslow faults the traditional values systems, both religious and secular, for failing to address it adequately. He sees the current period in history as an interregnum between the old values systems and the one for which he hopes to serve as midwife, to be born and nurtured through the humanistic psychology movement, as well as through fellow travelers from a wide variety of academic disciplines and vocations. And he identifies what is needed for the transition: "a validated, usable system of human values, values that we can believe in and devote ourselves to because they are true rather than because we are *exhorted* to 'believe and have faith.'"[34]

31. Hoffman, *Right to Be Human*, 225.
32. Elkins, *Beyond Religion*, 18.
33. Maslow, *New Knowledge*, vii.
34. Maslow, *New Knowledge*, viii (emphasis in original).

Referencing the research necessary to accomplish this, Maslow observes that much remains to be done, adding optimistically that the pathway toward the goal of individual and societal improvement has been made clear. In a letter of invitation to the conference speakers, he identifies its scope as encompassing the totality of human values, including the spiritual, and their application toward advancing social goals. He hoped that out of the broad diversity of participants representing a wide cross section of the academic world, a convergence of thinking would emerge around these issues. What he did not know was that biologist Julian Huxley, a continent away in London, was also assembling a cadre of scholars to address the same topics. Their contributions would be published under the title *The Humanist Frame*, to be explored in a later chapter.

Who were the MIT conference participants, and what aspirations did they bring to the table? A sampling suggests both the commonalities and the diversity of those embarking on this quest for new knowledge in human values. Pitrim A. Sorokin, director of the Harvard Research Center in Creative Altruism, wrote of the need for a "moral transformation of man and the man-made universe [as] the most important item on today's agenda of history."[35] He did not expect this transformation to emerge through political change; as a former prisoner of both czarist and Soviet Russia, he knew well the limitations of political responses. Instead, he believed reformation would spring from the embrace of creative love, and he referenced the lives of the saints as exemplars.

Robert S. Hartman, philosopher and researcher at the University of Mexico and founding sponsor of the American Association for Humanistic Psychology, focused on the creation of a science of values and predicted that "there will come a time when the problems and conflicts that now plague us will be as forgotten as the tortures of the Middle Ages and the clubs of the cave men."[36] Zen master Daisetz Teitaro Suzuki, through whom humanistically oriented psychoanalyst and pioneering feminist psychologist Karen Horney was introduced to Eastern spiritual practices, emphasized the essential goodness of the created world and the necessity of the inner transformation of the person through the harnessing of moral and spiritual resources.

Harvard psychology professor and noted existentialist Gordon Allport called for more research on altruism, cross-cultural studies to discern human values that are intrinsic to the species rather than purely cultural ones, an emphasis on inclusion to confront egocentricity, and philosophically

35. Sorokin, "Powers," 3.

36. Hartman, "Science of Value," 34.

based research that would plumb the depths of intellectual thought. Erich Fromm, who had recently published *The Sane Society*, a work sometimes described as a response to Freud's pessimistic *Civilization and Its Discontents*, highlighted what was becoming a signature tenet in the humanistic psychology canon, namely, that values are rooted within the essential nature of the person, not generated from an external source.

Brandeis University psychology professor Kurt Goldstein, who first used the word *self-actualization* as a biological principle, emphasized that values are identifiable with that which is healthy to the organism—with that which promotes the species' survival—an insight fundamental to John Morgan's term *ethical humanism*, the understanding that "moral behavior is a biologically derived code of conduct generated from the inevitabilities of genetic and speciel survival."[37] And closing out the conference, theologian and Harvard professor Paul Tillich wondered where we might locate "the source of the ought-to-be in being"[38] and answered, as many before him had, that values must be located within the essential being of the person. A consensus was building: we are a values-making species.

As noted, these presentations occurred at the First Scientific Conference on New Knowledge in Human Values in 1957. Unfortunately, there is no record of a second conference, and the values institute that Maslow labored for never materialized due to lack of funding—which typically translates to a lack of sufficient interest beyond the core true believers. Of course, Maslow would not allow the defeat of so promising a project as this to set him back. With or without funding and professional support, he would proceed in his work on values together with whoever would care to join him.

Out of this intensity of effort would develop the new *psychology of Being*, humanistic psychology, founded in response to the values-free ideology of the world of science and the need to identify fundamental human values that transcend all cultures, healthy values that suggest the best that humanity has to offer. Throughout, Maslow's frequently offered lists of B-values continued to expand: "truth, beauty, justice, goodness, wholeness, perfection, uniqueness, simplicity, order, aliveness, self-sufficiency, necessity, completion, richness, effortlessness, playfulness, and dichotomy-transcendence."[39]

In fact, Maslow appeared to be emboldened by his inability to gain support for the values initiative. He began to get the sense of a grand mission and felt compelled to proclaim it in messianic fashion, as was his wont—"I have so much to give the world—the Great Message. . . . Before I die, I must

37. Morgan, *Beyond Divine Intervention*, 9.

38. Tillich, "Is a Science," 193.

39. Hoffman, *Right to Be Human*, 264.

say it all."[40] He continued reading the stories of history's sages, saints, and, increasingly, mystics—all those who reported peak-experiences of either the spiritual or secular variety. In time, the distinction he saw between spiritual and secular experiences faded into insignificance.

While Maslow's work with peak-experiences was leading him to a greater appreciation of the spiritual dimension of life, religious groups—liberal Protestants, ecumenically minded Catholics, and "a few maverick rabbis"[41]—began to take notice, no doubt much to his surprise. Erich Fromm also referenced religious groups taking notice, and with his sociopolitical orientation ever present, he noted the contributions of "the radical wing of the Catholic Church, as well as . . . the various non-Catholic Christian denominations, [which] shows a marked return to the prophetic principle . . . that spiritual aims must be applied to the political and social process."[42] Ever the experiential learner, Maslow realized that his early childhood experiences had blinded him to the wisdom available within the various religious traditions, including his own. The Old Testament prophet-in-the-making was emerging.

FORMULATING A PSYCHOLOGY OF BEING

Maslow's prominence within the growing movement that was beginning to define itself with the words *humanistic psychology* accelerated with the 1962 publication of *Toward a Psychology of Being*, which begins with the enticing words, "There is now emerging over the horizon a new conception of human sickness and of human health, a psychology that I find so thrilling and so full of wonderful possibilities that I yield to the temptation to present it publicly even before it is checked and confirmed, and before it can be called reliable science."[43] Maslow experienced frustration in finding the words he needed to fully describe his emerging "psychology of Being," by which he meant the study of "the range of exalted emotions like awe, bliss, ecstasy, euphoria, reverie, and wonder."[44]

In *Toward a Psychology of Being*, Maslow attempted to describe his vision despite the difficulty, noting that what he is proposing is "a larger jurisdiction for psychology," as a chapter title proclaims. He outlines nine basic assumptions guiding his work, at the core of which is his insistence that the

40. Hoffman, *Right to Be Human*, 263.
41. Hoffman, *Right to Be Human*, 264.
42. Fromm, *Revolution of Hope*, 30–31.
43. Maslow, *Toward Psychology of Being*, 14.
44. Hoffman, *Right to Be Human*, 289.

person's inner nature is good, or at least neutral, and becomes tainted only through the frustration of the natural growth process. He observes that if "these assumptions are proven true, they promise a scientific ethics, a natural value system, a court of ultimate appeal for the determination of good and bad, or right and wrong."[45] Maslow's work was no mere theoretical musing; he was on a mission to change the world.

In keeping with his health- and growth-oriented approach, Maslow reinterprets neurosis as a deficiency disease, an illness resulting from the absence of certain basic needs, namely, safety, love and belonging, and respect and prestige. He adds that we need love and belonging in the same way the body needs vitamins: without them, we become ill. For Maslow, "belonging and affection were fundamental needs in their own right—not reducible to safety or sex,"[46] as Freud would have it. Once these basic needs are met, the individual can cross the threshold from deficiency motivation to growth motivation, an advance in personality development that Maslow refers to with the now-familiar term self-actualization. At the level of self-actualization, the focus is no longer on tension reduction; instead, tension is welcomed, as it relates not to needs fulfillment but to the experience of growth. It is the tension or stress associated with, for example, engagement in a major project or anticipation of a significant life change.

Homing in on the peak-experiences of self-actualizing persons, Maslow explores what can be learned about people at their best—that is, when they choose healthy values—instead of when they are in the grip of neuroses. He distinguishes between the state of Becoming, which is means-focused, and that of Being, which is ends-focused and values-focused. He places special emphasis on tolerance, patience, and equanimity in the face of dichotomies as an aspect of self-actualizing people—the ability to hold opposites in tension, to avoid either-or formulations, to transcend the dialectic and allow for a third way to develop naturally. Creative people appear to be able to see connections that others don't, according to Maslow, because they avoid dichotomizing reality and are more open to paradox.

At the close of *Toward a Psychology of Being*, Maslow pulls together all the sundry ideas he's placed before the reader into a compelling formulation of forty-three basic propositions, beginning with the recognition that the person possesses an inner nature that is observable both objectively (scientifically) and subjectively (through inner search and psychotherapy). Further, this inner nature is good (or at last neutral), and it has a will toward

45. Maslow, *Toward Psychology of Being*, 15.

46. Kaufman, *Transcend*, 37.

health and growth that social factors can either frustrate or promote. The goal of all this is, of course, self-actualization.

With a stirring summary statement on the importance of identifying his scientifically verifiable system of human values, Maslow concludes, "The human being needs a framework of values, a philosophy of life, a religion or religion-surrogate to live by and understand by, in about the same sense that he needs sunlight, calcium or love."[47] And he looks to self-actualizing people—historical figures, such as Socrates, Meister Eckhart, Baruch Spinoza, Harriet Tubman, Frederick Douglass, Thomas Jefferson, and Abraham Lincoln; persons in the public eye, such as Albert Einstein and Eleanor Roosevelt; and personal acquaintances, such as Max Wertheimer and Ruth Benedict—as models for discovering and promoting this new values system, which he expects to be transformative.

Critics of Maslow's attempt to identify universal values were quick to point out that his selections of models for what it means to be a self-actualizing person reflect his own necessarily limited worldview. That worldview expanded through the years as his life experiences accumulated and as more individuals from different cultural settings took up the banner for a universal values system. No doubt, were he alive today, he would propose a broader spectrum of individuals, more representative of our diverse world. Nonetheless, the critique remains a cautionary reminder of how difficult it is to identify universal values while at the same time respecting the various ways different peoples might approach them. Humanists today would agree that the continuing struggle to identify values that promote the well-being of Homo sapiens and the future of the planet itself is both essential and challenging. Various approaches to this will be reviewed in the chapter on Julian Huxley.

FOCUSING ON RELIGIONS, VALUES, AND PEAK-EXPERIENCES

In 1964, two years after the publication of *Toward a Psychology of Being*, Maslow published his signature work on spirituality and values, *Religions, Values, and Peak-Experiences.* All of his studies, research, interaction with mentors, and varied life experiences had led him to the point at which he could develop his own synthesis of psychology, spirituality, religion, values, and the universally experienced moments of awe, wonder, reverence, and connection that he referred to as peak-experiences. *Religions, Values, and Peak-Experiences* is Maslow at the top of his game as a creative thinker, a

47. Maslow, *Toward Psychology of Being*, 169.

philosopher as well as a psychologist, and a prophetic voice that critiques the blandness of mid-twentieth century American psychology and culture while at the same time challenging men and women of science and religion to come together for the sake of our future as a species. Customarily, Maslow had much to say.

In the editorial introduction to the 1994 edition, E. I. F. Williams of Kappa Delta Pi Publications states that "there has been a growing movement toward the establishment of a world philosophy in the social and physical sciences."[48] The Association of Humanistic Psychology had been formed in 1961, but it was not recognized as an official field by the American Psychological Association until 1971, which perhaps explains Williams's failure to name the "growing movement." He also references the 1962–65 ecumenical council of the Catholic Church, noting the increased communication among the various religions as a hopeful sign for the final decades of the twentieth century. These were clearly heady times, in which "a world philosophy" could be imagined, and a 1900-year-old religious institution could throw open its windows, in Pope John XXIII's inviting metaphor, and welcome the wisdom of the rest of the world.

In Maslow's preface, he speaks of this new psychology as "holistic, integrative, and inclusive."[49] His words are strikingly contemporary and suggestive of psychological and spiritual movements that would soon be inspired by humanistic psychology, such as his own transpersonal psychology and contemporary philosopher Ken Wilber's integrative psychology. He discusses the dangers of polarization, seeking instead to unite the mystical/individual and the legalistic/organizational wings of religion by encouraging persons of faith to enjoy their rituals, which often provide a meaningful and unitive purpose to life. At the same time he advises against the temptation to reduce their faith either to the ritual forms and symbols or to their private, mystical experiences—an advanced level of faith development in James Fowler's schema, to be explored in a later chapter.

Introducing themes that will resonate throughout the humanistic psychology literature, Maslow bemoans how the original illumination and the "charismatic seer who started the whole thing"[50] were often lost in later legalisms, leading to religion's losing its ability to transform both the individual and society. The mystical, too, has its traps, he adds, such as reducing all to the experiential as the only criterion of right and wrong, potentially leading to solipsism or egocentrism. Maslow highlights what was becoming

48. Maslow, *Religions, Values, and Peak-Experiences*, v.

49. Maslow, *Religions, Values, and Peak-Experiences*, vii.

50. Maslow, *Religions, Values, and Peak-Experiences*, viii.

a key humanistic formulation, namely, that the sacred is found within the ordinary, not limited to a particular class of people or specific places and settings. Arguing for a "small 'r' religion,"[51] he intends to focus less on the external dimensions of religion and more on the ability of people, both individually and interpersonally, to develop to their fullest potential and live lives of consciously chosen values.

Maslow explores these sentiments throughout this small but seminal work, emphasizing that the spiritual values he is calling for are not reducible to theological concepts, nor are they the exclusive property of churches; they are identifiable through psychological inquiry, verifiable through scientific processes, and, ultimately, accessible to all. He upbraids both scientists and professional religionists for excluding values from scientific analysis and criticizes the behaviorists for ignoring the question of values altogether, Freud for his sole focus on the pathological, and pre-World War I humanists for their relativism. As an alternative, he presents this newly developing third force in psychology, one that embraces the question of values and is willing to distinguish, through scientific methods, between those that are healthy and those that are not.

Maslow sees both science and religion as "too narrowly conceived . . . too exclusively dichotomized and separated from each other," leading to a value-free science with "nothing to say about ends or ultimate values or spiritual values . . . a purely technological, amoral science."[52] We have seen the results of valueless science, observes Maslow: two world wars, genocide, and nuclear destruction, all of which, he hastens to remind us, the previous definers and protectors of values—the world's religions—failed to prevent. This dichotomy of knowledge and values has not served religions any better than it has served science, instead "cutting them off from facts, from knowledge, from science, even to the point of making them enemies of scientific knowledge" and closing their minds to any further learning.[53]

The absence of discourse or openness to mutual learning on the part of both the religious and scientific communities has dulled the ability of each to contribute to the greater good: Science is reduced to a cold, technological force with no appreciation for ethical responsibility, and religions—shunted to the sidelines of meaningful dialogue related to the development of common, humanistic, prosocial values—find themselves preaching only to their respective choirs. The result of that "preaching to the choir" has increasingly led to narrowness and intransigence that further isolates religions from the

51. Maslow, *Religions, Values, and Peak-Experiences*, viii.

52. Maslow, *Religions, Values, and Peak-Experiences*, 11.

53. Maslow, *Religions, Values, and Peak-Experiences*, 12.

larger cultural milieu: as a bumper sticker popular in the American Bible Belt some years back put it, "God said it. I believe it. That settles it." Without the presence of a healthy, scientifically minded community, religion runs the risk of descending into irrationality.

At the same time that Maslow was advocating for robust dialogue among men and women of science and religion—that, indeed, very little is "settled," the Bible Belt notwithstanding—Julian Huxley was developing the same set of ideas as the cornerstone of his own scientific methodology. In a scientific humanist worldview, humanity is on a continuing quest to learn and redefine its values to meet societal changes. For both Maslow and Huxley, religion and science were past due for a new definition of science that included the study of values and that opened religion to changes in accordance with new discoveries.

Maslow extends his vision to include an expanding definition of faith that eschews the traditional religionist understanding that faith is something possessed by a specific, often exclusive, group—"we have the faith; you do not." Faith, he proposes, is more a belief *in* a person or a principle rather than a belief *of* certain specific, closed statements. Further, he argues for a broader understanding of the sacred, one that defines it as an ever-present reality that anyone can enter at any given moment, not as the sole prerogative of religious institutions. He decries the narrow, rigid, and dichotomizing view of religion and science, with the former reduced to the abstract and pietistic and the latter to the concrete and amoral—and never the twain shall meet. Nineteenth-century atheism, of which Freud is one emphatic example, did nothing to heal this, often discarding the religious questions with rigid responses. Maslow, in contrast, considers those questions to be valid and worthy of serious consideration; both the religious questions and the religious quest are welcome in humanistic psychology.

In Maslow's spiritual worldview, at the core of religion is "the private, lonely, personal illumination, revelation, or ecstasy of some acutely sensitive prophet or seer,"[54] followed by its codification and communication to the mass of humanity—which, over time, often results in the formulation of beliefs and practices in direct opposition to those of the founding leader. Maslow appreciates these original revelations as examples of peak-experiences, and he wonders if these could be recognized as purely natural experiences available to us all. Author Steven Nadler, writing forty years after Maslow, suggests the same about the gift of prophecy, which he describes as "a perfectly natural, if unusual, phenomenon [that] arises from

54. Maslow, *Religions, Values, and Peak-Experiences*, 19.

the excellence of certain human faculties,"[55] not from the divine. Perhaps the boundaries separating the natural from the mystical are more permeable than we have heretofore imagined.

Furthermore, Maslow continues, if all peak-experiences, all experiences of the sacred, are essentially the same—all involving a sense of awe or wondrousness or sheer delight—would it not then follow that all religions are the same, with perceived differences being attributable to localisms of time and place? And is the difference between the prophet who shared the great truth and the follower who organizes, codifies, and institutionalizes it reducible to that between one who is attuned to peak-experiences and one who is not? With Maslow, we have traveled far from Freud's militant dismissal of all things religious and behaviorism's unwillingness to engage the transcendent—and, of course, from Maslow's own early rejection of religion as pietistic and superstitious—arriving at a place where the spiritual can be accepted as a valid subject of psychological discussion and investigation.

Maslow characteristically addresses these questions from the perspective of values: there is religion that promotes healthy values and religion that promotes unhealthy values, and both can be found within any particular religious denomination. Likewise for science, which can function in the service of both healthy and unhealthy values. As noted, the word *value* is itself value-free; it can be positive or negative, and the principal social goal of humanistic psychology is to promote systems and structures—in the therapy office, the family, the place of worship, the business community, the civic community, the nation, the world—that foster positive, healthy, life-affirming values. All values are not created equal.

Maslow criticizes the practice of "'religionizing' only one part of life"[56] while secularizing the other parts, arguing that all of life can be "religionized." For those who appreciate a more humanistic religious attitude, heaven is always available, always a possibility through peak-experiences. He asks how we can be more open to heaven's ready availability, to see the here and now "under the aspect of eternity . . . to see the sacred and symbolic *in* and *through* the individual here-and-now instance"[57]—words familiar to the contemporary practitioner of mindfulness meditation.

Maslow observes that as we focus more on values as qualities intrinsic to the person, the need for supernatural sanctions declines, as Freud suggested in *The Future of an Illusion*. Saintliness itself becomes more natural, more normalized. Referencing Fromm's humanistic faith and the new

55. Nadler, *Book Forged in Hell*, 73.

56. Maslow, *Religions, Values, and Peak-Experiences*, 31.

57. Maslow, *Religions, Values, and Peak-Experiences*, 32 (emphasis in original).

humanistic psychology that was just beginning to be named, Maslow embraces the challenge of arguing for humanity's higher nature and presenting his "new knowledge in human values." He sees it as his mission, his life's goal, to present an alternative to the values-free science and sterile psychology of the nineteenth century that presented "a lopsided picture of human nature which omits most of what human beings value, enjoy, and cherish in themselves, in fact, what they live for."[58]

Fearlessly engaging the most fundamental question of theology, Maslow calls for a new definition of God as "'Being itself,' . . . 'the integrating principle in the universe,' . . . 'the whole of everything,' . . . 'the meaningfulness of the cosmos,'"[59] all of which invite nontheists to the spiritual dialogue. He hopes to transcend the dichotomy between that which restricts the realm of values to organized religion, leaving science and the secular world with little to say about them, and that which restricts knowledge or reason to those in the secular world, with religion relegated to matters of faith. He proposes a new understanding of religion and science, one that frees religion from the exclusive domain of the churches and opens science to the acceptance of the mysterious as a natural part of the human experience.

Differences of opinion and approach would, of course, remain but not as dichotomous, opposing domains; instead, they would exist as shades of distinction along a continuum. Debate would not have to pit scientists against religionists but would focus instead on levels of basic needs fulfillment, personality differences, and personal preferences relating to one's comfort and interest in these higher spiritual principles. Maslow understands that it will take a different understanding of the person to accomplish this transcendence. He sees it as the primary goal of this new psychological movement "to aid the person to grow to fullest humanness, to the greatest fulfillment and actualization of his highest potentiality, to his greatest possible stature . . . to become *actually* what he deeply is *potentially*."[60]

What gets in the way of this growth? What temptations might frustrate our advance toward self-actualization, toward our fullest potential? Maslow's response serves as a handy summary of the humanistic orientation of his thinking: attempting to live a value-free life, trying to live a purely technological life (defined as focusing on means to the exclusion of ends), trying to live one's life exclusively in terms of old traditions and habits rather than embracing living values, and seeing education—and learning

58. Maslow, *Religions, Values, and Peak-Experiences*, 43.

59. Maslow, *Religions, Values, and Peak-Experiences*, 45.

60. Maslow, *Religions, Values, and Peak-Experiences*, 49 (emphasis in original).

in general—in terms of the indoctrination of old values to the exclusion of those identified through one's own experiences.

Key to all this, in the eyes of contemporary humanistic psychologist Scott Barry Kaufman, is Maslow's emphasis on ends over means: "*end experiences* (such as wonder, laughter, and connection), *end-values* (such as beauty, truth, and justice), *end-cognitions* (such as efficient perception of reality and newness of appreciation), *end-goals* (such as having an ultimate concern or purpose), and with *treating people as ends unto themselves*, not means to an end."[61] Kaufman, author of *Transcend: The New Science of Self-Actualization*, has assumed the role, and deservedly so, of present-day baton carrier for Maslow.

Throughout *Religions, Values, and Peak-Experiences*, Maslow strives for inclusiveness regarding the "religious experience," by which he means the sense of the holy, the sacred, the awe-inspiring, the mysterious, all of which can be accepted as real by "theists and non-theists, . . . by individuals of every political and economic persuasion."[62] With his signature optimism and magnanimity, he notes that the road to spiritual discovery beckons all who are willing to seek truth in spite of differences and limitations; it is a road for "all profoundly 'serious,' 'ultimately concerned' people of good will."[63] Expanding on his road metaphor, Maslow identifies two options at a fork near the road's end: the supernatural approach, offering an afterlife and a transcendent God, and the humanistic, nonreligious option, understood simply as the natural end to one's existence. He imagines the scientist and the theologian walking arm in arm along that road, having worked together throughout their lives to solve the world's problems through identifying and promulgating healthy values. At the fork, they part agreeably—one to God, the other to an eternal sleep.

Maslow closes the main body of his work by reviewing and highlighting the centrality of values in his worldview. Reiterating that they transcend any particular religion, he adds that they serve as the common core of all religions, including nontheistic ones. He sees the identification of healthy values as the goal of religion, education, psychotherapy, family life—indeed, all dimensions of society—and reminds the reader, lest we forget, that any "philosophy that permits facts to become amoral, totally separated from values, makes possible in theory at least the Nazi physician 'experimenting'

61. Kaufman, *Transcend*, xxiii–xxiv (emphasis in original).

62. Maslow, *Religions, Values, and Peak-Experiences*, 55.

63. Maslow, *Religions, Values, and Peak-Experiences*, 54.

in the concentration camps, or the spectacle of captured German engineers working devotedly for whichever side happened to capture them."[64]

In a series of appendices, Maslow, who could barely contain his enthusiasm to share all he was discovering with the reader, expounds further on the intersection of religion, values, and peak-experiences—as if his hyperactive mind would not allow him to place a final period on the last sentence of the book. He notes commonalities between peak-experiences and experiences typically considered to be religious, including the oceanic feeling (which Freud had famously addressed and discarded in *Civilization and Its Discontents*), the intense concentration of the senses (what today we might call mindfulness), and the sense of the world as good, with evil nonetheless present yet somehow reconciled. Further, he highlights the universal spiritual experiences of awe, wonder, and reverence attendant upon the birth of a child, falling in love, standing atop a mountain peak after a daylong trek, or being in the presence of a rare celestial event.

While listening to news reports on the eclipse that graced much of the United States in August 2017, I was struck by the response of a thirteen-year-old middle school student interviewed about what it was like to witness it. Reportedly, she smiled and breathed the simple word *ooh*, stretching it out for maximum effect. *Ooh* expresses an encounter with the spiritual, the peak-experience of wonder, poignancy, and sheer delight that words can rarely express. For Maslow and many others, this is the essence of the religious, the spiritual, the divine.

Peak-experiences by their very nature are subjective—they reside in the eyes of the beholder and are often experienced as miraculous. In *The Psychology of Science*, Maslow observed that "any oak tree or baby or pretty girl is a fantastic and unbelievable, unassailable miracle if seen for the first time (or if it is seen *as if* for the first time) . . . for any person as soon as he has sense enough to realize that it is more fun to live in a world of miracles than in a world of filing cabinets and that a familiar miracle is still a miracle."[65]

Continuing with examples of the intersection of religion, values, and peak-experiences, Maslow references the sense of being and acting as one's true self, life-changing shifts in perception, encounters with the ineffable, the "I-Thou" relationship, and experiences of becoming more loving, accepting, and grateful. He notes the discovery of unity and integration within life's apparent polarities and the experience of heaven, "which exists all the time all around us, always available to step into for a little while at least."[66]

64. Maslow, *Religions, Values, and Peak-Experiences*, 57–58.

65. Maslow, *Psychology of Science*, 82.

66. Maslow, *Religions, Values, and Peak-Experiences*, 66.

The peak-experience is a window into heaven for Maslow, and though we may rarely experience it, a "single glimpse of heaven is enough to confirm its existence even if it is never experienced again."[67]

Never hesitant to provide specifics regarding what he means by healthy, life-affirming values, Maslow offers a list of fourteen, with multiple synonyms, expansions, and further-nuanced versions of each. These range from truth, goodness, and beauty to self-sufficiency, and they transcend religious and philosophical beliefs. Understood as identifiable throughout the human species, these values buttress Maslow's conviction that measurable improvement in the person and society is possible and within reach. He welcomes the objection that although the organism biologically knows what is good for it, experience shows that "in several species, there are 'good choosers' and 'bad choosers.'"[68] Further, environmental conditions can mitigate against the wisdom of both body and soul. Nevertheless, he remains optimistic that these objections can be addressed through the spread of humanistic psychology throughout society.

Maslow closes *Religions, Values, and Peak-Experiences* by highlighting the importance of embracing the enhanced awareness of a life lived at the level of the B-values. He offers an enticing picture of what that kind of life is like: "In this way, the eternal becomes visible *in* and *through* the particular, the symbolic and platonic can be experienced *in* and *through* the concrete instance, the sacred can fuse with the profane, and one can transcend the universe of time and space while being of it."[69]

FINAL YEARS

Nineteen sixty-six was a banner year for Maslow: he was named president of the American Psychological Association—the same association that had ignored his early work and had taken ten years to even recognize humanistic psychology as a legitimate field of study—and was presented the Humanist of the Year award by the American Humanist Association. Both Maslow and the humanistic psychology he championed finally received the professional recognition they deserved. At the same time, he found himself increasingly intrigued by spiritual, transcendent issues, which led to his work on a "fourth force" approach he called transpersonal psychology. He even hinted at a *fifth* force—transhumanism, "that would transcend human interests

67. Maslow, *Religions, Values, and Peak-Experiences*, 75.
68. Maslow, *Religions, Values, and Peak-Experiences*, 101.
69. Maslow, *Religions, Values, and Peak-Experiences*, 116.

and focus on species-transcendent values."[70] In addition, Maslow became more in touch with his Judaism; biographer Hoffman quotes him as observing in later life that "my work was determined unconsciously by the Jewish passion for ethics, utopianism, messianism, the prophetic thundering."[71]

In secular terms, that word *messianism* suggests passion, fervor, and zeal, typically related to a cause or a movement understood as a societal imperative, which certainly describes Maslow's approach to the new psychology he was advancing. David Bakan, in *Sigmund Freud and the Jewish Mystical Tradition*, places this within a historical perspective by observing that "one of the critical features of Messianism is its goal of leading people out of slavery and oppression."[72] It could be argued that through his rediscovery of ethical Judaism, Maslow understood his mission as offering a uniquely humanistic path away from the slavery and oppression of the unfulfilled life and toward a spiritual freedom characterized by and facilitated through self-actualization and self-transcendence. He even began to imagine the highest states to which humanity could aspire, occasionally entertaining the idea of a utopian society, "Eupsychia," characterized by a maximum number of fully self-actualized persons.

As Maslow grew in the understanding that individual healing demands corresponding sociopolitical healing, he became more politically conscious and, as was his custom, messianic in his attempt to address the needs of America and the world. His daughter Ellen readily embraced those humanitarian concerns and joined the Freedom Riders, the 1961 integrated bus rides through the American South to confront racial segregation laws, one of the most dangerous activities a young person could engage in at that time: the freedom rides resulted in a number of martyrs to the cause, men and women whom history has been late to recognize and appropriately honor.

Maslow's interests in the political domain, however, never rose to the level of Fromm's, whose writings on sociopolitical subjects caught the eye of at least one president (John F. Kennedy) and one pope (John Paul II), or to that of Rogers, who became actively involved in peace processes in Northern Ireland, South Africa, and other hotspots in the world at that time. Further, unlike others in the broad humanistic psychology movement, Maslow was no apologist for the counterculture excesses of the 1960s. He had a "paternalistic, almost rabbinic quality that challenged their 'I do my thing, you do your thing' approach to values and social behavior."[73] When

70. Kaufman, *Transcend*, 251.

71. Hoffman, *Right to Be Human*, 306.

72. Bakan, *Sigmund Freud*, 170.

73. Hoffman, *Right to Be Human*, 318.

it came to values, Maslow was no relativist; he had no illusions about the difference between healthy and unhealthy, between right and wrong.

Abraham Maslow died at his home in Menlo Park, California, in 1970 at age sixty-two—far too young and with so much on his mind. In the preface to his biography, Edward Hoffman references "the intriguing work that Maslow left unfinished [and] Maslow's fascinating unfinished products."[74] Central to these were his further forays into spiritual themes that resulted in his cofounding of transpersonal psychology, quite a journey from the behaviorism of his early years. He had begun to speak not only of peak-experiences but of *plateau-experiences*: lengthier, more pervasive periods of awe, wonder, and reverence—"being able to see the miraculous in the everyday."[75] He was entering deeper waters here, and one can only imagine what he would have accomplished had he lived another ten or twenty years.

If humanistic psychology was "a rather lumpy collection" of ideas, as referenced earlier, transpersonal psychology was something of an amorphous jumble, barely classifiable, that focused on "unitive consciousness, mystical experience, and cognitive blissfulness"[76] and emphasized the conscious engagement of spiritual practices such as meditation. In 1969, Maslow, psychiatrist Stanislav Grof, and psychologist Anthony Sutich launched the *Journal of Transpersonal Psychology* and formally christened their new psychological approach.

At least in part, transpersonal psychology developed out of Maslow's frustration with the adverse effects of the countercultural movement on humanistic psychology, which tended to emphasize the hedonistic, escapist, and nonrigorous dimensions of a life lived free of externally imposed values, conveniently forgetting the importance of living a life immersed in personally identified humanistic values. As Maslow observes regarding consciousness-raising through drugs, "to have a peak-experience, you need to sweat."[77] But of greater weight than the effect of the excesses of the 1960s was Maslow's continuingly developing spirituality; transpersonal psychology developed naturally out of a life lived in pursuit of spiritual values.

It is probably better to appreciate transpersonal psychology less as a separate branch of psychology than as an offshoot of the larger humanist movement, a deeper focus on the spiritual emphasis that humanistic psychology had brought to the surface largely through Maslow's work. Today,

74. Hoffman, *Right to Be Human*, xvii.

75. Scott Barry Kaufman, *Psychology Podcast*, Apr. 12, 2022 (further bibliographic information unavailable).

76. Grogan, *Encountering America*, 250.

77. Hoffman, *Right to Be Human*, 266.

its mission is continued by the Association for Transpersonal Psychology in Palo Alto. Its best-known representative is Ken Wilber, whose *Grace and Grit*, the story of his wife's struggle against the ravages of breast cancer, is one of the most existentially wrenching love stories of all time. As for his musings about transhumanism, Maslow anticipated the work of contemporary biologists, like E. O. Wilson, who advocate a species-wide approach to the problems that plague our planet. As in other areas, Maslow was far ahead of his time.

Abraham Maslow was a beloved teacher, an expansive thinker, a groundbreaking psychologist, and a messianic cheerleader. Most of all, he was a human being who celebrated his and others' humanity. He delighted in people; as noted earlier, "he was irrepressibly compelled . . . to view people as resplendent." A quote at the close of Hoffman's biography well describes Maslow's humanistic spirit: "There was something otherworldly [about Maslow]. He could have talked to Plato with ease, but would have felt just as elated in conversing with a janitor about the virtues of grandchildren."[78] Abraham Maslow fully embodied what it means to be human. He became what he advocated for all humanity: the fully self-actualized person.

78. Hoffman, *Right to Be Human*, 334.

Chapter 4

Experience and Encounter

The Improbable Spiritual Journey of Carl Rogers

[When] I am closest to my inner, intuitive self, when I am somehow in touch with the unknown in me, when perhaps I am in a slightly altered state of consciousness, then whatever I do seems to be full of healing. Then, my *presence* is releasing and helpful to the other . . . [and] it seems that my inner spirit has reached out and touched the inner spirit of the other. Our relationship transcends itself and becomes part of something larger. Profound growth and healing and energy are present.

—Carl Rogers, *A Way of Being*

In contrast to Abraham Maslow's "prophetic thundering," Carl Rogers offered a quiet, tentative, almost ethereal presence that worked its magic slowly, almost imperceptibly. He was the counselor's counselor, intent on providing a warm, nurturing atmosphere within which the client might experience his or her own capabilities and personal significance, thereby seeing the self as one worthy of personal growth and fulfillment. He was the teacher who created lasting relationships of mutual respect with his students. And he was the community developer who, after performing his magic, exited quietly, leaving the group somewhat uncertain about what they had experienced, yet energized and empowered—and likely believing they had figured it out all by themselves. More than any of the thinkers reviewed in this work, Carl Rogers emphasized the importance of one's unique, personal experience—in counseling, teaching, group formation, community development, moral decision-making, indeed, all dimensions of life. Appropriately, it was a personal experience that first led me to Rogers—even though I was unaware until some dozen or so years later that it was to him and to his approach to working with people that I was being led.

In April 1991, I attended a three-day training program designed to address the problems of the contemporary American family and to empower the participants—largely marriage and family therapists, clinical social workers, and a scattering of men and women in ministry—to work with parents and teachers on developing more healthy family and school relationships. At the time, I was a school principal who had long observed the correlation between what was going on in the classroom and what was occurring at home, and although I believed I had the skills to address the former, I was feeling inadequate about the latter. Somewhere I had gotten the notion that it was my responsibility to address the latter, so off I went to the training. The reference to an experience as having changed one's life has become too commonplace to communicate the desired effect. Nonetheless, no other expression will do: that training altered the direction of my life, beginning a process that would result in my leaving education and embracing a new career, one I had never before considered: counseling.

Titled "Developing Capable People" and created and led by psychologist H. Stephen Glenn, the training challenged us, within the safety of a structured and supportive environment, to confront our learned behaviors about interpersonal relations and open ourselves to healthier, more affirming, and more effective approaches. It quickly became apparent to all of us that what we were learning went far beyond the reasons we had signed up for the training, whether it was to enhance one's counseling effectiveness, to provide better support services for the community, or, in my case, to address family issues more effectively within the school environment. What we were learning affected all dimensions of our interpersonal lives, and by the third day we were on fire, poised to change the world, one person at a time. Both the medium (the workshop leader and the group dynamics he helped us create) and the message (a new way of being and working with people, one centered on deep listening, authentic sharing, supportive feedback, personal affirmation, and encouragement) were exactly what so many of us in attendance needed, whether we were aware of it going in or not.

On the morning of that third and final day, a young lady, who hailed from a traditional Catholic background, asked to share her experience upon arriving home the previous evening. She related that she had described to her husband in exquisite detail everything that she was learning at the training with such enthusiasm and at such length that the husband, somewhat concerned, stopped her midsentence and asked, "But are you still Catholic?"

Each of us at that training could relate to her story: what we were learning was transformational, paradigm-shifting, nothing less than a new way of being. A few in attendance, who represented a particularly insular religious tradition (not unlike that of the home in which Rogers was raised), were unable to fit this new thinking into their understanding of how the world works and how we are to relate to one another, and they left disoriented and confused. But for most of us, our old ways of thinking, feeling, and relating would no longer do. We were affected at the most profound level of our beings, at our spiritual cores, and things would have to change.

Brian Thorne, emeritus professor of counseling at the University of East Anglia in the UK, observes in his intimate biography *Carl Rogers* that "the 'secular' experience of person-centered groups, in particular, seems for some people to open up a channel into spiritual terrain which has previously remained unexplored and whose very existence had been denied."[1] Whether or not that terrain had been previously unexplored by the participants, most of us left that training—in effect, a person-centered group—with a new appreciation of the spiritual and the interpersonal.

In *A Way of Being*, published in 1980, seven years before his death, Carl Rogers offers a reflection on his long life, adding frank commentary on both his successes and his failings and, directly pertinent to the theme of this book, insights into his newly developing thoughts on the spiritual dimension of life. He introduces his musings on spirituality by first discussing consciousness, which he understands from an evolutionary perspective: Consciousness is the natural development of the life force coming to fruition within the human person. It is the fullness of our growth potential, of the "actualizing tendency," Rogers's term for the internal organic drive, the directional tendency inherent within the organism that points toward fulfillment of one's nature. However, recent research—and Rogers mentions Stanislav Grof, one of the founders, along with Abraham Maslow, of transpersonal psychology—has led to an "advance beyond the ordinary level of consciousness . . . that picture[s] the individual self as being dissolved in a whole area of higher values, especially beauty, harmony, and love . . . confirming the mystics' experience of union with the universal."[2]

Rogers adds that he, too, experiences those phenomena, particularly in his work with clients and intensive, person-centered groups. In words suggesting nothing short of a shift in how one views the world, Rogers notes

1. Thorne, *Carl Rogers*, 113.
2. Rogers, *Way of Being*, 128.

that when he is at his best as a therapist or facilitator of groups, he encounters a fourth condition of therapeutic change, beyond his signature triad of personal congruence, unconditional positive regard, and empathy:

> [When] I am closest to my inner, intuitive self, when I am somehow in touch with the unknown in me, when perhaps I am in a slightly altered state of consciousness, then whatever I do seems to be full of healing. Then, my *presence* is releasing and helpful to the other . . . [and] it seems that my inner spirit has reached out and touched the inner spirit of the other. Our relationship transcends itself and becomes part of something larger. Profound growth and healing and energy are present.[3]

Continuing, Rogers quotes one of the participants in his groups, who observed how he had

> found it to be a profound spiritual experience . . . [in which he] felt the oneness of spirit in the community . . . [and] the power of the "life force" that infuses each of us.[4]

Biographer Thorne said of Rogers that "the clue to the essential continuity in his development as a person lies in the hiddenness of his spiritual pilgrimage,"[5] suggesting that Rogers's spirituality was subtler, one that came to fruition of its own accord and in its own good time. Thorne, who references Howard Kirschenbaum's biography, *On Becoming Carl Rogers*, throughout, had the advantage of time: Kirschenbaum's book was written in 1979, eight years before Rogers's death, while Thorne's was written in 1992 (with a revision in 2003), five years after. Additionally, Thorne had known Rogers intimately during the last ten years of his life and had witnessed his movement toward the spiritual more closely. It is to Thorne that we owe thanks for illuminating Rogers's spiritual journey.

However Rogers's spiritual development could be described, it was certainly of a different sort from the living, breathing, ethnic Judaism of Abraham Maslow, a Judaism that any efforts to dismiss would have been erased with every look in the mirror. Maslow's was an identity of skin and bones, culture and heritage, language and custom, myth and song and story. It could be denigrated but never denied. We will observe the effects of this influence again in our chapter on Erich Fromm.

Though not as pervasive and visceral as Maslow's and Fromm's Judaism, Rogers's American Protestantism nonetheless formed him, giving him

3. Rogers, *Way of Being*, 129 (emphasis in original).

4. Rogers, *Way of Being*, 129–30.

5. Thorne, *Carl Rogers*, 21.

something to both cling to and rebel against, as we all need in our youth. In his short yet impactful biography, Thorne highlighted Rogers's development from the harsh evangelistic Protestantism of his upbringing, through his dismissal of his parents' religion, and, in his final years, to a discovery of the spiritual, mystical dimension of life, characteristically through his own personal experiences.

Thorne identified three turning points in Rogers's spiritual journey—a trip to China during his college years; a near emotional breakdown related to the counseling of a woman suffering from psychosis (specifically, schizophrenia); and the death of his wife, Helen. Through the China trip, Rogers experienced the universal connectedness of people from widely different backgrounds and the inadequacy of the insular religion of his youth to accommodate that diversity. Through the woman afflicted with psychosis, he got in touch with his own personal struggles with connection and—as a result of entering counseling himself with a therapist trained in his own methods—with the power of healing. Finally, with Helen's death and through the influence of his daughter, Natalie, he began to open himself to the mystical and spiritual—tentatively, no doubt.

A SEPARATIST FAMILY

Carl Rogers was a Midwesterner, born in 1902 in a Chicago suburb to parents whose roots in America are traced to the seventeenth century. In that regard, he differed markedly from most of the significant psychological trailblazers of his time, who were mainly of European Jewish ancestry. Rogers's ancestry can be traced to the English Separatist movement, the most representative images of which are the Pilgrims of 1620 and the English Civil War of the 1640s.

The word *separatism* describes Carl's upbringing as well as it does his religious roots—the family preached and practiced a sense of being of the elect, an elitist separatism from what it considered the temptations of the world, among which were dancing, drinking, theatergoing, card-playing, and engaging in premarital sexual activities. In Rogers's own words from *A Way of Being*, written at age seventy-eight, "In a narrowly fundamentalist religious home, I introjected the value attitudes toward others that were held by my parents"[6]—as, of course, we all do in our youth. The message he and his siblings received about those outside the family was "to keep away from any close communication with them and to live your life within the family: 'Come ye out from among them and be ye separate' is a good biblical

6. Rogers, *Way of Being*, 27.

text to follow."[7] He added that he was not sure he really believed what he had learned, but he knew he acted out of those learnings.

Separatism, which primarily evolved into the Congregational and Baptist churches and tended toward a fundamentalist Evangelicalism combined with a prototypically American Protestant work ethic, affected all dimensions of Rogers's upbringing. His was a family environment characterized by rituals and routines, from family meals and family worship to the ever-present chores around the farm, experiences often absent in today's families. Prayer and Bible-reading were daily family activities of the highest priority, with productive work a close second.

It was also a family of love—not the intimate love that Carl so desperately needed but a patriarchal/matriarchal love that kept things together. It was a substantial, character-forming love that affected him both positively and negatively. Brian Thorne, who saw deep religious strivings in Rogers throughout his life, wondered what course his life would have taken had the family atmosphere been characterized by a more embracing theology and less separatist religious experience. Perhaps he would have become a "much-loved pastor and theologian whose life could have transformed the face of the Church."[8]

Carl was the fourth of six children. His parents, both educated, enjoyed a long family association with the University of Wisconsin, from which his father had graduated with an engineering degree and which would become Carl's alma mater as well. As a result of both personal temperament and the family's disinclination to engage with others, Carl was a lonely child who, like Maslow, took comfort in books. The move thirty miles west to a spacious farm—a decision made at least in part on the desire to insulate the children further from the world's temptations—did nothing to alleviate Carl's loneliness or his craving for intimacy, an emptiness that he would not be able to articulate until much later in life. He reported only a single high school date—to a requisite class dinner.

Lacking close interpersonal relationships, Carl occupied his time with nature and science. He was fascinated with the exotic moths that inhabited the woods around his farm, breeding them, learning the life cycle from moth to caterpillar, and waiting patiently for nature to take its course. He also raised chickens and livestock and pored through Frank Barron Morrison's classic *Feeds and Feeding: A Handbook for the Student and the Stockman*, learning everything he could about experiments, control groups, randomizing procedures, and hypothesis testing. One could have imagined a long and

7. Rogers, *Way of Being*, 28.

8. Rogers, *Way of Being*, 28.

productive life as an agricultural scientist; it would have been much more difficult to imagine a life as a world-famous psychologist who craved intimacy and focused on interpersonal communication and personal growth.

COLLEGE YEARS—THE WORLD OPENS

After high school graduation, Carl followed the predictable path by entering the University of Wisconsin, where he dormed with his brother Ross and majored in scientific agriculture. However, in short order, events began to impinge on the trajectory of Carl's life. An agricultural group he joined introduced him to the camaraderie of like-minded friends who shared a common interest. More significantly, the group was led by a professor who encouraged the students to assume leadership and make their own decisions. Carl would later refer to what he experienced in that class as his first exposure to facilitative leadership, a skill for which he would become world-renowned.

He also became involved with YMCA meetings, camps, and conventions, creating further opportunities for conviviality and leadership experiences, both of which he found himself readily, and at times surprisingly, drawn to. Carl's personal growth in college took a life-changing turn when he met Helen Elliott, with whom he discovered that "private thoughts and dreams of the future could actually be shared on a mutual basis with another person."[9] In just a few years, Helen would become his wife. In addition, he decided on a career in ministry and changed his major to history, hoping that would be more suitable for ministerial life.

As Carl became more comfortable with the enjoyment and naturalness of having friends outside the family and his experiences in student leadership, the first of the three spiritual turning points noted by Brian Thorne occurred: he was selected as one of only twelve American students to participate in a World Student Christian Federation-sponsored six-month trip to China. One can only imagine the impact on a college student, whose life had been insular, predictable, and uneventful, upon finding himself interacting with hundreds of other students from around the world in a culture so radically different from his own. Indeed, if this trip was intended, at least in part, as an evangelizing venture, something akin to the opposite was happening: Carl was being "evangelized" by others and by all that he experienced, including the independence—intellectual, psychological, and spiritual—that he was encountering. Thankfully, he shared his thoughts and feelings in his diary and in letters to Helen and his family, all of which reveal

9. Rogers, *Way of Being*, 31.

an introspective young man deeply committed to processing and learning from his experiences. Experiential learning would become Rogers's lifelong friend.

Among the many things Rogers learned on the China trip was that "it is possible for sincere and honest people to have very different religious beliefs and perceptions."[10] In addition, his social conscience was developing as he confronted the grinding poverty of Chinese factory workers and others he encountered, and he possessed enough wisdom and maturity to recognize that this existed in his own country as well. As a result, he came to see the value of religion far more in its actions than its beliefs; indeed, he began to question whether the beliefs were essential to the actions, and whether one needed to believe in religion at all to be a person of virtue.

In a remarkably short space of time, Carl Rogers was confronting deeper and more challenging questions about ultimate matters, life's larger concerns, to which he was not finding answers to in his religious formation. And the more he asked and pondered, the more he doubted the value of religion itself. After all, what does religion have to offer for finding solutions to society's ills that is not already being taught in the more socially progressive schools? Further, how can one reconcile the distinction between the scientific approach to responding to social ills, which relies on experiential learning, and the answers provided by religion, which seem to be fixated on "eternal truths" that it is unwilling to question?

Placing priority on truth discovered through experience rather than on dogma proclaimed by authority, he began questioning everything he had previously learned. The floodgates had opened, freeing him to think the hitherto unthinkable. Much in line with many on the outskirts of traditional Christianity then and now, he began to question the uniqueness of the divinity of Jesus, directing his attention instead toward the *person* of Jesus and seeing him as a man who came closer to being Godlike, or to being God, than any other—something of a model for the humanist person. Interestingly, all this thinking appeared to flow quite naturally for Carl; it "did not involve much of the internal conflict, guilt, and rebellion that often accompany achieving independence from one's parents."[11]

Unsurprisingly, Carl's letters to his parents scandalized them. He was forming new—and to them, dangerous—ideas about God and one's relationship to God. He was learning, as we all must, that the microcosm of the family is just that, a tiny subset of all that is and all that can be thought and imagined. Upon his return home, he and Helen decided to marry

10. Thorne, *Carl Rogers*, 4.

11. Kirschenbaum, *On Becoming Carl Rogers*, 25.

and, against their parents' wishes that they wait until they were financially settled, did so in just two months. Following their wedding, they moved to New York City, where Carl would attend Union Theological Seminary, reportedly the most liberal in the country. From the insularity of the family farm to the largest city in the United States, the city that epitomized more than any other the liberal, free-thinking lifestyle his parents feared, and then on to the most progressive seminary in America, Carl Rogers's journey had in a few short years taken him to a place as different as one could imagine from that of his upbringing. He was becoming his own person.

For some seminarians, immersion in a progressive theological learning environment might lead to a coveted role as a professor at a like-minded university or the pastorate of a large metropolitan church. But Carl, like many others at Union, as it is familiarly known, found himself increasingly uncomfortable in a situation where he was required to believe certain things that were not directly experienced. The value of one's experiences was becoming increasingly foundational for Rogers, personally and professionally, as he became more conscious of who he was and what he believed.

To respond to this need for a more experientially based program, Rogers began taking courses at the nearby Teachers College of Columbia University. Enjoying what he was learning there, he left the seminary and enrolled at Columbia in psychology, where the dominant orientation was behaviorism, and the methodology was scientific and statistical. Carl excelled, even developing a test for measuring personality adjustment in children that continued to be sold and used throughout his lifetime. He earned both his MA and PhD at Columbia.

EARLY PROFESSIONAL WORK AND OHIO STATE—FINDING A SENSE OF PURPOSE

Upon graduation, Rogers was awarded a fellowship at the Institute of Child Guidance, which favored a psychoanalytic approach in its counseling. Among the many things he learned about himself through that experience was a disinclination toward the behaviorism he had studied at Columbia and the psychoanalysis practiced at the institute; however, as was his style, he appreciated and benefited from his experiences with both.

In 1928, he was awarded a position at the Rochester (New York) Society for the Prevention of Cruelty to Children, where he would remain for twelve years, eventually becoming director. His experiences in Rochester led to his first book, *The Clinical Treatment of the Problem Child*, published in 1939, in which he focused mainly on the process of the therapy employed rather than specifically on child guidance—on the *how* more than on the *what.* At a time when counseling was still a new and untested concept, Rogers believed it needed to be subjected to rigorous scientific inquiry to identify what worked and what did not. Impatient with careless thinking and uncritical acceptance of inherited opinions, he needed to verify the processes that produced the desired results for himself.

A critical event in Rogers's growth as a therapist was his encounter with the mother of a child with whom he was working who casually inquired if he would work with her on her own personal concerns, not regarding her parenting. Up to that point, Rogers had focused on working with children; any interaction with their parents was directed toward addressing the children's needs. In working with the woman on her own personal issues, Rogers discovered that if he directed his efforts toward listening intently to what she was saying, a sense of internal peace, even insight, would occur—for both therapist and client. Through this and other experiences at Rochester, Rogers learned the importance of methodology over theory. More importantly, he began directing his thoughts toward forging his own path in the therapeutic world. In 1939, his growing reputation having preceded him, he was offered a full professorship at Ohio State.

Rogers wasted no time adjusting to his new position. He dove into teaching, counseling, supervising, writing, establishing the first university practicum program in America, and rapidly developing his own distinctive approach to psychotherapy, which was characterized by empathic listening. He quickly developed a reputation as an energetic, innovative professor with a pronounced love for his students, whom he insisted on treating as adults; his love for those students would be fully reciprocated.

Rogers's successes at Ohio State led to a lecture invitation at the University of Minnesota in December 1940, which he titled "Newer Concepts in Psychotherapy." A critique of directive therapy, it was Rogers's first public lecture on his new ideas about replacing the current problem-solving focus of therapy with an encouragement model that highlighted the client's own developing resources. Rogers credited that lecture as seminal to the formulation of client-centered therapy, "the first indigenous American challenge to psychoanalysis."[12] In emphasizing self-reflection, growth, the emotional dimension, attention to the present moment, and the therapeutic relationship itself, Rogers was proposing a groundbreaking approach to therapy, one that flowed seamlessly out of his own personal experience. In today's parlance, he was finding his voice. And he would speak that voice with the

12. Taylor, *Shadow Culture*, 262.

passion of an evangelist; as his brother Walter commented, "[Both] Carl and Mother are somewhat Billy Graham types at heart."[13]

Two years after moving to Ohio State, Rogers published his second book, *Counseling and Psychotherapy: Newer Concepts in Practice*, which received praise from Irvin Yalom, noted existentialist and emeritus professor of psychiatry at Stanford University, for helping "to shape the future of a humanistically oriented therapeutic approach."[14] In that 1942 book was his first published reference to the word *client*; it also included the first published transcript of an entire course of therapy.

Having identified the approach of client-centered therapy, Rogers set it as his task to scientifically evaluate the process's effectiveness. In the first fully recorded, transcribed, and published therapeutic sessions in history, involving the use of 78-rpm disks that had to be replaced every three minutes over a period of fifty hours, Rogers set the standard for intensity of purpose and persistent work ethic, no doubt traits that were honed on the family farm. Reflection of feelings—the core of this emerging psychotherapy—and Rogers's soft voice and welcoming presence helped to establish nondirective, client-centered therapy as both a novel and well-tested approach worthy of attention. And attention it got, along with fame—except from the psychological establishment, a continuing thorn in Rogers's side and a repetitive theme in the history of humanistic psychology.

GLORY AND DISAPPOINTMENT

In 1945, Rogers accepted a position at the University of Chicago, to which he was recruited to establish a counseling center, both for the students and the larger community. Though not yet a household name, he was making his mark in academia for his teaching and counseling prowess, as well as for his writing. By then, he and Helen had been married twenty-one years and had two children, David, nineteen, and Natalie, seventeen. For Carl Rogers at age forty-three, life was good.

The Chicago years, a period of rapid professional growth for Rogers, were filled with teaching, counseling, administrating, serving on councils, writing books and articles, giving speeches, and receiving honors. Yet with all that he was doing, in biographer Kirschenbaum's succinct statement, "[most] important[ly] he was a counselor, a therapist."[15] He saw his work with his clients as providing a living laboratory through which he could

13. Kirschenbaum, *On Becoming Carl Rogers*, 32.

14. Irvin Yalom, in Rogers, *Way of Being*, ix.

15. Kirschenbaum, *On Becoming Carl Rogers*, 156.

continuously evaluate the effectiveness of the concepts that were becoming increasingly clearer to him. These concepts, which would become synonymous with his name, were congruence (genuineness, authenticity, transparency in one's feelings), unconditional positive regard (acceptance, receiving the person as he or she is), and empathic understanding (making an effort to see the client's world through his or her eyes and accurately communicating that to the client).

None of this suggests that Rogers's approach to counseling was passive. Within this atmosphere of congruence, unconditional positive regard, and empathy, Rogers had no hesitancy in offering comments to his clients. In *On Becoming a Person*, he reports that what his clients found most helpful was when he "clarified and openly stated feelings which the client had been approaching hazily and hesitatingly."[16] The key is that what Rogers offered was *the clients' own feelings* reflected back to them in a manner that honored both the feelings and the clients. His goal was not to offer explanations to his clients; rather, it was to help them better formulate their feelings, thereby taking greater ownership of them.

Undergirding these concepts was the emphasis on counselor attitude over technique and the conviction that clients possess the inherent ability to comprehend their struggles and move toward self-actualization, toward fulfilling their potentialities. That conviction regarding the client's capabilities was a self-imposed limitation on Rogers's counseling: in working with clients, he assumed what he referred to as a state of psychological contact in the counseling relationship, meaning that the client is capable of giving full and informed consent to the relationship and that he or she can be fully present—not entering counseling under duress, or suffering from psychosis, or experiencing learning difficulties that would limit involvement, etc. Of course, not all who would benefit from counseling would fit those requirements. Absent those limitations, however, if the client experiences the counselor's congruence, unconditional positive regard, and empathy, change will occur.

Rogers's therapeutic approach evolved out of the person he was. It was a felicitous congruence of personality and vocation characterized by his efforts to enter the client's subjective world and reflect what he observed as accurately as possible. In addition, he exuded unwavering optimism about the nature of the person that constitutes "a revolutionary departure from almost all of Western tradition—a more optimistic view than Western culture from the Old Testament through Freud has held on this subject."[17] That

16. Rogers, *On Becoming a Person*, 43.

17. Kirschenbaum, *Carl Rogers Reader*, 399.

optimism fueled both his work ethic and his personal life: he is described by biographer Kirschenbaum as a hard-driving, disciplined advocate for what he believed to be right and one who demonstrated deep caring in his relationships. As an introvert, he found the slow, quiet, intimate process of one-on-one therapy to be a perfect fit for his personality. Concomitantly, outside the counseling room, he often came across as distant, with awkwardness at social gatherings and a strong need for privacy—the introvert's personal cross to bear.

Rogers, growing in stature with each new publication, was now positioned to advance person-centered psychotherapy as the most studied, researched, and vetted counseling methodology ever developed. But first, he had to confront his own "dark night of the soul," which materialized in the form of a near mental breakdown resulting from his work with a particularly demanding schizophrenic client. Biographer Thorne identified this second major turning point, which was occasioned not so much by Rogers's work with the troublesome client but by his own experience as a person in therapy.

Wisely knowing when to seek counseling for himself, he did so through a therapist he had trained. As a result, he received the level of empathic, attentive care that he offered his clients—but, significantly, he had not experienced it in his family of origin. If Rogers had any doubts about the value of his therapeutic approach, they were erased, and he emerged from that experience with an increasing appreciation for what he was discovering and its power to heal. As Thorne notes, "It is not, perhaps, too fanciful to suggest that Carl Rogers was led to create client-centred therapy because he himself so badly needed the kind of healing it offered."[18] He learned that his work healing others also applied to himself, "that at the deepest level [he] was by no means free of the insidious conditioning of his childhood and adolescence,"[19] which had resulted in a profound sense of unworthiness and self-rejection. His abandonment of Christianity and all institutional religion was finalized at this time, according to Thorne, and only in the final years of his life, with the death of Helen, would he open himself again to the spiritual, including the possibility of life after death.

Rogers refined his thinking on congruence, unconditional positive regard, and empathic understanding throughout his life but never wavered from the conviction that they are both necessary and sufficient for therapeutic growth. When the client experiences the counselor's relating as a real person (rather than as a distant expert), accepting the client regardless of

18. Thorne, *Carl Rogers*, 15.

19. Thorne, *Carl Rogers*, 22.

what is being presented, and making an effort to enter the client's subjective world, the client gets more in touch with his or her inner strength and self-worth and is more able to confront whatever challenges are presented. Rogers argued that those attitudes of authenticity, positive regard, and deep, empathic listening for understanding were both essential and sufficient for the client to grow. Nothing more than these attitudes on the part of the counselor was needed for therapeutic change, and anything less would be insufficient.

During his twelve years at Chicago, Rogers permanently shifted "from the *method* to the *attitudes* to *relationship* as the key ingredient in the therapeutic process."[20] Through congruence, unconditional positive regard, and empathy, he would forever change the world of psychotherapy. For Rogers as therapist, what mattered were the necessary and sufficient conditions of personality change, not the particular theoretical orientation; for Rogers as scientist, it was more about what works: "Facts are friendly" was the mantra that governed his ongoing commitment to research on effective therapy.

Years before these concepts were clarified in his mind, Rogers, through his close attention to work on the farm and later in his own garden, learned that there are identifiable conditions for growth. Provide those healthy conditions—water, sunshine, nutrient-rich soil—and plants will grow; deny them, and they won't. Likewise, persons need growth-enhancing conditions, which he identified as authenticity in relationships, mutual appreciation and liking, and being listened to. He believed that he had discovered how change occurs:

> Without knowing it, I had expressed an idea whose time had come . . . the individual has within himself vast resources for self-understanding, for altering his self-concept, his attitudes, and his self-directed behavior—and that these resources can be tapped if only a definable climate of facilitative psychological attitudes can be provided.[21]

In 1951, Rogers published his third book, *Client-Centered Therapy*, a significant challenge to the dominant psychoanalysis and behaviorism of the time. It was met with wide acclaim—except within the psychological establishment. Shortly after that, he served as editor of a fourth book, *Psychotherapy and Personality Change*. And in 1953, he and two colleagues received the first Distinguished Scientific Contribution Award from the American Psychological Association in recognition of the quality of the research they had conducted, which resulted in client-centered therapy being

20. Kirschenbaum, *On Becoming Carl Rogers*, 202 (emphasis in original).

21. Rogers, *Way of Being*, 49.

supported by more research than any other counseling orientation at the time. Rogers was deeply affected by this award, as it recognized the value of his methodological diligence and scientific orientation. The following year, his star continuing to rise, Rogers was offered a full professorship at the University of Wisconsin at Madison, where he would work in both the psychology and psychiatry departments.

At the top of his profession, Carl Rogers left Chicago for Wisconsin, ostensibly to have a more significant impact on an expanding field of interests. Like Maslow before him, he evidenced "a crusading spirit which saw in the Wisconsin post an irresistible opportunity for spreading the message."[22] He was also attracted to the promise of being able to work in both the psychology and psychiatry departments. Much to his dismay, however, he discovered that if it is difficult to navigate the politics in one university department, it is next to impossible to do so in two.

The Wisconsin years did not go well for Rogers. Years later, he placed significant blame on himself, noting that he had violated one of his own most treasured principles: he had, in keeping with his custom, given over authority to the group he was working with but then tried to pull it back when things appeared to be going astray. Discouraged by his experiences, he resigned from the university and accepted a position at the Western Behavioral Sciences Institute in La Jolla, California, formally ending all further association with the academic world. In 1964, one year after leaving Wisconsin and assuming his new position, he was named Humanist of the Year by the American Humanist Association.

Carl Rogers and Martin Buber: Person-Centered Counseling Meets the I-Thou Relationship

Between the publications of *Client-Centered Therapy* and, a decade later, *On Becoming a Person*, Carl Rogers was invited to the University of Michigan to meet and converse with one of the most treasured and enduring spiritual and philosophical icons of the twentieth century, Martin Buber, known worldwide for his promulgation of the I-Thou relationship. Buber's classic formulation of God's personal relationship with humanity and our relationships with each other, titled *I and Thou*, was published in 1923; the dialogue between Rogers and Buber took place in 1957. Who was Martin Buber, and how did these two giants in their respective fields come to share a stage in Ann Arbor, Michigan?

22. Thorne, *Carl Rogers*, 16.

Born in Vienna in 1878, Buber was a full generation ahead of the humanistic psychologists. Like many European Jews of his generation, he was educated both within the traditions of his ancient faith and the European intellectual corpus characterized by philosophically oriented thinkers such as Kant, Kierkegaard, Nietzsche, Goethe, and Freud. In addition, he was much influenced by the Hassidic tradition, which "emphasizes man's direct, mystical, spontaneous and joyful relationship with God,"[23] an understanding of relationship that would find its way into his own classic formulation some years later.

Upon Hitler's rise to power in Germany, Buber, unlike so many of his generation, fled not to America but to Jerusalem, arriving in 1938, ten years before Israel declared itself a nation-state. An early Zionist, he became prominent in Israel's formation, specifically advocating for a national self-definition along the lines of a "believing humanism"—a Jewish state founded on humanistic principles. Those principles extended to the sociopolitical realm: Rogers's biographer Howard Kirschenbaum, in *Carl Rogers: Dialogues*, notes that before even arriving in Israel and throughout his life, Buber was a consistent advocate for the rights of the Palestinians and that upon his death "Arab students at the Hebrew University laid a wreath at his bier as he lay in state."[24] Once settled in Israel, Buber became a professor of social philosophy at Hebrew University.

In 1963, Buber was awarded the Erasmus Prize, bestowed by the Praemium Erasmianum Foundation in the Netherlands in honor of the sixteenth-century Dutch humanist and awarded to one who represents the humanistic spirit through "an exceptional contribution to culture, society, or social science."[25] Through his presentation in receipt of the award, titled "Believing Humanism," Buber advocated for a worldview in which humanity and faith relate to each other not as two separate realms but as spheres that "penetrate each other . . . work together . . . are so centrally related to each other that we may say our faith has our humanity as its foundation, and our humanity has our faith as its foundation."[26]

At a time when humanistic psychology was dominating the psychological and psychotherapeutic conversations, offering a largely secular path to growth and self-actualization, Buber advocated for the recognition of God's intimate relationship with humankind and the depth of the person-to-person relationships that might ensue from that. The message to his

23. Kirschenbaum and Henderson, *Carl Rogers*, 41.

24. Kirschenbaum and Henderson, *Carl Rogers*, 43.

25. www.erasmusprijs.org.

26. Buber, *Believing Humanism*, 117.

fellow humanists was a warning of the consequences of failing to recognize the importance of that relationship: a world in which "a type of man predominates who prefers to observe and make use of the beings whom he encounters on his life way instead of turning soul and deed toward them."[27] Noting the existential dangers of the atomic age and all it has wrought, he wondered if the potential for crisis might serve as the incentive for humankind to turn away from its current trajectory and embrace his call for a new humanism, a specifically *believing* humanism.

Needless to say, the humanism Buber espoused was not the same as the humanism of Erasmus, much less of contemporary humanists. Between Erasmus (late fifteenth and early sixteenth centuries) and Buber, the West gave birth to the Enlightenment, with its emphasis on liberty and autonomy, both personal and political, and those basic concepts of classical liberalism were incorporated over time within the humanistic sense of self. And whereas contemporary humanists are largely nontheistic, Buber spoke consistently of the centrality of the place of God in our lives.

That being said, we can discern from Buber's 1963 address in reception of the Erasmus Prize a number of commonalities with humanistic psychologists then and now. In a chapter titled "Religion and God's Rule" in *A Believing Humanism*, Buber differentiates between the biblical understanding of the kingdom of God and religion as he observes it in the present day. Emphasizing that "Moses, the prophets, and Jesus do not mean a religion but a kingdom, a condition of the world in accord with God," he observes that "one can have a great deal of religion and be far from God, even godless."[28] Fully and freely displaying his frustration with much of what passes for religion, he notes that the "largest part of what is today called religion is perverted . . . in its whole structure."[29] And echoing the insights of Maslow, Frankl, and others that happiness, contrary to the United States Declaration of Independence, cannot be pursued directly but, rather, must ensue from living a meaningful and purposeful life, he offers the same caveat about religion: it is not religion that we must pursue, but God; pursue God and perhaps religion will emerge as a pathway toward that; focus only on religion and "what sorts of malformations must come together there!"[30]

Buber exhorts his readers to embrace God wholly, lest the specific form of religion that we substitute for God be lacking and, over time, find its "rituals [replaced] by art, its commands by ethics, its revelations by

27. Kirschenbaum and Henderson, *Carl Rogers*, 121.
28. Buber, *Believing Humanism*, 109.
29. Buber, *Believing Humanism*, 110.
30. Buber, *Believing Humanism*, 110.

science"[31]—just as theorists from Freud through Maslow and Fromm, and many contemporary humanists, have both predicted and, at times, advocated for. Buber's impassioned advocacy for the centrality of God in our lives did not blind him to the very human shortcomings of the religious establishments whose mission it is to promote God's word. Although a committed believer in the God of Israel, he was not slavishly devoted to the rituals and traditions of his faith; according to Southern California-based Old Testament scholar Michael Leo Samuel, "he wasn't the most observant Jew"[32]—as his words above well suggest. Buber closes his speech with words of encouragement to all those who would join him in his efforts to promote a new humanism, one in stark contrast to the form it was taking in his day: "From the land of Erasmus I greet the *believing* humanists in all the world—those who are already active and those who are only ripening."[33]

According to translator Ronald Gregor Smith, the central question Buber raises in his spiritual classic *I and Thou* is "How may I understand my relation with God?"[34] For Buber, "God is one pure relation . . . [who] enters into a direct relation with us men in creative, revealing and redeeming acts, and thus makes it possible for us to enter into direct relation with him."[35] God's relationship with us is the sine qua non of our relationships with others, "essential for the recovery of true humanity in all spheres."[36]

I and Thou is no easy read, as Buber himself confesses in a postscript written some thirty years later, in which he observes that in spite of numerous responses to questions regarding clarification, "it has turned out that by no means everything has been sufficiently clarified. Again and again readers have turned to me to ask about this and that."[37] More than a theological or philosophical work, *I and Thou* is a mystical reflection on God-in-relationship and persons-in-relationship. It moves and affects the reader more than instructs, and it must be experienced with the heart rather than understood by the mind. In the words of translator Smith, *I and Thou* is a poem that "must be read more than once, and its total effect allowed to work on the mind."[38]

31. Buber, *Believing Humanism*, 111.
32. Samuel, "How Does One Build."
33. Buber, *Believing Humanism*, 112 (emphasis added).
34. Buber, *I and Thou*, 7.
35. Buber, *I and Thou*, 124.
36. Buber, *I and Thou*, 8.
37. Buber, *I and Thou*, 116.
38. Buber, *I and Thou*, 10.

Adding to the difficulty in understanding Buber's mystical, spiritual, and theological reflection is the problem of translation, specifically in reference to the English word *Thou* for the German *Du*. Many years ago I read John Steinbeck's *Tortilla Flat*, in which he used *thou* as the translation of the Spanish *tú*, the personal form of address used among friends instead of the more formal *usted*. It came across as awkward and artificial to me, a disruption to the flow of the narrative—no one refers to their friends in English as *thou*! Although *thou* at some point in the history of the English language likely suggested a more personal, more intimate form of address, it has long since lost that meaning and is now used only in reference to God in prayer.

The combined effects of the book's use of the word *thou* as a cognate for *you*, its theological profundity, its poetic rather than prosaic style, and its having being written as a series of reflections rather than as a linear narrative or thesis add to the challenges faced by the contemporary reader. Helpfully, there is a clearly defined structure to the book—it is divided into three parts, the first a definition of the difference between the I-Thou and the I-It relationships, the second somewhat of a commentary on the society in which Buber and his intended audience are living and the various frustrations that society poses toward being in I-Thou relationship, and the third a reflection on the current state of religion. It is in this third part that we find Buber expounding on many of the themes the humanistic psychologists addressed regarding authoritarian, inauthentic forms of religion, as he did in his Erasmus Prize acceptance speech.

Rather than define what I-Thou means, Buber intimates what it looks like, what it feels like: "If I face a human being as my *Thou*, and say the primary word *I-Thou* to him, he is not a thing among things . . . [he is] whole in himself, he is *Thou* and fills the heavens [and] . . . all else lives in *his* light."[39] The I-Thou takes place in the present and it involves the whole being, one to another. There is no object in I-Thou relationships, only two subjects, two persons in the fullness of their being. And the relationship that takes place between the two is not an I and a Thou but an I-Thou, as a single unit, with the hyphen representing the interconnectedness, the unity, the intimacy of the relationship. One is fully engaged in an I-Thou relationship.

For Buber, recognizing the other as *Du*/Thou suggests a relationship of being, intimacy, encountering. When we relate to others as *Thou*, we are offering our full presence to them, accepting them as they are. Recognizing the other as *It*, on the other hand, is about interacting, passing the time, doing business, exchanging information, all somewhat transactional.

39. Buber, *I and Thou*, 23–24 (emphasis in original).

This is not to dismiss the I-It experience, however. It is the stuff of everyday life. When I order my *caffe misto* at the local coffee shop each morning and the barista and I exchange casual greetings, that serves as no more than an I-It experience. Not much occurs in that exchange except a credit card and a perfectly made *misto*, for which I am most grateful. But we have not touched each other; we have not encountered the being of each other; we have done little more than "pass the time of day," hopefully in a manner that at least affirms the place of the other in our lives. A world limited to I-It relationships is a world of alienation and loneliness, and the solution is a world that seeks and embraces the I-Thou.

Into this world of Martin Buber and the I-Thou relationship, in 1957, stepped Carl Rogers. At the time of their meeting at the University of Michigan, Rogers was fifty-two and director of the counseling center at the University of Chicago, and Buber, seventy-nine, was professor of philosophy at Hebrew University in Jerusalem. The conversation that ensued was initiated and moderated by Maurice Friedman, philosophy professor at Sarah Lawrence College in Bronxville, New York, and author of *Martin Buber: The Life of Dialogue*, who took advantage of the opportunity presented by a conference on Buber's work to bring Buber and Rogers together.

The dialogue between Buber and Rogers serves well as an example of what can be accomplished when conversation is guided by the quest for mutual understanding. These men came from distinctly different backgrounds and perspectives, the one a nonreligious psychotherapeutic innovator and proponent of a counseling relationship based on the equality between persons and the other a man of deep faith whose closeness to God, and whose prescription for humanity, is epitomized through the intimacy of I-Thou. Their differences notwithstanding, both were committed to fostering relationships characterized by personal authenticity and respect for the personhood of the other—Buber through the I-Thou relationship and Rogers through "a way of being" first identified in the counseling office and, through the years, expanded to include all realms of interpersonal relations from parenting and education to international affairs.

Rogers opened the conversation—after first apologizing for any impertinence in his words—by inquiring how Buber could have formulated an approach to interpersonal relationship that is as intimate as the I-Thou without having had formal experience as a therapist. Working under the assumption that the only path to relationship that touches the inner core of the other is through the conditions fostered in person-centered counseling, Rogers was curious to know how Buber, not having been a psychotherapist, had come to learn so deeply about interpersonal relationships. True to his commitment to person-centered relationship as "a way of being," the ever-curious Rogers was intent upon getting to know Buber as a unique, subjective person and learning about the processes and experiences through which his ideas were formed.

With that opening, the dialogue proceeded apace. Buber responded that he too had a background in psychology, having studied under the tutelage of Eugen Bleuler, an associate of both Freud and Jung and the coiner of the word *schizophrenia*, adding that through the years he had experienced "a certain inclination to meet people . . . [and] to change if possible something in the *other*, but also to let me be changed by him."[40] He also referenced an experience of losing a friend to political violence after the close of the First World War that changed his approach to working with people—away from intellectualism and toward a more experiential approach, one more focused on being with the other and experiencing the other's personhood.

The topic of discussion having been set—the experience of relationship in both person-centered counseling and the I-Thou relationship—and the common ground on which they stood defined, Rogers and Buber explored what differences, if any, exist. Rogers began by describing the person-centered therapeutic relationship in terms of subjectivity of experiencing, transparency, acceptance of who the other is, and the clients' sensing of those attitudes on the part of the therapist, then asked Buber how that description fits with his own ideas regarding the meeting of two persons in an I-Thou relationship. Buber's response came in the form of a challenge to Rogers, one that cast doubt that the counseling relationship, even one characterized by transparency, unconditional acceptance, and empathic understanding, could be equivalent to the I-Thou relationship, which assumes the complete equality of persons. Rogers countered that his own experience in counseling suggests "a real sense of equality between us . . . a meeting of two persons on an equal basis,"[41] particularly in moments of real change. Buber, testing the limits of Rogers's confidence, questioned whether this ability to reach full equality can extend to work with psychotics, specifically those suffering with schizophrenia. And Rogers, after cautiously noting that his opinion on this is opposed by many in the field, asserted that "there is no difference in the relationship that I form with a normal person . . . I don't really feel any difference . . . there is this same kind of meeting of persons no matter what the psychiatric label."[42]

To Buber's response that Rogers's motivation to help the client, which drives the therapeutic session, is not necessarily reciprocated, thereby not

40. Kirschenbaum and Henderson, *Carl Rogers*, 46 (emphasis in original).

41. Kirschenbaum and Henderson, *Carl Rogers*, 51–52.

42. Kirschenbaum and Henderson, *Carl Rogers*, 53.

constituting what takes place in the I-Thou relationship, Rogers contended that his intent is less about offering assistance and more about mutual understanding: the *meeting* of the two persons is paramount, not the *helping*, which is only a by-product. And in that there *is* reciprocity: "I am able to see this individual as he is in that moment and he really senses my understanding and acceptance of him. And that I think is what is reciprocal and is perhaps what produces change . . . what I give him is permission to be [and to be in] relationship to himself."[43] Although Rogers may not have convinced Buber that person-centered counseling, at its best and during its most sublime moments, is an example of the I-Thou relationship, there is no doubt that he believed it himself. And believed it not as an intellectual formulation but as a result of his lived experience.

Rogers then took the opportunity to expand on his experiences in the counseling office, observing that "when you get to what is deepest in the individual, that is the very aspect that can most be trusted to be constructive or to tend toward socialization or toward the development of better interpersonal relationships"[44]—a reference to one of the central principles of humanistic psychology, the forward-moving process of the organism, now being applied to relationship. Buber responds that what he experiences in those moments is not so much the person moving toward personal betterment or advancement—self-actualization, to the humanistic psychologists—but as a "*polar* reality . . . with the worst in him and the best in him . . . dependent on one another,"[45] and his responsibility is "to change the relation between the poles."[46] He adds that the poles he is speaking of "are not good and evil, but rather yes and no, rather acceptance and refusal."[47] For Buber, good and evil are not defined substances but directions on a continuum, and it is the movement toward acceptance, toward the positive pole, that most interests him.

In a concluding statement, Buber returns to the core of the discussion at hand—the comparison of the I-Thou and the person-centered approaches to relationship—by highlighting the distinction between the words *person* and *individual*, the latter signifying mere uniqueness and the former one who is "living really with the world . . . in *real contact*, in real reciprocity with the world in all the points in which the world can meet man."[48] Leaving

43. Kirschenbaum and Henderson, *Carl Rogers*, 55–56.

44. Kirschenbaum and Henderson, *Carl Rogers*, 58.

45. Kirschenbaum and Henderson, *Carl Rogers*, 59 (emphasis in original).

46. Kirschenbaum and Henderson, *Carl Rogers*, 59.

47. Kirschenbaum and Henderson, *Carl Rogers*, 59.

48. Kirschenbaum and Henderson, *Carl Rogers*, 63 (emphasis in original).

no doubt about the importance of the distinction between the I-Thou relationship (and, by extension, the person-centered relationship) and any form of personal interaction that objectifies the other, Buber pronounces, "I am *against* [relating to others as] individuals and *for* [relating to others as] persons"[49]—with which Rogers would no doubt heartily concur.

BEYOND THE COUNSELING OFFICE—ON BECOMING A PERSON

Four years after his dialogue with Martin Buber, Rogers published *On Becoming a Person*, in which he moved beyond a *client-centered* orientation toward one that he now referred to as *person-centered.* It is now about more than therapeutic change—it is about becoming a person, the inherent desire to grow into that which one is meant to be, the "urge which is evident in all organic and human life—to expand, extend, become autonomous, develop, mature."[50] Significantly, this process of "becoming a person" leads "not only toward enhanced *personal* development but in the direction of constructive contribution to *the whole species*."[51]

Rogers made only a brief reference to the I-Thou relationship in *Becoming a Person*, in a chapter titled, significantly, "Persons or Science? A Philosophical Question." After referencing the moral neutrality of scientific knowledge and the responsibility of persons regarding its use, and reiterating the importance of "putting the subjective, existential person, with the values which he holds, at the foundation and the root of the therapeutic relationship and of the scientific relationship," he pronounces that "science too, at its inception, is an I-Thou relationship with a person or persons."[52] That single reference—one that proposes that the I-Thou relationship, like the person-centered relationship, applies to domains well beyond its original application—suggests that Buber's signature insight much affected Carl Rogers.

With each new book, Rogers further developed and expanded his understanding of what makes growth and change possible. In *On Becoming a Person*, the change that is encouraged is one that embraces the full equality of personhood itself. How does this change into full personhood occur, and what are the characteristics of the kind of relationship that can facilitate this growth? The answer lies, Rogers argues, not in the "truth" of a particular philosophy but in the encounter between two people. In a foundational

49. Kirschenbaum and Henderson, *Carl Rogers*, 63 (emphasis original).

50. Rogers, *On Becoming a Person*, 35.

51. Kirschenbaum, *Carl Rogers Reader*, 156 (emphasis added).

52. Rogers, *On Becoming a Person*, 224.

statement that is repeated in different formulations throughout the book, Rogers observes that when the client experiences someone "listening acceptingly to his feelings, he little by little becomes able to listen to himself,"[53] leading to a positive, realistic, mature change in personality and behavior—*the becoming of a person.*

For many, this understanding that personality change follows upon one's experience of acceptance by another is the most profound of Rogers's insights on human nature. In *On Becoming a Person*, Rogers relates what he discovered "from the thousands of hours I have spent working intimately with individuals in personal distress . . . that we cannot change, we cannot move away from what we are, until we thoroughly accept what we are;"[54] it is only when I accept myself just as I am, with all my imperfections, that I can see myself as worthy of change. In conversation with Paul Tillich at Saybrook University some years later, Rogers referenced this "paradox of change" in words that have become something of a mantra in humanistically oriented therapy today: "I can only accept the unacceptable in myself if I feel accepted by the other."[55]

It is no exaggeration to say that Rogers obsessed over the *how* of creating just the right atmosphere within which clients could accept themselves as they are. In a YouTube video titled "Carl Rogers Interviews: Richie," we can witness a five-minute segment of Rogers in a counseling session. He gently welcomes Richie and, after allowing a few seconds of centering, invites him to share his concerns. Leaning into his client, Rogers listens intently, interjecting only to help his client clarify a thought or feeling. This is Carl Rogers in action, doing what he does best: being fully present, fully entering the client's world. At the close of the short video, Rogers summarizes what he has learned about therapeutic change: "If I can create the proper climate, the proper relationship, the proper conditions, a process of therapeutic movement will almost inevitably occur in my client."[56] Those by now familiar descriptors of person-centered counseling (as well as of Rogers himself)—authenticity or realness, unconditional positive regard for the client, and empathic understanding—manifest through that brief look of the master at work.

Rogers expands on this in *On Becoming a Person*, in which he trains his lens on the person's internal experience, on his or her subjective world. For Rogers, it is not about asking what *others* might think or desire but

53. Rogers, *On Becoming a Person*, 63.

54. Rogers, *On Becoming a Person*, 16–17.

55. Laggner, "Dialogue with Carl Rogers."

56. Concord Media, "Carl Rogers Interviews: Richie."

about trusting one's own observations: "How do *I* experience this? What does it mean to *me*?"[57] Further, the therapist's role is not about empowering the client in the literal sense of giving the client power. For Rogers, all power already rests within the client: "It is not that this approach gives power to the person; it never takes it away."[58]

What happens when the client shifts from wondering what others might think to asking what he or she is encountering in the moment and reflecting on personal meaning? Rogers identifies four characteristic trends he was observing: an openness to accepting one's own experiences as capable of providing accurate information; trust in one's organism (one's internal self; one's thoughts, feelings, and bodily sensations) as a valuable presenter of experience; an internal locus of evaluation; and a willingness to be in process, "a continually changing constellation of potentialities, not a fixed quantity of traits."[59] In emphasizing process and potentiality over the identification of specific traits, Rogers was differentiating himself from Maslow. Their goals were the same, but they took different paths—Maslow as the innovative psychologist, Rogers as the groundbreaking therapist.

What is the ultimate goal? As defined by Rogers, in words that Maslow would second, it is "to be that self which one truly is."[60] It is the process of growth in being and knowing—and, ultimately, accepting—the person one is, of becoming more aware of what has been denied in oneself and more willing to embrace it. The result of this is "the good life," which for Rogers is not a philosophical concept arrived at deductively but one that comes to awareness experientially, within the psychotherapeutic process. Its characteristics include openness to experiences (which was increasingly taking center stage in Rogers's descriptors of the true self), living fully in the moment (existential living), and increasing trust in what feels right within the self when we are open to what we are encountering. Rogers observes, as did Maslow before him, that the good life, the self-actualized life, is not pain-free, is not "for the faint-hearted. . . . It involves the courage to be."[61]

Rogers turns his attention toward the conflict he experiences within himself between the scientist and the person-centered therapist, a conflict he comes to accept as an unresolvable paradox that can nonetheless provide insight into the purpose of science—"a way of preventing me from deceiving

57. Rogers, *On Becoming a Person*, 103 (emphasis in original).

58. Rogers, *Carl Rogers*, xii.

59. Rogers, *On Becoming a Person*, 122.

60. Rogers, *On Becoming a Person*, 163.

61. Rogers, *On Becoming a Person*, 196.

myself in regard to my creatively formed subjective hunches."[62] Science is not a dogma for Rogers; it is a means, a method through which one's experiences can be verified dispassionately. The result of that commitment to validate his own "subjective hunches" during person-centered therapy would be the conclusion that the necessary and sufficient conditions of change can be observed, measured, and, more significantly, translated into effective therapeutic practices.

Rogers was too broad a thinker to allow his insights to remain locked within the narrow world of therapy. With some trepidation, acknowledging that his views on counseling had resulted in a reputation of controversy in that field and not wanting to extend the controversy into another, he considered sharing his thoughts about the world of teaching and learning. Once he made the decision to do so, he set caution aside and confronted head-on the fundamentals of schooling: examinations, grades, credits, degrees, and the value of formal instruction itself, not so much in order to be controversial but to encourage reflection and discussion.

Rogers's first opportunity to present his emerging ideas on education took place at Harvard. In a speech to educators titled "Classroom Approaches to Influencing Human Behavior," he offered several learnings from the counseling process that might also make a difference in the classroom: identifying a problem to solve; being congruent or authentic as a teacher; having unconditional positive regard for the students; making the effort to understand the students' internal worlds; and being conscious of the importance of the students' perceiving that congruence, regard, and understanding. In a quote that encapsulates Rogers's devotion to the value of one's subjective experience, he concludes his revolutionary and challenging words to the assembled educators with an invitation to personal exploration: "I want to know primarily whether anything in my inward thinking, as I have tried to describe it, speaks to anything in your experience in the classroom as you have lived it, and if so, what the meanings are that exist for you in *your* experience."[63]

What was it like to have Rogers for a teacher? One of his former students, Samuel Tenenbaum, PhD, contributed a chapter to *On Becoming a Person* in which he describes that experience. He paints a picture of Rogers entering the room, casually taking a seat at a round table with the students, and opening with, "It would be nice if we stated our purpose and introduced ourselves."[64] Then . . . silence, much to the assembled students' befuddle-

62. Rogers, *On Becoming a Person*, 218.

63. Rogers, *On Becoming a Person*, 278 (emphasis in original).

64. Samuel Tenenbaum, "Carl R. Rogers and Non-Directive Teaching," in Rogers, *On*

ment and growing discomfort. Throughout the course, which was titled "The Process of Personality Change," Rogers offered no structure, no syllabus, no scope and sequence. Instead, by listening to the students' words, respecting their contributions, and offering unconditional positive regard, he directed his energies toward creating a supportive atmosphere, a psychological climate within which they might feel valued and empowered. The result? A student-centered learning environment about which, Tenenbaum concludes, "I never had a classroom experience from which came such warmth and closeness."[65]

Having taken the risk of introducing his ideas to the world of education, Rogers next directs his attention to family life, offering a mini-treatise on what encourages and what gets in the way of communication. He identifies judgment and disapproval as the major barriers and offers listening with understanding as the corrective. He reaffirms his developing theory that empathic understanding is "the most effective agent we know for altering the basic personality structure of an individual, and improving his relationships and communications with others."[66]

Further, the more there is a congruence of experience and awareness ("I am aware of what I am thinking, feeling, and sensing") and of awareness and communication ("I am willing to take the risk of honestly communicating what I am experiencing") in at least one of the two parties in the relationship, reciprocity and interpersonal congruence results, leading to a strengthening of the relationship. Throughout, Rogers reflects on what has been learned in research about person-centered therapy and the correlation of the necessary and sufficient conditions with values such as self-perception, confidence, openness to experience, and mature behavior.

Taking a more global perspective in the closing chapters of the book, Rogers addresses the power of the behavioral sciences to do either good or ill in the world, as did Maslow before him. He sees in our hands the ability to use the behavioral sciences to control humanity in the service of, for example, a destructive ideology, or to free humanity by helping individuals become more accepting of their growth potential, a direction in thinking that the sociologically oriented Erich Fromm would much appreciate.

By way of providing a philosophical foundation for his discussion, Rogers offers two points: 1) We have the ability to make personal, subjective, values-based choices about our future, which we may then effectuate

---

Becoming a Person, 300.

65. Samuel Tenenbaum, "Carl R. Rogers and Non-Directive Teaching," in Rogers, *On Becoming a Person*, 312.

66. Rogers, *On Becoming a Person*, 332.

through the use of science; and 2) Science itself cannot make those choices; science is values-neutral. Science, therefore, is an effective tool for evaluating whether a particular course of action results in the desired outcome, but it cannot of itself determine the value of that outcome—a healthy reminder of science's limitations. In a later chapter, we will see those limitations challenged by men and women of science both in Rogers's day and the present.

Rogers closes the book with a stirring summary of the values he believes worthy of encouragement. He wants to direct his attention not to static elements but to process—the *how* to be the people we can be rather than the specific behaviors required. Like Maslow, he advocates for self-actualization, emphasizing the achievement of self-worth, living creatively in an ever-changing world, and engaging in meaningful and mutually satisfying relationships. As always, he encourages continuing research into the fundamentals of effective counseling, and he closes with a reaffirmation of responsible personal choice as the most important element in becoming a person.

A NEW DIRECTION

The Western Behavioral Sciences Institute (WBSI), to which Rogers turned after his difficulties in Wisconsin, was a nonprofit organization in La Jolla, California, concerned with humanistically oriented research related to interpersonal relations. Among other activities he engaged in through the institute, Rogers immersed himself in the encounter movement, through which "he became markedly more expansive of his own feelings and more prepared to risk being vulnerable in relationships."[67]

The encounter movement, which provided one of the more enduring iconic images of the 1960s, was an umbrella term for group experiences in which the free expression of the participants was considered not only the process but the goal itself. In the hands of less experienced leaders—or leaders with less-than-benevolent intent—they tended to descend into unrestrained, no-holds-barred, in-your-face confrontations, often with strong sexual undertones. In Rogers's hands, they focused on authentic exchanges tempered by respect for all involved and sincere attempts at empathic understanding, all toward the goal of personal and interpersonal growth. These experiences further encouraged his openness to person-centered opportunities outside the therapy room. Rogers also experimented more with group-therapy sessions at this time, and, in 1969, a session conducted by Rogers was nominated for the Academy Award for short films.

67. Thorne, *Carl Rogers*, 19.

In 1967, Rogers's restless spirit, combined with a concern that WBSI was not following its mission after a leadership change, led to the founding of the Center for the Person, which still exists today in La Jolla as the Center for Studies of the Person. Through the center, Rogers was able to expand beyond counseling to confront the full range of life's challenges—individually, regionally, nationally, and globally. Issues of world peace and cultural and racial reconciliation—in places such as Northern Ireland, South Africa, Poland, Russia, and Brazil (for which he was nominated for the 1987 Nobel Peace Prize)—increasingly occupied his time.

The Center for the Person also provided opportunities for Rogers to facilitate workshops with his daughter, Natalie, who had received psychotherapeutic supervision from Maslow and who would later become an advocate for what she would call person-centered expressive arts therapy. Natalie also encouraged her father to revisit the spiritual terrain that he had set aside in his youth when he abandoned Christianity. As referenced in this book's introduction with regard to my own experience as a parent, although it is true that parents give birth to their children biologically, children often give birth, or rebirth, to their parents spiritually; this certainly appears to have been the case in Natalie's relationship with her father.

The extension of the term *person-centered* to the workshops Carl and Natalie co-facilitated effectively communicated that their work applied not only to the therapy room, or even to education and business, but to all social gatherings—organizational, political, cultural, religious—through which people interact and, as a result, experience interpersonal growth. Unsurprisingly, central to Rogers's approach to change regarding all those entities was his triad of congruence, unconditional positive regard, and empathic understanding. More than being understood exclusively in terms of the core elements of his nondirective, person-centered counseling, they now constituted, in Rogers's eyes, a new way of life, a new way of being, one that provides a pathway toward healing in education, family life, religion, business, medicine, politics—all the helping professions and all areas of life in which people work together to solve mutual problems. The ability to be whole and genuine, to be in touch with one's thoughts, feelings, and organic striving (congruence), to appreciate the good within the person—"the spark of the divine," in spiritual terms—and to feel a liking, a prizing for that person (unconditional positive regard), and to experience the ability, however imperfect, to place oneself in the shoes of the other (empathy) are distinctly human capabilities that lead to healing in all areas of life.

It is clear that Rogers's spirit lives through the Center for Studies of the Person, as a visit to its website confirms.[68] The center offers experiential training in person-centered psychotherapy and sponsors workshops, conferences, and other programs designed, as Rogers intended, to extend into all dimensions of life. Although it doesn't specifically reference a mission statement, the home page suggests their purpose by noting that they are "a face-to-face community of people for whom the Person-Centered Approach plays an important role in our personal and professional lives—as a way of being and doing." The center celebrated its fiftieth anniversary in 2016.

In 1979, Helen, Carl's wife of fifty-five years, died. This marked the third turning point in Rogers's spiritual journey as identified by biographer Brian Thorne: after Helen's death, Rogers became more purposeful and intentional in his spiritual, ethical, and political explorations. He was certainly a deeply religious man in his youth, while at the same time a person willing to wrestle with theological questions. The result of that wrestling was his renunciation of Christianity, understandable given the harsh theology of his upbringing, which is described as "negative and guilt-inducing . . . enshrined in the severe interpretation of the doctrine of Original Sin."[69]

Through his work with clients in counseling and later through his experiences in group work, Rogers found that persons are essentially forward-looking, creative, and responsible, not corrupt and fallen. Further, through his own counseling related to his experiences with the psychotic client noted earlier, he was able to get more in touch with the negative effects of that religious upbringing on himself. In his last years of life, he opened himself, slowly and methodically, to an acceptance of events and experiences typically considered outside the bounds of scientific inquiry, such as psychic events, the possibility of life after death, and Eastern spiritual practices. In his last published description of a therapeutic encounter, he wrote that his current experiences "involve the transcendent, the indescribable, the spiritual. I am impelled to believe that I, like many others, have underestimated the importance of this mystical, spiritual dimension."[70]

Rogers imagined in *A Way of Being* a possible fourth condition of therapeutic change—a mystical, spiritual presence he would encounter in counseling and workshops when he was at his best, when he was in the flow, we might say. Thorne muses that "had he lived, we might have heard much more of the 'presence' of which he speaks,"[71] and he detects a direct line

68. www.centerfortheperson.org.

69. Thorne, *Carl Rogers*, 21.

70. Thorne, *Carl Rogers*, 130.

71. Thorne, *Carl Rogers*, 40.

connecting the religious milieu in which Rogers was raised and his later embrace of the transcendent.

How did this develop? If there is a direct line from Rogers's fundamentalist Christian upbringing to his late-life openness to the spiritual, how do we account for it? We can look at that early upbringing and imagine several paths that could have developed from it, one being the default response of repeating it exactly as learned, living out his parents' script and extending their teachings to yet another generation. Another classic response would have been that of the rebel or maverick who chooses the opposite path, the life of the libertine, for example. But Rogers was a sensitive, reflective, thoughtful youth, whose response to life was characterized by, for example, his insight during the China trip that good people can come to very different conclusions about questions of philosophy, theology, and God. The more he observed and, significantly, recorded—his journals and letters during that trip were voluminous, illustrative, and therapeutic—the more he discovered a way of being that was distinct from what he had learned growing up. He was too introspective a person to replicate without question what he had received and too careful and honest an observer to take the path of unreflective rebellion. He was a learner, and followed what he learned—and it took him far afield of what he had been taught.

In addition, it must be noted that in every description of Rogers's family, we learn that home was a place where love was experienced and wherein each child knew he or she had an important role to play in the household. In counseling related to parenting, a familiar model distinguishes between loving/control and loving/autonomy, understood as opposite directions on a continuum. (There is also a continuum of harsh/dismissive control and neglectful autonomy.) Rogers's upbringing was toward the loving/control end of the continuum, and the most distinguishing feature of it was that it was, indeed, loving—at least the kind of loving that his parents were able to give, which was more patriarchal/matriarchal than connective and intimate. There was love in the Rogers home, even if it was not demonstrated in ways Carl might have needed. He would find the love he needed years later in the counseling office, in the roles of both counselor and client.

What did he learn? And how did it eventually lead him to matters spiritual? Within each of us, Rogers came to observe, there is an actualizing tendency, "the built-in motivation present in every life-form to develop its potentials to the fullest extent possible"[72]—to be that which we are meant to be. Sometimes, like the light-seeking potato in the cellar noted in the first chapter, the odds against actualization are high. Nonetheless, that tendency

72. Morgan, *Damaged Self*, 35.

remains, and with it the striving to attain the fullest state of personhood of which we are capable. Rogers offers various names for this internal striving besides actualizing tendency—organismic tendency, syntropy, morphic tendency, evolutionary flow—and he observes that those who embrace this tend "toward a transcending experience of unity . . . higher values, especially beauty, harmony, and love . . . at one with the cosmos."[73] Rogers was on a path of self-discovery, striving to articulate his own emerging spiritual voice.

How is that internal striving encouraged? Through his own experiences, and through his close and extensive research, Rogers located the answer to the *how* in the three necessary and sufficient conditions essential to personal growth. He saw empathy as the most powerful of the three factors in bringing about change, noting that empathic understanding reinforces one's sense of personal identity. With a stronger sense of identity, clients can take "a prizing, caring attitude toward themselves . . . [and] listen more accurately to themselves, with greater empathy . . . [allowing for] new facets of experience which become part of an accurately based self-concept."[74]

Rogers referenced the power of the three conditions of change that he observed in his work with schools, businesses, and cultural and political groups as well—perhaps even more so than in counseling. Noting changes in the value choices of those he worked with in multiple settings—changes that suggested a more internal than external orientation—he began to describe the experience of participants in spiritual terms. Rogers, unlike Maslow, expressed little interest in identifying healthy values for the world—through the process of person-centered counseling, clients will discover those values for themselves. He further observed that in person-centered communities, values are less rigidly held because they are based on what the person experiences, which can change over time—"they are held more tentatively, less rigidly. They are not carved in stone, but written by a human heart."[75]

While Maslow was busy identifying specific values, Rogers was more process-oriented, interested instead in the growth from an external locus of evaluation to an internal one, trusting that when we look within our hearts for our deepest values, we will discover them. It is interesting to note, however, that in *A Way of Being*, written when he was seventy-eight, Rogers included at the end of the book a list of twelve traits common to what he referred to as "persons of tomorrow," persons who "enlarge our view of the person . . . [due] to their growing interest in the spiritual and transcendent

73. Rogers, *Way of Being*, 128.

74. Rogers, *Way of Being*, 159.

75. Rogers, *Way of Being*, 195.

powers of the individual."[76] This list includes openness, authenticity, wholeness, intimacy, caring, internalized authority, and spirituality, words synonymous, and sometimes identical to, Maslow's own words. For Rogers, the identification of these words—these traits or values—finds expression at the culmination of his life's work, as if they describe what he has been searching for all his life; for Maslow, as we have seen, they were what set his life's work in motion.

Rogers had immense faith not only in the person but in the wisdom of the group, and he spoke appreciably of the transcendence and spirituality that he discovered in the community-forming process. Regarding those words *transcendence* and *spirituality*, he confessed his surprise: "These are words that in earlier years I would never have used. But the overarching wisdom of the group, the presence of an almost telepathic communication, the sense of the existence of a 'something greater,' seem to call for such terms."[77] Furthermore, he decried those who are so confined by a belief system that they cannot participate as real people, as persons in their own right, but instead, participate only as representatives of a party line to which they are bound—as was the experience of several attendees at the training described earlier in this chapter.

It is in words like *community-forming* and *person-centered community* that we can more clearly identify Rogers's movement toward the spiritual. Personal congruence, caring, prizing, and empathy seemed to take on greater power for him when more persons were involved, and it was particularly in these settings, upon which he focused almost exclusively in his later years, wherein the presence of the spiritual emerged. For Rogers, the responsibility of the counselor (or of the group or community leader) is to provide the three conditions of change, and a fourth, the spiritual, will emerge naturally.

Biographer Brian Thorne, who is a founder of the Norwich Centre for Personal, Professional and Spiritual Development in the UK, notes that he sees in Rogers and the work he engaged in "the re-emergence of a spiritual tradition which has its origins in the early writers of the Old Testament and continues through Jesus, the early Christian theologians and many of the great medieval writers, not least Dame Julian of Norwich."[78] Julian, whose life spanned the second half of the fourteenth and the early years of the fifteenth centuries, was the author of *Revelations of Divine Love*, in which she describes her visions of God. She is much revered today in spiritual circles,

76. Rogers, *Way of Being*, 343–44.

77. Rogers, *Way of Being*, 196.

78. Thorne, *Carl Rogers*, xi.

particularly within the Anglican Church. For Thorne to reference this saint of Christianity in the same sentence as Carl Rogers speaks of the largeness of spirit of both Thorne and Rogers.

Thorne observes that although Rogers never embraced the understanding of a personal God himself, the discovery of the spiritual dimension through counseling or person-centered group work often does result in a movement toward God. Thorne clearly wants this for Rogers, whom he befriended during the last decade of Rogers's life. He further hopes that Rogers's path toward the spiritual can serve as a model for all those who have been disillusioned by their early or present religious experiences. Rogers found no need to embrace the fourth force work of transpersonal psychology that Maslow and others were exploring during the latter years of the 1960s and beyond, even as their expressions of what they were discovering overlapped. For Rogers, the spiritual arose spontaneously within the relationships he experienced in the counseling office and in person-centered groups.

Jessica Grogan, in *Encountering America*, references the attraction of many in the pastoral counseling community to Rogers. As she wryly observes, "While Rogers may have been done with religion, it wasn't done with him . . . pastoral counselors took to Rogers like fish to water."[79] In his necessary and sufficient conditions for therapeutic change, many in the Christian churches saw the human characteristics of Jesus—a person who spoke with consistency and authenticity, who offered forgiveness and unconditional love (even reducing the Ten Commandments to two, love of God and love of neighbor), and who, through his own behavior and the stories he shared, revealed a deep empathy for all humanity. Men and women in ministry who had shunned the harsh God of their youth and yearned for a gentler message that emphasizes "original blessing," in theologian Matthew Fox's inviting words, rather than original sin, saw in Rogers a psychologically validated alternative, one they could wed to the Christian message. The message spread, and in 1963 the American Association of Pastoral Counselors was formed, inspired by Rogers's person-centered approach and hopeful of linking pastoral counseling to this emerging message of authenticity, unconditional acceptance, and empathy through which one might experience being listened to, heard, and understood.[80]

79. Grogan, *Encountering America*, 153–54.

80. For more on the relationship between Rogerian therapy and pastoral counseling, and the influence of the former on the latter, see Lundy, "Serving Spiritual Independents." Dr. Lundy's article, supplemented by personal correspondence four years later, convincingly demonstrates both the role of spiritual direction in the healing arts and the debt it owes to Carl Rogers's person-centered approach to counseling. Lundy is a spiritual director and pastoral counselor whose approach to those with whom she works

The attraction was mutual. The more opportunities Rogers had to experience the close, intimate, face-to-face, empathic encounter characterized by the three conditions of therapeutic change, the more he experienced and appreciated the spiritual. Though he would not come to accept a personal God, he found what he needed through the human encounter, through the experience of intimacy. If Maslow's spiritual journey could best be defined within the context of his search for universal human values, Rogers's developed in and through his increasingly intense encounter with the person. His research on the conditions that make therapeutic change possible validated his own experiences both as a counselor and client, but it was the encounter itself that led him to the spiritual. It was transformational, for him and for others.

Rogers actively encouraged the humanistic, person-centered transformation of religion whenever and wherever he had the opportunity, even diving into disputes in traditions other than his own. James Kavanaugh's 1968 bestseller, *A Modern Priest Looks at His Outdated Church*, which scandalized many Catholics with its frank description of a worn-out, unwieldy, and authoritarian Church and its call for radical institutional change, carries a lengthy endorsement by Rogers on the back cover that refers to the book as "one of the most moving human documents I have ever read." He was never hesitant to jump into the fray, giving his support to any who would have the courage to confront cold and impersonal institutionalism wherever it might be found.

Rogers's spiritual musings and extension of his theories into the world of religion were not met with universal acceptance. A former student, Bill Coulson, saw Rogers's person-centered approach as posing a secular humanist challenge to Christianity, one that eliminated the need for a theology of redemption and expiation. In arguing against Union Theological Seminary professor Reinhold Niebuhr's teaching on original sin, Rogers had emphasized instead the more hopeful self-actualizing principle that, with the support of the necessary and sufficient conditions, would make external redemption superfluous. Coulson feared that Rogers was intent upon remaking religion in his own person-centered image and likeness,

---

is described in words like "compassionate companionship" and "pure presence," suggesting a level of attentive care characterized by the deep, empathic listening championed by Rogers. Having arrived at some of the same conclusions about the importance of attuned, attentive presence through her work as a spiritual director, as did Rogers through his person-centered counseling, Lundy found herself drawn to learn more about Rogers and how he came to develop his celebrated conditions for personal growth. She found that both she and Rogers had discovered that when persons experience a relationship characterized by warmth, acceptance, and a calming presence, healing and growth will occur, whether that be in the psychological domain or the spiritual.

and after Rogers's death, he went on the offensive against the threat he saw to traditional Christianity.

Troubled by the prospect of Rogers's approach becoming, for some, a new religion, Coulson railed against humanistic psychology's inroads into domains traditionally within the purview of the church. As Thorne observed, "Experiences of personal growth and interpersonal intimacy akin to those recorded by participants in person-centred contexts have in the past commonly been associated with a religious and spiritual reality."[81] As the personal story that opens this chapter suggests, person-centered groups may indeed become surrogates of religion for some.

Referencing the work of Rogers and other humanistic psychologists, University of Dallas psychology professor Robert Kugelmann, author of *Psychology and Catholicism: Contested Boundaries*, notes that once psychology moved from a role focused on the psyche to the art of counseling itself, thereby impinging on pastoral counseling and spiritual direction, it was bound to open wounds. Due to his emphasis on the internal locus of values formation and his anti-authoritarian inclinations, Rogers was not well-received within some Catholic psychological circles; for Rogers, the organismic, internal valuing process was a given, an absolute—one might say *infallible*, a commanding and consequential word in Catholic thought. Nonetheless, Kugelmann adds, Catholic psychologists were largely favorable to Rogers's approach, appreciating it as "preparation for spiritual direction, in that the acceptance the client experiences prepares the way for a mature relationship with God . . . [and] human relationships that are based upon respect for human freedom."[82]

Although the roots of Rogers's spiritual journey can be traced to a particular religious heritage—as was Maslow's, Fromm's, and May's—in the form it was developing, it could not be reduced to that religious heritage, any more than could Maslow's, Fromm's, or May's. Where Rogers was going was not about a common creed or dogma. In his own words, he was "too religious to be religious,"[83] words that evolutionary biologist Julian Huxley, who redefined the word *religious* in humanistic terms, would have applauded. The direction in which Rogers was moving during his later years was in response to "the mysterious paradox of our uniqueness and our membership one of another"[84]—it was about connection, intimacy, and relationship.

81. Thorne, *Carl Rogers*, 113.

82. Kugelmann, *Psychology and Catholicism*, 312–13.

83. Thorne, *Carl Rogers*, 115.

84. Thorne, *Carl Rogers*, 115.

Carl Rogers died of a heart attack in 1987 at age eighty-five. In his final years, as his spiritual life was continuing to mature, he opened himself to the possibility of an afterlife: "I now consider it possible that each of us is a continuing spiritual essence lasting over time, and occasionally incarnated in a human body."[85] Was Rogers coming full circle, back to his roots, back to the spiritual grounding of his youth?

Although Rogers's late-life spiritual awakening did not return him to the Christianity of his youth, it did bring him to a deeper understanding of his life's path. Always the lifelong learner, Rogers eagerly embraced this new world that he was experiencing through his ever-deepening relationships. It was not a return to the past; rather, true to Rogers's expansive spirit, it was an opening to the infinite possibilities of that which lies beyond the present.

85. Thorne, *Carl Rogers*, 92.

Chapter 5

Humanistic Religion

The Prophetic Zeal of Erich Fromm

The humanistic promise is that every person carries within himself all of humanity; that within ourselves we are saints and criminals, although in varying degrees, and hence that there is nothing in another person which we cannot feel as part of ourselves. Compassionate and empathic knowledge requires that we get rid of the narrowing ties of a given society, race, or culture and penetrate to the depth of the human reality in which we are all nothing but human.

—Erich Fromm, *The Revolution of Hope*

If Maslow's path to the spiritual evolved out of his impassioned search for universal human values and Rogers's through the depth and intensity of the interpersonal encounter, Erich Fromm's took shape within the long tradition of prophetic Judaism and increasingly assumed a humanistic, sociopolitical agenda. Fromm was the thundering Old Testament prophet confronting a world that had turned its back on authentic freedom and was bending its knee to the golden calf of authoritarianism. In its place, he called for the rediscovery of a humanistic religious attitude, a spirituality that recognizes the primacy of the person in his or her own right and rejects the many temptations and roadblocks that the world places between the person and the full realization of freedom.

Fromm's story is one of many lives, as Lawrence Friedman suggests in the title to his comprehensive biography, *The Lives of Erich Fromm: Love's Prophet*, published in 2013. He was a sociologist, psychoanalyst, social reformer, modern-day prophet, apostle of love, professor, therapist, researcher, bestselling author—and "the voice of reason during the troubling years of social unrest in America during the 1960s and 1970s."[1] It is also a story that is eerily contemporary, and even the casual observer of the present day will identify with Fromm's critique of his own. The themes he explored during his long and productive life—authoritarianism, demagoguery, freedom, security, fear, love, religious and ethnic hatred, a being-centered life (one that celebrates the full development of the person versus one focused on marketing, consumerism, and accumulation)—are themes relevant to us today, and many of the answers to our current travails can be found in the pages of his books. Three of his major works will be examined to highlight those themes—*Escape from Freedom*, his first book; *Psychoanalysis and Religion*, his most succinct statement on humanistic religion; and *To Have or to Be?*, a summation of his life's work written four years before his death.

Fromm's Roots

Erich Fromm, born in 1900 to an observant Jewish family in Frankfurt in what was then the German Empire, fits comfortably into the story of the foundations of contemporary psychological thought, many of whose leaders hailed from a similar background. His was a world within a world, a tightly knit Orthodox Jewish community located within a liberal, bourgeois city. It was a world that valued study and learning over commerce, an influence that stayed with Fromm throughout his life, serving as both a defining factor in his ethical formation and a template for his insightful critique of societal norms and structures. He would come to reject both the Jewish orthodoxy (but not its heart and soul—he remained intimately connected to the songs, stories, vision, and values of his Jewish heritage) and the bourgeois liberalism.

Erich was the only child of Naphtali and Rosa Krause Fromm, descendants of a long line of rabbis and talmudic scholars, whose home was "dominated by religious ritual and fraught with religious angst."[2] Embarrassed by his father's status as a wine merchant and his apparent disinterest in matters beyond the commercial, Erich sought adult mentors who could respond to his intellectual curiosity, naturally gravitating toward talmudic scholars. We

1. Morgan, *Clinical Psychotherapy*, 333.
2. Funk, *Erich Fromm*, 37.

observed this instinctual gravitation toward mentors and father figures in Maslow as well, in his case more toward the left-leaning scholars, almost exclusively Jewish, who dominated academic circles in New York.

Erich attended the Wöhlerschule in Frankfurt for his elementary and secondary education, graduating in 1918, upon which he enrolled at the University of Heidelberg. During his years at the Wöhlerschule, he encountered his first influential mentor, Rabbi Nehemiah Nobel. Several years later, at Heidelberg, he met Dr. Salman Rabinkow, who built on the earlier tutelage of Dr. Nobel by introducing or further developing insights from the great wealth of Jewish tradition, including Hasidism, "a popular reaction against the excessive legalism and rationalism of mainstream rabbinic orthodoxy."[3] From Rabinkow, we can trace Fromm's developing economic, political, and spiritual interests, perhaps most notably a sense of Jewish law as responsive to universal human needs.

Fromm completed his studies in 1922 with a major in sociology; his doctoral dissertation was titled "Jewish Law, a Contribution to the Sociology of Diaspora-Judaism." Sociology, or social science, formulated by Émile Durkheim in France during the late nineteenth and early twentieth centuries, was still in its infancy, not yet meriting its own academic department; at Heidelberg, it was considered part of National Economy. Through the success he achieved teaching and writing, Fromm was instrumental in helping sociology become a respected academic field. Two years after graduation, he added another credit to his broad academic interests by beginning studies in psychoanalysis in Berlin.

Frieda Fromm-Reichmann

Another major early influence on Fromm was the German neurologist and psychiatrist Frieda Reichmann, through whom he was introduced to psychoanalysis and with whom he fell in love. Their marriage in 1926 was destined to fail: she was his analyst and eleven years his senior. They separated in 1930 and formally divorced ten years later, nonetheless remaining personal and professional friends throughout their lives—and Frieda, who never remarried, forever maintained that hyphenated name. There was a motherly aspect to Frieda that attracted Fromm, an inclination that would manifest soon afterward in a relationship with another older woman, the humanistically oriented psychoanalyst Karen Horney. Erich's relationship with Frieda influenced him in several important ways, including his identification of patriarchy as one of his central critiques of Freud, his approval of

3. Burston, *Legacy of Erich Fromm*, 13.

the Catholic Church's emphasis on Mary as an all-loving and all-forgiving mother, and his deep appreciation for maternal kindness in both men and women wherever he found it.

In 1924, Erich and Frieda opened a psychoanalytic sanatorium for Jewish patients in Heidelberg, focusing largely on repression, both in its individual and societal dimensions. In short order, their experiences in learning and practicing psychoanalysis affected their religiosity, and together they decided to set aside their Jewish orthodoxy for good—ritualistically, by eating leavened bread in a Heidelberg park on Passover. However, like Erich, Frieda remained committed to the ethical teachings of Judaism throughout her life.

Frieda Fromm-Reichmann would become a towering presence in the developing field of psychotherapy in her own right. Biographer Gail A. Hornstein, in her aptly titled *To Redeem One Person Is to Redeem the World*, notes as the core principle of Fromm-Reichmann that "no patient, however disturbed, was beyond the reach of psychotherapy."[4] Since Fromm-Reichmann worked almost exclusively with schizophrenic patients, that is quite a courageous stance, one that would undo all but the most persistent of therapists. But she was nothing if not persistent in her efforts to cure her patients, and references to her work ethic abound in Hornstein's biography.

Like Erich, Frieda was born in Germany to an Orthodox Jewish family. Denied the quality of educational opportunities that were allowed for boys, she was homeschooled by her mother. But in 1908, the medical schools opened their doors to females and Frieda began classes, soon gravitating toward neurology and psychiatry, popular specialties in European medical schools at the time; Sigmund Freud's specialties, out of which he developed psychoanalysis, were in neurology and psychiatry. Receiving her degree in 1913, a year before the outbreak of the Great War, she would soon receive ample opportunities to practice her craft on soldiers suffering from brain injuries.

After the war, Frieda worked in Frankfurt under the guidance of Kurt Goldstein, whose studies of brain-injured soldiers led to his coining the word *self-actualization*, which was destined to become the cornerstone of the humanistic psychology movement thanks largely to Maslow's adoption of the word for both the process of growth and the goal of personal development. Throughout her life, Fromm-Reichmann attributed her patients' healing to their own inner strength and internal striving for actualization; she saw her own role in terms of "helping to marshal the recuperative processes

4. Hornstein, *To Redeem One Person*, xiii.

already present in the nervous system"[5]—a familiar theme throughout the humanistic psychology movement. Following her work with Goldstein, Frieda moved to Berlin to learn psychoanalysis under Karl Abraham, a close collaborator of Freud, and later, as noted earlier, met, married, and divorced Erich Fromm. Like so many of her contemporaries, she left for America upon Hitler's rise to power.

In 1935, Chestnut Lodge, a sanitarium for patients suffering from psychiatric conditions, recruited Fromm-Reichmann due to her developing reputation as a psychoanalytically trained therapist with the rare intuitive gift for discerning exactly what each client most needed. Psychiatrist Harry Stack Sullivan, whom she befriended during her years at the lodge, also famously demonstrated that skill which, like the gifted musician's ability to play a musical instrument "by ear," is largely unteachable. Fromm-Reichmann would spend the rest of her life, twenty-two years, at the lodge, during which time she would achieve international fame, largely for her work with schizophrenic patients.

Fromm-Reichmann was a practitioner, not a theorist, one who would fearlessly try anything she thought might help—"an empiricist in the literal sense of the word."[6] Like Sullivan, she used a direct, interpersonal approach with her patients. More importantly, and also like Sullivan, she intuitively understood the loneliness of mental illness, particularly schizophrenia, a notoriously solitary disease. Freud had argued that psychoanalysis was not for patients suffering from psychosis, only for neurotics, but Fromm-Reichmann thought otherwise (as did Sullivan, who was described as "like a Zen master, totally present to the patient").[7] For both Fromm-Reichmann and Sullivan, schizophrenia was considered and therefore treated as an affliction less of biogenic origin than as one resulting from a frustrated interpersonal environment. Fromm-Reichmann could not imagine that any patient, no matter how shackled by mental illness, would be undeserving of her full attentiveness and responsiveness, and she would never give up on a client. As a result, as Hornstein observes, "her work inspired a whole generation of young psychiatrists to try to create truly therapeutic environments for people assumed to be beyond reach."[8]

For Fromm-Reichmann, the lodge was a therapeutic community "where even the sickest patients could get better"[9] through psychoanalytically

5. Hornstein, *To Redeem One Person*, 30.
6. Hornstein, *To Redeem One Person*, 38.
7. Hornstein, *To Redeem One Person*, 127.
8. Hornstein, *To Redeem One Person*, 172.
9. Hornstein, *To Redeem One Person*, 174.

themed psychotherapy. It was an understanding dramatically different from other psychiatric hospitals at the time, who saw their patients as wards to control through shock treatments and lobotomies, not as persons to connect with through the art of psychotherapy. All doctors at the lodge—and many of the nurses—underwent psychoanalysis themselves so as to better serve their patients.

Fromm-Reichmann's most famous patient, Joanne Greenberg, immortalized Frieda in her 1964 pseudonymous book, *I Never Promised You a Rose Garden*, a nonfiction work marketed as fiction, in which "Dr. Fried" healed "Hannah Green" of schizophrenia. Greenberg, freed from the grip of mental illness, would go on to publish several other books and become a professor of anthropology.

Fromm-Reichmann died in 1957. Fromm, always in and out of her life and a dear friend to the end, was the executor of her will. Her *Principles of Intensive Psychotherapy*, written in 1950, compares favorably to the works of Carl Rogers and Rollo May in its descriptions of the therapeutic art during the early days of the profession's formation, as well as serving as something of a bridge between Freud's psychoanalysis and the newly developing humanistic psychology. Most importantly, as noted earlier, Fromm-Reichmann inspired legions of therapists to never give up on a client, no matter how challenging.

On to America

Erich Fromm's experience eating leavened bread with Frieda on Passover might have been the end of his formal participation in the religion of his ancestors, but it was certainly not the end of his attraction to and celebration of the long prophetic tradition of the Jewish people. Unlike Maslow, who rejected the rich heritage of his ancient religion along with its practice, reconnecting with his cultural patrimony only late in life, Fromm made a distinction early on between religious formalism, which he rejected, and the cultural traditions that provide for a sense of identity, which he embraced.

In 1929, Fromm joined the Frankfurt Institute for Social Research, which promoted an interdisciplinary, humanistic Marxism integrated with Freudian psychology. It was at this time that he began developing his concept of "social character," which emphasized the influence of societal conditions as transmitted by the family on personality formation and with which his name is frequently identified. For Fromm, trained as a sociologist, the formation of personality could not be understood solely in terms of intrapsychic dynamics; account must also be taken of the larger social context within which the person was born and raised and lives his or her life. Fromm's association with the Frankfurt institute eventually ended as a result of this developing accentuation of the sociocultural approach over the more Freudian, instinctual one.

Though Fromm increasingly charted his own psychoanalytic course, he consistently demonstrated what Daniel Burston in *The Legacy of Erich Fromm* refers to as "Freud piety,"[10] a sense of reverence for the one who started it all. His reverence for the prophetic and cultural dimension of his Jewish heritage endured as well. In 1932, the Frankfurt institute moved to Switzerland, then on to New York's Columbia University in response to the increasingly menacing situation in Germany.

Alarmed by the rising popularity of Nazism, Fromm engaged in a study of German workers to discern their psychological character and level of possible resistance to Hitler. An exhaustive research project, it indicated, to Fromm's dismay, that a vast majority of the respondents were consistently authoritarian in their attitudes and values. Some two decades later, Fromm would attempt a second sociological study of social character, this time among Mexican peasants. By then more consciously humanistic, he hoped to enhance their quality of life through sociological research, something he discovered takes many generations.

In 1933, Fromm accepted an invitation from Karen Horney, who was distinguishing herself as a psychoanalyst and feminist pioneer, to visit the Chicago Psychoanalytic Institute and present several lectures. Horney, fifteen years his senior, became a longtime intellectual (and sometime romantic) companion. The opportunity to present at the Chicago event proved to be pivotal in providing Fromm entrée to the American psychoanalytic community, and in May 1934, like so many other Jewish professionals in his native land, he immigrated to America. This east-to-west brain drain resulting from Hitler's rise to power would become one of the most enduring positive influences on America's intellectual and cultural life over the years.

Offered a teaching position at Columbia, Fromm settled comfortably into the New York academic world, rapidly assimilating and making new friends, including the psychiatrists Clara Thompson and Harry Stack Sullivan and the anthropologists Margaret Mead and Edward Sapir. He spent much of the next ten years helping family members leave Germany, and the intensity of that activity, according to biographer Friedman, accounts for much of the power and energy found in his first book, *Escape from Freedom.*

10. Burston, *Legacy of Erich Fromm*, 1.

Escape from Freedom

"If humanity cannot live with the dangers and responsibilities inherent in freedom, it will probably turn to authoritarianism." These much-quoted words, from the back cover of my 1994 paperback edition of *Escape from Freedom*, neatly summarize Erich Fromm's motivation for writing the book that established him as a major force in American social psychology. It was first published in 1941, well into the Second World War, with totalitarianism and militarism threatening to destroy the Europe that had nurtured his youth, educated him in sociology and psychology, and, seven years previously, forced him to escape to America. In this book, Fromm engages in no abstract theorizing; he was writing while freedom itself was in peril.

In *Escape from Freedom*, Fromm analyzes the factors in the character structure of the modern human that result in the failure to embrace personal freedom and the corresponding willingness, when faced with disorientation and the fear of insecurity, to abandon it. He asks why freedom appears too heavy to bear for some and what accounts for their apparent readiness to submit themselves to an external authority. Recognizing that freedom carries with it certain responsibilities, he notes that if we cannot learn to live with those responsibilities, we will turn to the false security of authoritarianism. And he laments, writing eight years after Hitler's ascent to power, that "millions in Germany were as eager to surrender their freedom as their fathers were to fight for it."[11]

Defining his terms, Fromm asks if freedom is understood solely as the absence of external control (freedom *from*) or if it is more about a movement toward something (freedom *to*), and if the latter, how that something might be identified. Freedom *from* is chronicled through the many rights movements of the past several centuries, from the "rights of man" celebrated during the closing years of the eighteenth through the emancipation of enslaved persons in the nineteenth and on to the various civil rights and liberation movements of the twentieth and twenty-first. It is the freedom from arbitrary and unjust restrictions, discriminatory laws and practices, and cultural and political roadblocks that frustrate efforts to promote the equality of treatment. It is the bedrock of the classical liberal order that exists, while occasionally threatened, in our modern democracies.

But this freedom is fragile, according to Fromm, unless it evolves into a freedom *to*. Freedom *to*, he argues, is characterized by the movement toward self-actualization, the fulfillment of one's potentialities, the living of an authentic life (a life based on freely chosen values), and a connectedness

11. Fromm, *Escape from Freedom*, 3.

with all of humanity. Fromm's lifework could be encapsulated by reference to his championing of freedom *to*, the positive, humanistic understanding of freedom.

Fromm, a practicing psychoanalyst and a faithful admirer of Freud (even as he veered from traditional psychoanalysis), sought to apply Freud's insights to the larger society and elucidate the effect of the social conditions of a given time and place on the psychological development of the personality. Just as Freud labored to make manifest the unconscious forces of the psyche, Fromm endeavored to reveal the unconscious forces of the social/economic/political order. With a greater understanding of those forces, we might respond to life's choices from a position of maximum freedom—from the fullness of our beings, not out of fear or intimidation. This social conditioning factor—this interplay of social, economic, and political conditions on the personality—is the context within which Fromm's arguments in *Escape from Freedom* make sense.

In the opening chapter, Fromm presents his central challenge: the more we gain freedom from societal restraints, the more we must learn to use that freedom in an altruistic, cooperative, and productive manner. If we fail to do that, the social character of the community is threatened, and conditions are created that lead to the perceived need for an external provider of security, an authoritarian response that results in compromises to our integrity and, ultimately, to our freedom. Fromm's approach is sociological and historical: his lens is trained on the relationship between socioeconomic factors and characterological change throughout history and the effects of that relationship on freedom.

Fromm begins his socioeconomic review with a look at the late Middle Ages and the Renaissance, an era characterized by the emergence of a new, ambitious, moneyed class engaged in rapidly expanding commercial enterprises, spurred by trade far beyond the borders of the medieval villages. As the solidarity of the old medieval structures with their protective guilds and stratified social restraints began to crumble, the individual was forced to confront the isolation and alienation that followed in the wake of this newfound freedom. The assumptions of the Middle Ages—fixed social positions, a single and unified religion, and trade understood as serving one's livelihood (rather than the accumulation of wealth)—were being replaced by what would come to be called the capitalist ethic, with its emphasis on work for its own sake, the accumulation of capital, material success, efficiency, effort, and competition.

For the poor, there was continuing exploitation and increasing poverty, and for the trade guilds, reduced solidarity and monopolization. For the urban middle class, results were mixed, with those who took advantage of opportunities to monopolize gaining strength, and those who did not, declining in status and security. The effect of this newly emerging capitalism was the freedom to become master of one's fate but at the price of increasing anxiety and possible economic destruction. In summary, the individual was freed from the bondage and economic and political ties of the medieval system but now lacked security and a clear sense of place, role, or position in the world.

The sixteenth-century Reformation offered the urban middle class, the urban poor, and the peasantry a new religious expression for the hunger for economic freedom and independence that had preceded it. Martin Luther and John Calvin accomplished two things, according to Fromm: they stripped the church of its sole claim to authority by emphasizing the individual's subjective experience and personal relationship with God, and they offered the individual, whose original depravity they had highlighted, the opportunity of God's salvific grace, a certainty of salvation that can override any lingering sense of isolation and anxiety. Any doubt that might arise regarding salvation is now addressed in terms of total submission to God—and, in short order, to the local prince as well—resulting in a characterological ambivalence manifested by both antipathy to and respect for authority combined with disdain toward the powerless, what Fromm referred to as the authoritarian character. In this schema, God became a tyrannical authority "who insisted on complete submission of man and annihilation of the self as the essential conditions to his salvation."[12] Freedom from the old order was effectively replaced by submission to a new one.

However, there was hope—through unceasing moral effort and a life of virtue one could demonstrate one's election, or salvation. As this concept developed over time, the surest demonstration of election became success in life as the world measures it, a philosophy that "may be assumed to be the most important psychological change which has happened to man since the end of the Middle Ages."[13] As a result of this change—a true paradigm shift—hard work and frugality became goals in themselves, even virtues, ushering in the development of modern capitalism.

Fromm observes that this newly developing system and practice, this emerging capitalist ethos, molded the personality by both increasing freedom and, paradoxically, creating a new dependency. Freedom had been associated with the destruction of the old societal forms, so the more those forms were attacked, the more people were assured they were moving toward freedom, unaware of the newly emerging assaults against it in the form

12. Fromm, *Escape from Freedom*, 81.

13. Fromm, *Escape from Freedom*, 81.

of isolation and insecurity. Membership in the medieval church—which, according to Fromm, restricted freedom but provided solidarity and security—was replaced by the Protestant emphasis on the individual facing God alone, a psychological preparation for the emergence of a more individualistic character. Having become no more than the means by which God manifests his power and glory—for the few, favorably, and for the many, not so—the person is sufficiently prepared spiritually to accept the role of servant, not only of God but of the new capitalist machine that emerged in conjunction with this new religious character. Furthermore, Fromm observes, prepared over time for the coming of a *Führer*. Needless to say, none of this was imagined, much less intended, by the Protestant reformers Luther and Calvin.

Fromm interprets Calvin's arbitrary, merciless God as "the projection of the middle class's own hostility and envy,"[14] a moral indignation toward both the successful above and the suffering below. Calvin had placed a wedge between glorifying God and loving and honoring the self, and the safest course was to demean the self. Fromm sees at the heart of this dichotomy a false understanding of the nature of love, a theme he introduces in *Escape from Freedom* and fully develops later with the publication of *The Art of Loving*. He describes love as emerging from a quality within the person—"an active striving and inner relatedness, the aim of which is the happiness, growth, and freedom"[15] of the other. And it cannot emerge from within a diminished spirit; a readiness for the love for all humanity, including the self, must be present within the person before he or she can turn to another in love.

Fromm posits a distinction between essential self-love and selfishness, the latter of which he defines as the exhaustive need to possess the other and fill the emptiness within the self. Selfishness springs from a lack of self-love, resulting in an absence of internal affirmation and security, and the narcissism that often follows is nothing more than overcompensation for that absence. This selfishness spills over into the world of work, with competitiveness becoming the rule of the market and the uncertainty of employment in a purportedly free market replacing the security of social role in one's trade. It is no longer a relationship of two human beings who are personally connected but a business transaction, with value reduced to salability.

Fromm asks what is normal and healthy for the individual within society and responds in terms of optimum growth and happiness while

14. Fromm, *Escape from Freedom*, 96.

15. Fromm, *Escape from Freedom*, 114.

fulfilling one's societal roles, adding that such a state could be achieved if the structure of society were ordered in a more supportive manner. Throughout his works, Fromm reveals his congruence with Maslow's passion for the identification of healthy, universal values. His definition of a "sane society," the title of one of his books, is based upon the assumption that there do exist "universal criteria for mental health which are valid for the human race as such, and according to which the state of health of each society can be judged."[16] Continuing on themes that Maslow would place at the center of his "third force" psychology, Fromm recognizes the importance of both physiological and psychological needs, placing emphasis on "the tendency to grow, to develop and realize potentialities which man has developed in the course of history . . . the biological tendency."[17] Rather than look to outside causes for this growth tendency (such as God or the "laws of nature"), Fromm, who of the four psychologists studied most embraced the appellation humanistic psychology, posits an internal dynamism as the source.

Unfortunately, as both Maslow and Fromm frequently observed, the quest for universal values is frustrated by the gravitational pull of the conventional and the mediocre, often resulting in the marginalization of those who strive for more humanistic responses to life's travails. Echoing sentiments often expressed by Viktor Frankl, Fromm observes that "the person who is normal in terms of being well adapted is often less healthy than the neurotic person in terms of human values."[18] Adaptation to social norms sometimes requires the renunciation of one's true self, an existential conflict that in extreme situations is resolved only at the price of martyrdom.

Turning his attention toward the anxiety and uncertainty that can attend to newfound freedom and the perceived need to escape its burden, Fromm identifies the emergence of the authoritarian response. He describes the effect of this response as sadomasochistic, with the masochistic element manifesting in terms of the submission to and admiration for an often-brutal authority and the sadistic in terms of the tendency to be contemptuous toward others and to crave absolute power over them, while at the same time displacing one's own suffering onto them. He identifies as the most prominent feature of this developing authoritarian character its division of humankind into the powerful and the weak, noting a fatalistic attitude in the latter's submission to destiny, fate, or "the will of God"—a pronounced external locus of control.

16. Fromm, *Sane Society*, 12.

17. Fromm, *Escape from Freedom*, 285–86.

18. Fromm, *Escape from Freedom*, 138.

In identifying the fatalistic attitude—an example of his concept of social character, which emphasizes the influence of societal conditions on personality formation—Fromm establishes a theme that has been explored by many sociological thinkers since. Kai Erikson, for example, established himself in the sociological field with his 1976 landmark study of a West Virginia Appalachian community that was destroyed by flood. Titled *Everything in Its Path*, it highlighted the sense of futility and fatalism of the townsfolk, going back generations to their first settlement in the area. Erikson, son of developmental psychology pioneer Erik Erikson, followed in the footsteps of Erich Fromm in illuminating a character type formed through its interaction with the prevailing culture.

Another avenue through which the individual might seek to escape or avoid the challenges posed by freedom is to set aside his or her sense of self and adopt, through the introjection of society's thoughts, feelings, and subsequent behaviors, the personality style expected by the culture. Once the gap between one's sense of self and the world's expectations closes, the fear of aloneness and powerlessness ceases. The result of this is what Fromm calls the automaton character type, defined in terms of the absence of a healthy ego. Sometimes referred to disparagingly as the herd mentality, it represents the unconscious, unquestioned identification with the prevailing culture and its ethos.

After delineating both the authoritarian and the automaton character types, Fromm describes the psychology of Nazism, which he defines as blind obedience to an authority figure combined with hatred for identified minorities, an exaggerated militarism, and an equally exaggerated ethnic nationalism. He wonders if this is simply an economic or political phenomenon, or if it is best understood from the perspective of psychopathology, with Hitler dismissed as a madman. Or should blame be placed on the post-World War I thirst for retribution, embodied in the Treaty of Versailles, or on the incompetence of the Weimar Republic, which was faced with the formidable task of picking up the pieces and rebuilding a country in tatters? Fromm concludes by positing Nazism as primarily a psychological problem molded by socioeconomic factors, and he focuses his inquiry on its human basis, the character structure to which it appealed and what made it so attractive to the German people. He points to the lower middle class, for whom Versailles had become a convenient object of projection for their devastating loss of social and economic status, and observes that Hitler, also of lower middle-class roots, emerged as the savior who articulated and gave credence to their anger—the singular talent of the demagogue then and now.

Formulating a response to authoritarianism by echoing a familiar humanistic theme, Fromm speaks of "organic growth, the unfolding of a nucleus that is peculiar for this one person and only for him."[19] He advocates for relationships of solidarity, not dominance, and he champions the humanistic person who lives authentically—by which he means embracing freedom with responsibility and living one's life through an internal locus of values formation. He speaks of the importance of ideals that promote growth and happiness, not dominance and submission, emphasizing, like Maslow, the universality of values: just as we know what foods and activities promote physical health, so too can we know what values and activities foster personal, interpersonal, and spiritual growth. He emphasizes the prominence of the spiritual, noting that sometimes it is necessary to sacrifice our physical self for the spiritual self, a theme that will take on greater prominence in *Psychoanalysis and Religion*.

Like Maslow, Fromm is optimistic about the future, anticipating the economic and social changes that would be critical to the support of personal growth, the goal of which is the realization of the true self, what Maslow often referred to as Being and which many today might define as soul. Fromm understands democracy, which promotes the full development of the individual as opposed to fascism's subordination of the person to the state, as the form of government best suited to ensuring societal protection from hunger, homelessness, and unemployment. Just as we have mastered nature, so too can we master these and other social problems, a challenge that societies who pride themselves on being humanistic should never shrink from.

Writer, Prophet, Therapist, Teacher

Writing *Escape from Freedom* reawakened the Jewish prophetic tradition in Fromm, to which Salman Rabinkow and others introduced him early in life, a tradition that melded well with the emerging humanistic psychology movement's emphasis on identifying intrinsic human values. This became his first of many publications, sparking a career marked by book sale numbers that are astounding—five million for *Escape from Freedom*; a million and a half for both *Man for Himself*, his second book, and *Psychoanalysis and Religion*, his third; and twenty-five million in fifty languages for *The Art of Loving*.

As a clinician, Fromm, like many therapists of his time, abandoned the couch and focused on open, mutual, authentic, and empathic communication. He "focused entirely on the 'humane side' of the therapeutic relationship"[20] and stressed that it must entail a connective, meaningful dia-

19. Fromm, *Escape from Freedom*, 262.

20. Funk, *Erich Fromm*, 130.

logue between two people. Through his psychoanalytic training, he worked with dreams, free associations, transferences, and whatever else he thought might help the client discover the core, authentic self—the deepest part of the person, from which values are lived freely and responsibly.

During the 1940s, in addition to his work at Columbia and tending to his counseling clients and supervisees, Fromm lectured at the New School for Social Research in New York, Bennington College in Vermont, and Yale; *Psychoanalysis and Religion* developed from his Yale lectures. In 1943, Fromm was instrumental in the founding of the William Alanson White Institute with Harry Stack Sullivan, Clara Thompson, and Frieda Fromm-Reichmann. The following year, he became an American citizen and married Henny Gurland, who had escaped from Germany with her son four years previously. In 1950, they moved to Mexico City, seeking a warmer, dryer climate for Henny, who struggled with painful arthritis. Although she died there two years later, Fromm continued to live in Mexico until 1973, frequently returning to the United States for speaking and teaching engagements. He established the Mexican Psychoanalytic Society, maintained a vibrant counseling practice in his home, taught at the National Autonomous University of Mexico School of Medicine, and wrote *The Art of Loving*.

Beginning in the 1950s, an emerging interest for Fromm was American politics. Firmly positioned on the left of the ideological continuum and beginning to describe himself in terms of humanistic socialism, Fromm applied his insights on freedom and authority, both intrapsychically and sociopolitically, to the contemporary political scene. He was frequently sought out for commentary by media mavens, including the pre-*60 Minutes* Mike Wallace, who interviewed Fromm in 1958 on the ABC program *Voice of America* on subjects ranging from the marketing orientation and authentic socialism to the meaning of the word *God* and the place of religion in society. He attracted the attention of political figures as well: biographer Friedman, observing that President Kennedy had read *Escape from Freedom*, wonders what effect Fromm's book might have had on Kennedy's momentous policy-changing speech at the American University in 1963, in which he passionately argued against nuclear proliferation.

As Fromm shifted his attention more toward political matters, particularly the arms race, he identified a necrophilic tendency in the human character that emerges when irrational fears overwhelm a society's sanity. In this context, he is using the word *necrophilic*, which has a specific meaning related to sexual stimulation through corpses, in a broader sense, as "a form of psychopathology in which death, violence, destruction, and the power needed to achieve them become worshipped at the expense of life and the moral values that seek to preserve it."[21] In response to necrophilic destructiveness, he coined the term *biophilia*, signifying a sense of connectedness to all of life and the need to promote life-giving, humanistic principles and policies—"the growth of man with all his potentialities, the affirmation of life in all its forms against death and mechanization and alienation."[22] *The Sane Society*, often referenced as a continuation of *Escape from Freedom*, was written during this period of his life; the antinuclear arms group SANE, founded in 1957 and now called Peace Action, took its name from Fromm's book. Through these activities, Fromm became one of the foremost spokespersons for a rational nuclear policy in America.

Psychoanalysis and Religion

Erich Fromm was a multidimensional man with a plurality of interests, from psychoanalysis and sociological analyses to political activism and the art of loving, often as these fields of study intersected. Yet he found himself continually returning to questions about religion and spirituality. In 1950, he wrote *Psychoanalysis and Religion*, in which he tackles the problem of how to understand and address religion and spirituality through a psychoanalytic/humanistic lens. He confronts both the sociopolitical issues of *Escape from Freedom* and the ethical issues advanced six years later in *Man for Himself*, and he proposes a pathway for a religious way of thinking that could serve as an effective response to authoritarianism.

Fromm begins his classic religious work by indicating the many technological improvements of contemporary society that suggest that the day may be near when the basic needs of food, clothing, and shelter will be met for all, while adding cautiously that "we have failed to make of ourselves beings for whom this tremendous effort would be worthwhile."[23] He questions whether future generations will have something to live for—a *why* to make possible the *how*, as Viktor Frankl would often say—and he indicts organized religion for failing to provide an answer to the sterility and soullessness of contemporary society. He expresses concern that matters of the soul are assumed by many to be the exclusive domain of those in organized religious groups, and he wants to reframe the conversation about the soul within a psychological, rather than strictly religious, orientation, a running theme throughout the larger humanist movement. In Julian Huxley, we will

21. Schimmel, "Judaism and the Origins," 35.

22. Fromm, *Revolution of Hope*, 142.

23. Fromm, *Psychoanalysis and Religion*, 1.

encounter a similar emphasis, one viewed through the lens of evolutionary biology rather than psychology.

Having established the purpose of *Psychoanalysis and Religion*, Fromm recognizes his debt to Freud. As referenced earlier, Freud discussed his views on God and religion in several of his works, notably *The Future of an Illusion*, in which he positioned the origin of religion within humanity's helplessness against the power and arbitrariness of natural forces and the disquieting instinctive forces that roiled within. Ultimately, Freud dismissed religion as illusory thinking.

Fromm, in contrast, promotes a more nuanced view, one that embraces a humanistic form of religion but rejects its authoritarian manifestations. He defines religion broadly as "any system of thought and action shared by a group which gives the individual a frame of orientation and an object of devotion,"[24] theistic or otherwise. By "frame of orientation," Fromm means our principles, beliefs, norms, rules, etc., and by "object of devotion," he is referring to that to which we direct our love, worship, dedication, and commitment. The key question for Fromm is *Does the specific religion further the healthy psychological development of the person, or does it frustrate it?*—with the measuring stick being the degree to which a religious orientation assists the person in channeling his or her energies toward the higher self.

Fromm observes that for many, power, success, and market capitalism have become their religion, while for others, worship of the nation-state has assumed that status, and he specifically references the "my country, right or wrong" attitude as an unhealthy form of religion. Twenty-seven years later, in *The Revolution of Hope*, he references the "noteworthy phenomenon that in the development of capitalism and its ethics, compassion (or mercy), which was a cardinal virtue in the Catholic-Medieval world, ceases to be a virtue. . . . The new ethical norm is 'progress,' and by progress is meant basically *economic* progress, the growth of production and the creation of an ever more efficient system of production."[25] From his earliest years, Fromm had a keen sense of not only the political and economic ramifications of socioeconomic change but also the moral and ethical.

Fromm observes that the more established religions, in spite of achieving status and respect, have failed to protect humanity from the cultlike worship of the state. Instead, as history indicates, they have cooperated with secular powers and failed to provide the prophetic voice that is called for, a voice he locates within the spirit of the Ten Commandments and the Golden Rule. Continuing to refer to the distinction between authoritarian

24. Fromm, *Psychoanalysis and Religion*, 121.

25. Fromm, *Revolution of Hope*, 87 (emphasis original).

and humanistic religion, he characterizes the former as emphasizing the control qualities of a higher power and the need for obedience, reverence, and worship, and the latter as emphasizing moral qualities, law, and justice, as well as the intrinsic strengths of the person. In authoritarian religion, disobedience is identified as the core sin and submission as the sole means through which one may escape the resultant loneliness and sense of personal disorientation. He references two approaches to the word *faith*, one that emphasizes assent to external propositions and the other pointing more to a certainty of conviction based upon one's own experiences, thoughts, and feelings, a theme that will surface again in the works of Rollo May and the stages of faith development proposed by James Fowler.

In humanistic religion, Fromm observes, "God is a symbol of *man's own powers* which he tries to realize in his life, and is not a symbol of force and domination, having *power over man*."[26] He finds this humanistic emphasis in early Buddhism, Taoism, the Hasidic tradition, and the teachings of Isaiah, Socrates, Jesus, and the seventeenth-century ethicist Baruch Spinoza, as well as in the mystical tradition and the philosophical underpinnings of the Enlightenment. The differences between authoritarian and humanistic religion cannot be reduced to that between the theistic and nontheistic; it is not about the thought systems as such but the attitudes that undergird them.

Fromm offers Judaism, as presented through the Hebrew Scriptures, as a fitting example of a religion wherein both authoritarian and humanistic elements might be recognized. After the flood destroyed all of life save that which Noah was appointed to preserve on the ark, God made a covenant with humanity never to destroy life again. God thereby bound himself "by a constitution to which both he and man must adhere; he is bound by a principle which he cannot violate, the principle of respect for life."[27] A capricious, authoritarian act of destruction is followed by a humanistic covenant between God and humanity.

Shifting his lens to the Christian Scriptures, Fromm notes that "Jesus's precept that 'the true kingdom of God is within you' is the simple and clear expression of nonauthoritarian thinking,"[28] adding, however, that this formulation was severely compromised when Christianity became the religion of the Roman Empire. Nevertheless, he sees its humanistic core perduring throughout history, and he credits the mystical tradition for keeping that humanistic element alive.

26. Fromm, *Psychoanalysis and Religion*, 37 (emphasis in original).

27. Fromm, *Psychoanalysis and Religion*, 44.

28. Fromm, *Psychoanalysis and Religion*, 48.

Humanistic religion interprets God as the image of "man's higher self, a symbol of what man potentially is or ought to become."[29] Authoritarian religion, in contrast, interprets God as "the sole possessor of what was originally man's: of his reason and his love. . . . The more perfect God becomes, the more imperfect becomes man."[30] With God in sole possession of that which makes one fully human, alienation ensues and a vicious cycle defines our lives: the more we praise God (thereby projecting our most deeply human qualities onto God), the emptier we become, resulting in a more profound sense of sinfulness. In turn, the more sinful we feel, the more we experience the need to turn our praise to God.

Recognizing psychoanalysis as a pathway through which we might identify a more humanistic approach to religion, Fromm notes a distinction between those in the field who understand their role as that of "physician of the soul," on the one hand, and those focused merely on social adjustment, on the other. He observes that psychiatry's original focus was on symptoms such as obsessions, compulsions, phobias, and paranoia, the causes of which were understood as psychic rather than organic. The goal was the removal of the symptoms, as it is in contemporary medicine. But Freud and others had emphasized that the symptoms were only the most conspicuous expression of a deeper neurotic disturbance and that analysis of the person's character was necessary for lasting cure. Fromm, who no doubt saw himself as a physician of the soul, took this a step further, suggesting that the neurosis has spiritual roots, and he set himself the task of applying his spiritualized psychoanalysis to identifying a religion he could believe in, a humanistic religion.

Fromm begins his psychoanalytic/spiritual review of religion with a reinterpretation of Freud's most prized discovery, the Oedipus complex. For Fromm, the Oedipus complex is a metaphor for the child's separation from the family ties, a task that is essential to the full expression of one's selfhood and one's truth. He interprets Matt 10:35, wherein Jesus tells his followers that he has come to set child against parent, in terms of cutting the emotional cords that prevent the full development of the person. Ever broadening his perspective beyond the mere psychoanalytic, Fromm sees in the parent/child dependence, which he describes as incestuous, the roots of nationalism and racism with their fixation on the "tribe, the nation, the race, the state, the social class, the political parties."[31] Arguing that humanity cannot progress without breaking such ties, he espouses an approach to moral

29. Fromm, *Psychoanalysis and Religion*, 49.

30. Fromm, *Psychoanalysis and Religion*, 49–50.

31. Fromm, *Psychoanalysis and Religion*, 81.

decision-making that highlights universal values rather than tribal particulars, concluding that "only the complete eradication of incestuous fixation will permit the realization of the brotherhood of man."[32] For Fromm, then, Freud's insights on the Oedipus complex become most significant when they are freed from their narrow formulation in sexual terms and given broader spiritual, cultural, and sociological significance.

Fromm interprets human history in terms of an initial act of disobedience, but he places emphasis not on the original sin narrative but on the emancipation of humanity from the restrictive security of the garden of Eden and the embrace of authentic freedom. Highlighting the significance of this insight, John Morgan, in *Clinical Psychotherapy: A History of Theory and Practice*, observes that this interpretation of the Adam and Eve exile story in terms of the liberation of the human species is "the cornerstone of Fromm's humanistic psychology."[33] This theme of freedom and liberation runs through the story of Israel, examples being Abraham's leaving his native land; Moses's leaving the bondage of Egypt; and the prophets' calls for truth, justice, and love.

Fromm prophesies that the nation-state "must perish if man becomes tied to it in such a way that the welfare of the state, its power, and its glory become the criterion of good and evil."[34] It is interesting to note that these words were written shortly after the creation of the state of Israel, which Fromm, unlike his contemporary and coreligionist Martin Buber, opposed, fearing that it would lead to the idolatry of the state rather than to the fulfillment of humanistic values. He observes that the arc of organized religions throughout history tends toward the bureaucratic, wherein it is "no longer God who is worshiped but the group that claims to speak in his name."[35] Perhaps he wanted something more for Judaism than the political freedom of statehood; perhaps he envisioned a more authentic freedom that does not lose itself within the authoritarian structure of the nation-state.

Unlike Freud, who discounted the injunction to "love thy neighbor as thyself," Fromm recognizes it as foundational to all humanistic religions. He sees this basic need for love as central also to psychoanalysis and, by extension, to all therapy: "Whatever complaints the neurotic patient may have, whatever symptoms he may present are rooted in the inability to love."[36] With his therapeutic lens focusing on the centrality of love, Fromm

32. Fromm, *Psychoanalysis and Religion*, 82.

33. Morgan, *Clinical Psychotherapy*, 305.

34. Fromm, *Psychoanalysis and Religion*, 84–85.

35. Fromm, *Psychoanalysis and Religion*, 85.

36. Fromm, *Psychoanalysis and Religion*, 87.

reframes his signature distinction between authoritarian and humanistic religion by reminding us that in authoritarian religion, sin is about disobedience and rebellion, with fear and trembling being the natural response to the possibility of getting caught in wrongdoing. It is not about following an ethical norm; it is about the fear of a punitive power. In contrast, in humanistic religion, the emphasis is on the discovery of one's own voice, "the guardian of our integrity which recalls us to ourselves when we are in danger of losing ourselves."[37] In humanistic religion, doing wrong is not met with retribution but with the invitation to right the wrong, an approach given contemporary expression in discussions about restorative versus retributive justice. Likewise, the goal of psychoanalysis for Fromm is not about criticism for any personality shortcomings but about helping the client become more aware of the voice of conscience and respond directly to that internal voice.

In the final chapter of *Psychoanalysis and Religion*, titled "Is Psychoanalysis a Threat to Religion?," Fromm concludes his study with an impassioned argument against any perceived incompatibility between the psychoanalytic tradition and religion properly understood. Always seeking a "yes/and" approach whenever possible—psychoanalysis *and* humanistic psychology, religious sensitivity *and* humanism, even strict monotheism *and* nontheistic ultimate concern, "two views which, though different, need not fight each other"[38]—Fromm was at heart a unifier who instinctively sought to transcend the various dialectics he encountered. Where he does see an unbridgeable chasm is between psychoanalysis (and, by extension, humanistic psychology) and authoritarian forms of religion, and in the final pages of the book, he shifts his focus toward a spirited defense of humanistic religion, one that honors the religious spirit and eschews all taint of authoritarianism.

Driven by the desire to reframe religion in humanistic terms, Fromm begins by drawing attention to four dimensions or perspectives through which religion can free itself from authoritarianism and the role that psychoanalysis might play in supporting that. These dimensions or perspectives are referred to as the existential, scientific-magical, ritualistic, and semantic.

Looking first at the issue from an existentialist perspective, Fromm observes that psychoanalysis serves to support a more humanistic form of religion through its promotion of existential themes such as consciousness, awareness, reason, freedom of choice, and responsibility. Through psychoanalysis, the client becomes more aware of the self and of the influence of

37. Fromm, *Psychoanalysis and Religion*, 88.

38. Fromm, *Art of Loving*, 67.

others within the larger sociocultural milieu. The client experiences an enhanced awareness of the *why* of behavior and is empowered to recognize and stand firm against the retreat from freedom that characterizes the inauthentic person. Further, the client is better prepared to ward off the threats to the person—and to religion itself—presented by the advance of the marketing orientation in society, which, through a subtle assault on conscious freedom, devalues the person, reducing him or her to the status of an automaton. An argument could be made that today's "theology of abundance" and its focus on the accumulation of wealth and possessions rather than existential themes such as personal "consciousness, awareness, reason, freedom of choice, and responsibility" is an example of what Fromm feared for religion.

Looking at the role that psychoanalysis might play in freeing religion from authoritarianism from the scientific-magical perspective, Fromm references the role religion has played through the centuries as an interpreter of natural phenomena: it was God who sent the tornado to that North Texas community (or God who spared that community while surrounding cotton fields were devastated), not natural weather forces involving thunderstorms and rotating winds. In response, Fromm, like Freud before him, celebrates science's replacement of God as an interpreter of nature, thereby freeing religion to focus on matters of the soul. He notes that most of the antireligious arguments that men and women of science have made over the years are not directed at religion itself but at religious claims to serve as the sole interpreter of both spirituality and science—authoritarian religion.

Turning his attention to the ritualistic perspective, Fromm distinguishes between rational and irrational rituals; ritual hand washing, for example, could be viewed as a spiritual symbol of an inner cleansing or as a superstitious attempt to ward off evil. Fromm sees rituals—greeting patterns, for example—as symbolic expressions that are essential to interpersonal living, and he views psychoanalysis as poised to distinguish between the rational and the irrational in both religious and secular settings. Authentic, humanistically oriented religion, according to Fromm, understands rituals as meaningful, symbolic formulations, not as purveyors of magic.

Finally, Fromm addresses the role psychoanalysis might play in freeing religion from authoritarianism from the semantic perspective. He observes that religion speaks in a language different from that of daily life; it is symbolic language, "the only universal language the human race has known."[39] Where religion often errs is in taking symbolic language as literal instead of understanding it as an expression of the soul's experience. The

39. Fromm, *Psychoanalysis and Religion*, 111.

psychoanalytic tradition finds profound wisdom in symbolic expression; so too does religion. In both cases, the key is to remember that the expression is symbolic. In his classic *Stages of Faith*, which will be reviewed in a later chapter, James Fowler has much to add about symbols as expressions of the soul's experience.

Fromm closes his study of the intersection of psychoanalysis and religion by lamenting that, since the Enlightenment, we have made belief in an external God the central religious question for believers, an emphasis that he sees as preventing the development of a fully humanistic religion. He advocates retaining the symbol of God and the word *God* but giving it a meaning different from that which it has within the monotheistic tradition represented by the prophets and the medieval Christian and Jewish theologians. He proposes an alternative understanding of God as a "symbol of all that which man is not, a symbol of a spiritual reality which we can strive to realize in ourselves and yet can never describe or define."[40] He poetically describes God as "like the horizon which sets the limitations of our sight"[41]—God cannot be grasped, is always out of reach, is undefinable. He interprets the "I am that I am" of Exodus in terms of the *process* of being, rather than as a description of a finite entity (a distinction famously advanced by Harvard Divinity School professor Paul Tillich and, following him, Rollo May), and he enjoins us to avoid any reference to God that suggests certitude about one's definition or denunciation of another's. Again, following the lead of Tillich, who merits nomination as humanistic psychology's "designated theologian," Fromm sees the insistence on forcing God into definitive statements as a new form of idolatry, an idolatry of words comparable to primitive people's idolatry of stone figures.

THE SUMMATION OF FROMM'S LIFEWORK—TO HAVE OR TO BE?

In 1966, Fromm had a massive heart attack, after which he repaired to Lozano, Switzerland, for a more serene environment. But certainly not an inactive one: while there, he attended a *Pacem in Terris* conference in Geneva, where he praised Pope John XXIII as "a spiritual ally in the struggle against nuclear weapons and warfare"[42] and immersed himself in meditation, the spirituality of Meister Eckhart, and Zen Buddhism. *To Have or to Be?*, the culmination of his major contributions to social psychology, was published

40. Fromm, *Psychoanalysis and Religion*, 115.
41. Fromm, *Psychoanalysis and Religion*, 115.
42. L. Friedman, *Lives of Erich Fromm*, 269.

in 1976. An indication of the widespread influence that he enjoyed during his last decade was Pope John Paul II's reference to *To Have or to Be?* as "a great spiritual book with humane values—not the problematic values of consumption and the marketplace."[43]

To Have or to Be? was published thirty-five years after Fromm's groundbreaking *Escape from Freedom* and four years before his death. He was seventy-six years old, had had one heart attack, and would soon have another. He surely knew time was against him, adding more poignancy to his writing. If *To Have or to Be?* is more review and consolidation than provider of new insights, as biographer Friedman occasionally observes about Fromm's later works, it does that consolidation well, presenting a man who had dedicated his life to a well-defined mission and was now gathering and presenting his most mature thoughts.

In his foreword to the book, Fromm references the term *radical-humanistic psychoanalysis*, suggesting at this late point in his life a new understanding of his place in the larger humanistic world. His work is radical—it goes to the root of the matter, to the spiritual core, whether the healing needed is for the individual or the culture at large. It is humanistic—this is his religion, a humanism with a pronounced Old Testament prophetic tone. And it is psychoanalytic—it shines a light on our illusions and irrationalities so that we, both individually and culturally, may face ourselves and the world more directly, more authentically.

Fromm begins by criticizing both capitalism, for its exploitation of people and resources, and socialism, for its failure to recreate society and advance humanistic values. He argues for ethical principles rather than the law of the market as the proper guide to economic behavior, adding that we have turned our backs on the "Messianic vision of harmony between humankind and nature by conquering nature, by transforming it to our own purposes until the conquest has become more and more equivalent to destruction,"[44] words of much relevance today as we face the accumulating effects of climate change and our failures to be faithful stewards of the environment. He calls for a new humanistic ethos that advocates for social responsibility rather than personal success, referencing "Masters of Living," exemplars such as the Buddha, Jesus, the Hebrew prophets, the medieval mystic Meister Eckhart, the anonymous author of *The Cloud of Unknowing*, and Baruch Spinoza.

If Paul Tillich is humanistic psychology's "designated theologian," Baruch Spinoza is its philosophical forefather and patron saint. A few words

43. L. Friedman, *Lives of Erich Fromm*, 327.

44. Fromm, *To Have or to Be*, 8.

are in order regarding the frequent references to his life and works by humanistically oriented philosophers, psychologists, and theologians, particularly Erich Fromm.

A seventeenth-century Dutch philosopher of Portuguese Jewish ancestry, Spinoza emphasized a religion of reason, arguing that "there is *no* virtue whatsoever in believing with perfect faith. The virtue is believing because you *know*, which requires proof."[45] At that time, Amsterdam was considered a haven for religious outsiders, a relatively safe place from the religious wars and persecutions that ravaged much of Europe during the years following the Reformation. *Relatively* safe: at age twenty-three, Spinoza was expelled from his own Jewish community in Amsterdam because of his secular philosophy—a philosophy of reason that to the religious authorities smacked of atheism.

What so angered many in the Jewish community was that Spinoza, writing at the cusp of the Enlightenment, was arguing *against* religion as a guide to life and *for* its replacement by science, which was understood more broadly at the time to include reason, nature, and philosophy. Spinoza took aim at the Bible, particularly the Hebrew Scriptures of his own heritage, denying that it possesses a unique truth or exclusive claim to representing the word of God. For Spinoza, "the word of God" may be found in any book that promotes "virtue, happiness, and well-being in this world."[46] He further argued that the Bible should be used for the sole purpose of encouraging one another through "justice and loving kindness to your fellow human beings,"[47] a theology of right conduct, not right belief. In addition, he argued that "the difference between right and wrong is immanent within our human nature,"[48] not dependent upon religious decrees. "Love your neighbor" is the central message of the Bible, Spinoza argued, following on the long tradition of the Jewish scholar and rabbi Hillel the Elder, who articulated what we today refer to as the Golden Rule during the first century BCE. Further, Spinoza attacked the core of Jewish identity itself, the sense of specialness or "chosenness," arguing that "no group is more or less endowed with gifts or favor by God or Nature than any other group,"[49] and he railed against "the jealous fantasy that [God] loves us—our kind, our people—more than others."[50] Spinoza was advocating for a different kind of Judaism—indeed,

45. Goldstein, *Betraying Spinoza*, 86 (emphasis in original).

46. Nadler, *Book Forged in Hell*, 74–75.

47. Nadler, *Book Forged in Hell*, 120.

48. Goldstein, *Betraying Spinoza*, 53.

49. Nadler, *Book Forged in Hell*, 161.

50. Goldstein, *Betraying Spinoza*, 238.

a different kind of religion—centuries before Maslow and Fromm would address those issues.

That reference to "God or Nature," with the two words understood as synonyms and to be used interchangeably, is significant, and Spinoza argued that what he was denouncing was not the God he was identifying with Nature but the idea that there exists a personal God, *outside* of nature, who intervenes in human affairs. He rejected the charge that he was an atheist, insisting instead that God and Nature are one . . . and "the power of God *is* the power of Nature."[51] Defining nature's place in our lives in the *Theological-Political Treatise*, a political, theological, and philosophical work published in 1670, Spinoza observes that what we refer to as

> the edicts and commands of God, and hence of providence, are nothing other than the order of nature. That is, when the Bible says this or that was done by God, it simply means that it was done according to the laws and order of nature, and not, as most people think, that nature ceased to operate for a time or that its order was briefly interrupted.[52]

Needless to say, Spinoza's dismissal of the idea of a personal, external God and his identification of God with nature were not received well by the religious authorities in Amsterdam, and still today feelings about Spinoza remain strong in many quarters. He is quoted favorably by humanists and honored by many as a precursor to the Enlightenment, but, as a rabbi colleague once shared, "to Orthodox Jews he is lethal."

Interestingly, Spinoza spoke respectfully about Jesus as "the prophet who excelled all others."[53] His friends were largely Christians—renegades among their fellow Christians, but Christians nonetheless. Like the humanistic psychologists, particularly Maslow and Fromm, he understood religion not in terms of differing denominations, but according to their relative emphasis on universal values—like the Golden Rule and the commandment to love. For Spinoza, "true religion" hinges on "a simple code of moral behavior accompanied by an understanding of what constitutes the best condition for a human being and how to achieve it."[54] Further, as did Maslow, he understood religious feelings in terms of "a state of awe that is experienced when one appreciates the grand scheme of the laws of Nature."[55]

51. Nadler, *Book Forged in Hell*, 97 (emphasis in original).
52. Spinoza, *Theological-Political Treatise*, 89.
53. Nadler, *Book Forged in Hell*, 170.
54. Nadler, *Book Forged in Hell*, 52.
55. Yalom, *Spinoza Problem*, 268.

It is no accident that Maslow included both Spinoza and Jesus on his lists of models of self-actualization. And it is no surprise that in his final book, *To Have or to Be?*, Erich Fromm would pay tribute to Spinoza, a seventeenth-century antecedent to the humanistic psychology movement who argued for the naturalness, rather than the supernaturalness, of virtue; for science and philosophy over religious dogma; and for an understanding of the religious as that which provides a sense of awe, wonder, and mystery in our lives. Above all else, Spinoza strove to free science and philosophy from religious oversight. And like the humanistic psychologists, he consistently argued that he was not opposed to religion per se but to religion that considered itself beyond the reach of the laws of nature.

Indications of Fromm's debt to Spinoza abound in *To Have or to Be?*, in which he distinguishes between *having* persons, who resist change because it might dislodge a part of themselves, something they own that defines them, and *being* persons, who are open to new learning and the growth that flows from that. *Being* persons, like Spinoza, understand authority not in terms of power and exploitation but as a rational relationship directed toward helping others grow and becoming more fully human. Fromm further distinguishes between knowing as a process and knowledge as possession, the former beginning with the exposure of illusions and distinguished by the increasing revelation of truth, while the latter is limited to the accumulation of facts.

This having/being dichotomy has relevance to the word *faith* as well. In the having mode, faith refers to unprovable formulations that we accept out of submission to another and a desire to be part of a group that believes it possesses the truth. In the being mode, it is an attitude, an internal movement, an orientation toward another, that begins within the self. Faith in the having mode is about possession, while in the being mode, it is about relationship. In like manner, love in the having mode is about possessing; in the being mode, about relating.

Never far removed from the influence of the Jewish prophetic tradition on his life and work, Fromm observes that one of the themes of the Old Testament is letting go, freeing the self of possessions. He emphasizes that the opposite of possessing is being, or letting be, adding that the Sabbath—"the fountain of life for the Jews . . . one of the great innovations in human evolution"[56]—is properly understood as a day set aside to restore the harmony between humanity and nature, to take a pause in humanity's overuse of nature and to let it be.

56. Fromm, *To Have or to Be*, 50.

The word *messiah* itself takes on new meaning in this prophetic vision. For Fromm, the messiah is not a person but a historical period, one that transcends the Old and New Testaments and during which humanity will experience what it means to be truly human. Indeed, the word *God* is likewise metaphorical for Fromm: rather than representing an external deity, it depicts "a combination of ethical and spiritual ideals and societal aspirations that the Israelites developed with time, and called *God*."[57]

As in *Psychoanalysis and Religion*, Fromm addresses the creation story and Adam's disobedience, but now from a deeper perspective reflective of his spiritual growth. He notes that both church and state have highlighted Adam's disobedience as the original sin, doing so to protect their hierarchical power structures. But for Fromm, now deeply versed in the mystical tradition of Meister Eckhart and others, the original sin is not about disobedience but estrangement.

Before the fall, Adam and Eve experienced a state of unity; there was no shame in their nakedness because they did not see each other as separate. With the advent of sin, they—we, humankind—now face each other as isolated, disconnected, self-serving individuals. The choices that consequently confronted Adam and Eve are *our* choices: to submit and dominate or "to reach out and to *one* ourselves with the world.[58] Fromm highlights this word *one*, calling for atonement—"at-*one*-ment"—as the cure. This is Fromm as faithful, mature student of the mystical tradition.

Fromm understands religion not as reducible to specific doctrines or beliefs but as an integral part of our character structure—"We are what we are devoted to, and what we are devoted to is what motivates our conduct."[59] In the spirit of Maslow, he asks why we cannot identify and agree about our psychological and spiritual needs, just as we do about our biological needs. For animals, unencumbered by the psychological and the spiritual, instincts provide all that is necessary; for humans, a frame of orientation and an object of devotion that point to specific values through which to govern our lives are needed, and Fromm adds that there is often a disconnect between what we—both individually and societally—espouse as our values and what we truly value. He pays tribute to martyrs, those who lived their values within a nonsupportive socioeconomic structure, and contrasts them with the pagan hero, whose values are strength, victory, and exploitation. He asks why we hold on to Christianity, whose values are markedly different from the pagan values we actually honor, and responds in terms of

57. Schimmel, "Judaism and the Origins," 35.

58. Fromm, *To Have or to Be*, 124 (emphasis in original).

59. Fromm, *To Have or to Be*, 135–36.

the societal need for order, recommending that we substitute our *belief* in Jesus, who can carry our virtue for us, with *following* Jesus. We have made belief a substitute for behavior.

Fromm presents a summary list of humanistic values and, again reminiscent of Maslow, speaks of the arrival of the "New Man." He calls for hardheaded realism in this task of creating the new society, beginning with the shedding of illusions and identifying and confronting difficulties head-on. This cautionary approach does not dissuade him from describing this desired future in now-familiar messianic terms—"a united new humankind living in solidarity and peace, free from economic determination and from war and class struggle."[60] Having no illusions about what is at stake, he offers suggestions for establishing this humanistic society, from closing the gap between rich and poor and the liberation of women from patriarchal domination to nuclear disarmament—themes strikingly contemporary. Forgoing the binary choice between self-serving materialism and institutionalized religion, Fromm closes with the call for a new religious spirit, a new "nontheistic, noninstitutionalized 'religiosity' [that] is not an attack on the existing religions . . . [but a] synthesis between the spiritual call of the Late Medieval world and the development of rational thought and science since the Renaissance . . . *The City of Being*."[61]

A Humanistic Legacy

Fromm suffered numerous illnesses during his life related to a 1931 tuberculosis diagnosis. In 1977, he had a second heart attack, followed a year later by a third that resulted in brain damage, memory loss, hearing loss, and subsequent depression. In an interview late that year, he reminisced about his sense of estrangement and marginalization as a child, the positive and compensating influence of talmudic scholars and rabbis, and the humanist ethic—themes woven continually throughout the fabric of his life story. He died in Locarno, Switzerland, in March 1980, following a fourth heart attack. His third wife, Annis Freeman, died three years later. Lawrence Friedman closes his biography with reference to tributes to Fromm following his death, perhaps most significant of which is one referencing Fromm's own words prescribing love as "the only satisfactory solution to the problems of human existence."[62]

60. Fromm, *To Have or to Be*, 174.

61. Fromm, *To Have or to Be*, 202 (emphasis in original).

62. L. Friedman, *Lives of Erich Fromm*, 337.

Recognition of Fromm came from many quarters, including at least one pope, John Paul II, who, as indicated earlier, praised *To Have or to Be?* American politicians on the left of the spectrum read his books and sought his support. Luminaries in the great story of twentieth-century sociology and psychology called him friend and colleague. He touched a chord with the larger, universal public—the sales of his books routinely reached into the millions, and they were translated into dozens of languages.

Among the many challenges Fromm embraced was the interlacing of psychoanalysis and socialist humanism. He credited Freud with founding a science through which reason could unlock the irrational and the unconscious and, as a result, allow us to free ourselves from their control. He saw Freud as creating a synthesis of two historical movements, the Enlightenment (the rational element) and Romanticism (the nonrational element), and he understood his own task as the synthesis of socialism (the socioeconomic and political element) and psychoanalysis (the individual and psychological element).

Fromm countered Freud's pessimism with a long-term optimism, tempered by short-term doubts and frustrations. Freud had reason for his pessimism: he had seen his entire world—the bourgeois, liberal, patriarchal world of Austria-Hungary—collapse around him, followed by the barbarism of Nazism. Fromm too had experienced the onslaught of demagoguery and authoritarianism, and he occasionally expressed doubts about the ability of psychoanalysis to overcome individual and societal compulsions to repeat negative behavior. But Fromm was temperamentally opposite the pessimistic Freud; he was a lover of life with a humanist heart, within which pessimism could take up only temporary residence. It is no surprise that he wrote so passionately about love and freedom as the answers to individual and societal ills.

Like many in the broad humanistic psychology movement, Fromm was nontheistic. Yet he was a deeply spiritual man, steeped in the traditions of his Jewish ancestors, immersed in a Being-centered life. There was a bit of Victor Frankl in him: just as the devout Frankl honored and practiced his Jewish faith, closing himself in his study each morning with the black leather straps and boxes containing the Scriptures,[63] Fromm too repaired to his study daily to immerse himself in an hour's meditation. He was a prophetic peace-and-justice advocate in a postwar culture that paid little heed to peace or justice. And he preached a consistent message of love as the path to healing.

63. Klingberg, *When Life Calls Out*, 322–23.

Like his colleague and friend Harry Stack Sullivan, Fromm saw personality as relational, but whereas Sullivan emphasized the interpersonal, Fromm focused more on the societal. Through an emphasis on social character and his developing embrace of the oneness of all creation, he reminded us of John Donne's insight proffered three centuries before that "no man is an island, / Entire of itself"; each truly is a "piece of the continent, / A part of the main," and humankind is served only when we embrace and live out that truth.[64] As Fromm observes in *The Revolution of Hope* regarding what he refers to as the "humanist promise," "every person carries within himself all of humanity . . . within ourselves we are saints and criminals, although in varying degrees, and hence . . . there is nothing in another person which we cannot feel as part of ourselves."[65]

64. Donne, "No Man Is an Island."

65. Fromm, *Revolution of Hope*, 86–87.

Chapter 6

Ultimate Concerns

The Existential Humanism of Rollo May

We define religion as the assumption that life has meaning. Religion, or lack of it, is shown not in some intellectual or verbal formulations but in one's total orientation to life. Religion is whatever the individual takes to be his ultimate concern. One's religious attitude is to be found at that point where he has a conviction that there are values in human existence worth living and dying for.

—Rollo May, *Man's Search for Himself*

In 1939, thirty-year-old Rollo May, who had counseled students at Michigan State College in the mid-1930s, wrote *The Art of Counseling*, which was based on lectures he had given to student workers at Methodist Episcopal seminaries titled "Counseling and Personality Adjustment." The idea that the work of healing could be conceived as an art form, as a process, was in its infancy then, and May's book has the distinction of being the first in America to specifically address how that process works. Carl Rogers's *The Clinical Treatment of the Problem Child*, published the same year, also addresses the art of counseling, but its primary scope, as the title suggests, was toward the guidance of children in difficulty. Fifty years later, during which both May and Rogers worked to fine-tune the art of counseling, May published a revised edition, which Irvin Yalom praised as "still timely, wise, and, above all, immediately practical to both client and counselor."[1]

In a telling comparison of Rogers and May, Jessica Grogan observes that whereas "Rogers's religiosity seemed almost detachable, May's spirituality was his connective tissue,"[2] adding that May saw himself as "a public minister, aiming to treat the spiritual, philosophical, and psychological condition of the culture as much as of the individual."[3] Unlike Rogers, who discovered the spiritual dimension only late in life, May gives it a place of honor from the beginning. And like Fromm, he grappled throughout life with the distinction between healthy religion, which emphasizes personal freedom and responsibility and encourages an internal locus of moral decision-making, and unhealthy religion, which promotes obedience and submission to an external authority.

Through various projects and professional gatherings, May intersected regularly with Maslow, Rogers, and Fromm during the glory days of humanistic psychology, the 1950s through the 1980s. May was much drawn to Fromm, whom he saw as a fellow intellectual and student of the wisdom tradition, and he "loved Abe Maslow as a person"[4] but disliked the aloof Rogers, who expressed little interest in philosophical or theological deliberation. That dislike of Rogers did not prevent either of them from genuinely praising each other's work. At the William Alanson White Institute, May worked with Maslow and Rogers on producing *Existential Psychology*, a compilation of essays on the existentialist contribution to the new humanist direction in psychology; also working at the institute at that time were Erich Fromm and Harry Stack Sullivan.

The philosophically oriented May fit well within the larger story of the development of psychotherapy in the twentieth century, with all the various psychological stirrings that animated it, such as social psychology, existentialism, phenomenology, and the differing schools within the psychoanalytic tradition. He was influenced at an intimate level by the Lutheran theologian and recent German émigré Paul Tillich, who became his lifelong friend and father figure. May's most personal book, *Paulus: Reminiscence of a Friendship*, was written in 1973.

Like Maslow, Rogers, and Fromm, May was two generations removed from Freud and, as a result, more able to appreciate his genius while avoiding the drama around who was true to the master and who, having taken

1. May, *Art of Counseling*, back cover.
2. Grogan, *Encountering America*, 73.
3. Grogan, *Encountering America*, 74.
4. Abzug, *Psyche and Soul*, 234.

a separate path, had fallen out of grace. To May, Freud was always "the venerable Freud,"[5] and let each of us take of his teachings what fits while leaving the rest behind. A quote from *The Cry for Myth* suggests the respect May had for Freud's contributions, in addition to the respect he had for the spiritual calling of the counseling profession: "We cannot deny that we who are therapists deal with people's moral and spiritual questions and that we fill the role of father-confessor as part of our armamentarium, as shown in Freud's position *behind* and unseen by the person confessing."[6]

The Early Years: Family Conflict and Personal Growth

Rollo May was born in 1909 in Ada, Ohio, and grew up in Marine City, Michigan, in the southeastern part of the state. Like Rogers, he experienced "a typical small-town, midwestern childhood . . . [typified by] hard work, fidelity, honesty."[7] Unlike Rogers's upbringing, however, May's was troubled and unstable. The second of six children of Earl Tuttle (E. T.) and Madie May, his younger years were marred by his sister Ruth's struggle with schizophrenia; his mother's borderline-like behaviors—she is described as "unpredictable and often unhinged, snuggling with him one minute and screaming at him the next";[8] his father's infidelities; and his parents' eventual divorce.

In response to those challenges, May assumed responsibility for the well-being of his mother and sister, later helping them financially, and became something of a surrogate dad for his younger brother, Don. Whenever he sensed their need for his presence, such as when his parents divorced in 1934, he would hasten home, and the internal conflict he would experience between attending to his own responsibilities and the ongoing family drama would plague him throughout his life. Perhaps more than any other psychological theorist studied in these pages, Rollo May's life most represents the effects of the tangled interplay between nature and nurture, between biology and life experiences (especially early life experiences), on personality development. By nature, May was drawn to the darker, more introspective, more self-critical side of life, and so much of what he experienced at home made present to him, at an early age, the human failures, foibles, and occasional madness that plague the species.

E. T. worked as a field secretary for the YMCA, at the time a consciously Christian organization dedicated to both the physical and spiritual

5. May, *Man's Search for Himself*, 177.
6. May, *Cry for Myth*, 151 (emphasis in original).
7. Abzug, *Psyche and Soul*, 37.
8. Abzug, *Psyche and Soul*, 6.

development of young men. In addition, the Y promoted "a progressive reform program . . . [that] supported educational and moral uplift projects for African Americans, abolition of child labor, . . . the right of employees to organize and . . . the eradication of poverty."[9] Rollo worked at the Y throughout his early years in various capacities, and at age twenty-five, while a counselor at Michigan State University, he held the position of student secretary. Both the sense of religious mission and the sociopolitical engagement he experienced at the Y would affect May throughout his life.

While a student at Michigan State, May published editorials critical of the school administration that resulted in a decision to leave—a "decision" that bears the imprint of mutuality. An indication of what May wrote that so unsettled the administration may be surmised from a paragraph in *Man's Search for Himself*, in which he discusses his college years in the late 1920s—which sound much like college years in the late 1960s. He references the "sense of power we got from the causes and crusades, from knowing so staunchly what we were rebelling against, be it war, or sexual taboos, or companionate marriage, or booze, or prohibition, or what not."[10] One can easily imagine any one of those "causes and crusades" drawing a disapproving eye from 1920s academia.

May's spiritual struggles, tinged with a dose of moral superiority not unlike that of many students during the late 1960s, also surfaced around this time. He began to wonder if he was called to a life in the religious field, where he might transcend the stifling conformity of a rapidly technologizing American society. These strivings for an educational experience beyond the conventional led him to Oberlin College, a university known for its "excellence in the humanities and its long tradition of Christian activism."[11] Both a love for the humanities and social, if not Christian, activism would engage May's attention throughout his life.

May graduated from Oberlin in 1930 with a bachelor's degree in English. Like Rogers, he was drawn to missionary work in China, but his application did not survive the selection process. Nonetheless intent on spending his immediate postgraduate years overseas, he accepted a teaching post at a missionary school in Greece, Anatolia College, which allowed him to follow another of his passions at the time, art. When not engaged in teaching, May spent time studying and painting the indigenous people of Poland and traveling throughout Europe and Turkey.

9. Abzug, *Psyche and Soul*, 8.

10. May, *Man's Search for Himself*, 177.

11. Abzug, *Psyche and Soul*, 19.

Also during those years, May attended Alfred Adler's summer training program, an experience that influenced the direction of his professional work and writing, which is dotted throughout with Adlerian terminology. Introspective, ruminative, and self-critical, May readily related to Adler's teachings on the inferiority complex, which if successfully channeled might lead to personal empowerment and mastery. He was also being formed in a unique mix of spirituality, existentialism, and humanism, one that would not shrink from engaging the darker side of life; as philosophy professor Clement Reeves wrote in *The Psychology of Rollo May*, the "European experiences awakened in May an awareness of the tragic side of human being."[12] Those experiences overseas further served to intensify his sense of personal moral responsibility, and, like Rogers, he would soon start to question some of the religious teachings of his childhood. May was not yet ready to replace his Christianity with a more humanistic spirituality, but he was taking the first steps in that direction.

The eastern Europe trip affected the young Rollo May in ways comparable to the effect the China trip had on the young Carl Rogers. From a retrospective of over forty years, he wrote about it in *Paulus*, in words that accurately reflect the character he was developing:

> As a young man of twenty, I was impressed by the tragic sense of life which infused the culture of Europe, and especially that of ancient and modern Greece. It seemed to me that the delight in life and spontaneous joy which I had found a great deal more in Europe than in my years of growing up in Michigan had their source in depths which can be reached only by way of this tragic sense. Without it one experiences more superficial amusement and comfort. Europe meant for me in those early twenties not only a physical emancipation but a new spiritual and intellectual emancipation as well.[13]

Upon returning to the United States in the mid-1930s, May reconnected with Michigan State, where he would teach, advise students through the local YMCA, and serve in a youth minister capacity at an interdenominational church near the college. Shortly thereafter, he enrolled at Union Theological Seminary in New York, where he absorbed its liberal theology and learned existentialism under the tutelage of Paul Tillich.

As much as May was a humanist, so too was he an existentialist; existentialism would, to a large degree, differentiate his brand of humanistic psychology from that of others in the field. As referenced in the first chapter,

12. Reeves, *Psychology of Rollo May*, 254.

13. May, *Paulus*, 2.

May defined existentialism as "centering upon the *existing* person . . . on the human being as he is *emerging, becoming*." It's basic principle, in the words of John Morgan in *Post-Biblical Religion: Essays in Secular Spirituality*, is that we must take the initiative "in both self-defining and self-determining who we are, who we will be, and where we are going."[14] It does not concern itself with immutable principles or theories but with the person in the midst of his or her current struggles. As such, it focuses on the subjective experience of the person, typically addressing questions of freedom, responsibility, choice, meaning, suffering, and authenticity. The theologian influenced by existentialism, for example, would be less interested in proofs for the existence of God as in how one experiences God and what meaning is placed on that experience.

Taking the lead in adapting existentialism to the counseling office, May emphasized that the existentialist approach to therapy is one that focuses on "the experiences of the instantaneous encounter with another person who comes alive to us on a very different level from what we know about him."[15] Yes, May stresses, we need to know the basic data *about* the person—family of origin, marital status, interpersonal relationships, vocational information, etc.—but our attention must be directed to the person sitting across from us in the *here and now*, to the *encounter* that is in the present taking place, one human being to another. Existentialist therapy is *being-oriented* therapy.

When Abraham Maslow wrote *Toward a Psychology of Being*, he did more than introduce humanistic psychology to the world. He highlighted that often-elusive word *Being*, hitherto a concept more familiar to the world of philosophy, and introduced it to the world of psychology. For Maslow, *Being*, which he typically capitalized, represents the fullness of what we are capable of experiencing in life, the fullness of what it means to be a person, self-actualization. More accurately, *Being* is understood less as a noun than as a verb for Maslow, as it signifies the process of becoming that which one is meant to be. And the "psychology of Being" is the study of how to identify and maximize the factors that support that growth toward self-actualization.

Rollo May, who rarely failed to engage the opportunity to enter the philosophical domain, would second all that but add more. Agreeing with Maslow, he notes that "*being* is the potentiality by which the acorn becomes the oak or each of us becomes what he truly is."[16] But the person is more than the iconic acorn unfolding epigenetically toward its fulfillment in the oak tree. The person is self-conscious, "that particular being who knows

14. Morgan, *Post-Biblical Religion*, 81.

15. May, *Discovery of Being*, 88.

16. May, *Discovery of Being*, 93.

that at some future moment he will not be; he is the being who is always in a dialectical relation with nonbeing, death."[17]

Herein, May introduces a word, *nonbeing*, that is central to his—and, significantly, to Paul Tillich's—understanding of anxiety. The awareness of nonbeing serves as the ever-present recognition that being includes the certainty of death, both physical death at the close of life and spiritual death through, for example, a life of conformism to societal norms or the failure to integrate normal anxiety into one's life and make constructive use of it. The person must live his or her life in full recognition that it will come to an end and, therefore, must live that life fully and authentically, freely and responsibly, and with "courage in spite of imperfection."[18] It must be a life of *being*—always aware of, but never diverted by, *nonbeing*.

In addition to being influenced by Tillich, May also benefitted from an association with Kurt Goldstein, who familiarized May with his central concept of self-actualization and his thoughts on anxiety, which he understood as more existential than environmental. That juxtaposition of both the humanistic emphasis on self-actualization and the understanding of anxiety as central to life itself serves as a definitional statement of May's place in the larger story of twentieth-century psychology. He would ever be conscious of the delicate paradox between the positive orientation of the humanistic psychology movement and the tragic sense of life of which existentialism never fails to remind us.

May readily embraced the progressive atmosphere and teachings at Union, "the cutting edge of liberal Protestantism and Christian social action,"[19] that emphasized character formation and a social gospel response to societal wrongs over creeds and rituals. As such, Union stood in stark contrast to another manifestation of American Protestantism, one that found expression through the Dayton, Tennessee, Scopes trial, which had taken place just eight years before May entered Union. That historic and consequential trial pitted reformist political maverick and defender of fundamentalist Christianity (and three-time presidential candidate) William Jennings Bryan against prominent attorney and agnostic Clarence Darrow regarding the teaching of evolution. Belief in biblical fundamentalism was held up to ridicule, even as it won its case in court. It is a debate that persists to the present day in America—to the continuing frustration of men and women of science, as well as to those who strive for a more humanistically oriented religious experience.

17. May, *Discovery of Being*, 94.
18. Abzug, *Psyche and Soul*, 122.
19. Abzug, *Psyche and Soul*, 62.

May never lost the passion for progressive responses to societal ills that he had learned first through the YMCA, then at Oberlin, and later, with a more spiritual foundation, at Union Theological Seminary. A social justice advocate from his earliest years, he vigorously opposed the Vietnam War, participated in the 1965 civil rights March on Washington, financially supported the Student Nonviolent Coordinating Committee (among whose founders was John Lewis, the civil rights icon and United States Congressman from Georgia for over thirty years who passed away in 2020), and advocated for initiatives to reduce poverty. His was a persistent voice that lent both spiritual and intellectual gravitas to the peace and justice movements in America.

During his years at Union, May served in a ministerial position at a parish in Verona, New Jersey, just as Rogers had done at a parish in Vermont during his student days. A remark May made at that time to the effect that the only place he experienced personal authenticity in the parish was during the funerals says much about his existentially oriented view of life. Due to his vocal support for the left-leaning Popular Front government (the Loyalists) in Spain during the 1936–39 civil war and his friendship with the congregation at a nearby synagogue, the conservative parish did not work out well for May. He would need a much larger stage to proclaim his expansive message than that of a church pulpit.

Paul Tillich

Rollo May first met Paul Tillich in January 1934 at Union Theological Seminary. He knew nothing of him at the time, but was attracted by the titles of the lectures he was offering: "The Spiritual Implications of Psychotherapy" and "The Religious Meaning of Modern Art," for example. Tillich, recently arrived in America and halting in the English language, affected May deeply and immediately: "Despite the broken language, I felt I had been waiting all my life for someone to speak out as he did. His words called for truths in myself that I had known vaguely for years but never dared articulate."[20]

Tillich spoke of religion in terms of "ultimate concern," of deepest significance, and he never hesitated to deconstruct simplistic formulations about God and religion with challenging philosophical pronouncements such as, perhaps most famously, that "God does not exist. He is not one being over against other beings, but being itself."[21] Tillich directed May's bachelor of divinity thesis, which advanced his developing understanding

20. May, *Paulus*, 4.

21. May, *Paulus*, 4.

of the relationship that exists between religion and psychotherapy,[22] which he would expand upon in *The Art of Counseling*.

The American theologian and minister Peter J. Gomes provides a helpful biography of Tillich in his introduction to *The Courage to Be*, a masterful, esoteric work that is essential reading for an understanding of Tillich's philosophical and theological worldview. Born in Germany in 1886 to a family steeped in conservative Lutheranism (his father was a well-placed Lutheran pastor), Tillich was provided the opportunity and encouragement to pursue degrees in philosophy and theology, eventually earning a PhD in philosophy at the University of Breslau in 1911. A year later, he was ordained into the Lutheran Church.

During the First World War, Tillich served as a chaplain; following that, he taught theology at several universities, the last in Germany being the University of Frankfurt, where his outspokenness against the Nazis led to Hitler's depriving him of his position. Tillich has the distinction of being the first Christian to be dismissed from a university position for denouncing the Nazis. The American theologian and Union Theological Seminary theology professor Reinhold Niebuhr, a strong admirer of Tillich, reached out to him and invited him to come to Union and teach. He would remain there until 1955, at which time he accepted a position at Harvard. In 1962, Tillich moved to the University of Chicago, remaining there until his death three years later. At the interment of his ashes, it was Rollo May who delivered the eulogy.

In *Paulus*, May describes Tillich, who was twenty-three years his senior, as a "friend, mentor, and spiritual father . . . teacher and friend who gave me more than all other teachers I ever had combined."[23] He also describes him as a man of constant "built-in conflicts [which] kept him always psychologically open and dynamic. . . . His existence seemed like a man riding a bicycle who keeps his equilibrium by constant forward motion"[24]—traits not unlike those of May himself. Reinhold Niebuhr added his own perspective on Tillich, describing him as "trying to walk a fence between man's doubts and the traditions of man's faith . . . [and who] slips a bit to one side or the other"[25]—again, all of which could likewise be applied to May. Further, Tillich was plagued with guilt over his occasional moral lapses and, at the risk of overdoing the comparisons, so too was May.

22. Abzug, *Psyche and Soul*, 101.

23. May, *Paulus*, 23–24.

24. May, *Paulus*, 45.

25. May, *Paulus*, 72.

Referencing *The Courage to Be*, Gomes observes that "no one will ever argue that Tillich is an easy afternoon's read."[26] Further, it defies summarization. As noted, the God that Tillich sees is not the God that exists alongside all other beings, not the God we can anthropomorphize or even, some might argue, feel close to. God for Tillich is the God of the philosophers, the God above all essence and existence—the "God above the God of theism [who] is present, although hidden, in every divine-human encounter."[27] In the face of "no valid arguments for the 'existence' of God,"[28] we are called upon by Tillich to transcend the theistic idea of God, that God is a being among other beings, and to embrace "absolute faith . . . the accepting of the acceptance without someone or something that accepts."[29] For Tillich, God is not a being but *Being* itself, and he calls upon us to develop the courage to be, to affirm ourselves and the God above God in spite of our fears and doubts and anxieties.

While reading *The Courage to Be*, I was reminded of a larger-than-life philosophy professor I had had during my undergraduate years at a Catholic university in Texas. In discussing the works of Thomas Aquinas in a class in ontology (or metaphysics, as it was called then), he repeatedly used the word *being*, and occasionally *is-ing*, drawing both out for maximum effect while pacing the classroom as if it were his personal stage. *Being* was his word for God: God is *Being* itself, that without which there could be no things, no other being at all. Well beyond "the supreme being," the definition of God I had learned in my earlier years, the God of philosophy—and the God of Tillich's theology—is *Being* itself, one who both transcends and includes all being. I don't recall that professor—and he was one of those professors one never forgets—ever mentioning Paul Tillich, but he was clearly in sync with at least that part of his theology.

Tillich, whose progressivism embraced all spheres from the sociopolitical to the theological and philosophical, rapidly engaged with like-minded German intellectuals such as Erich Fromm, Kurt Goldstein, and Frieda Fromm-Reichman. He fit well into the vibrant academic world that America provided at the time, thanks largely to the influx of Jewish immigrants during the pre-World War II years and continuing thereafter. It was through Tillich that May came to know those luminaries, thereby expanding both his psychological and theological worlds.

26. Tillich, *Courage to Be*, xxxi.

27. Tillich, *Courage to Be*, 187.

28. Tillich, *Courage to Be*, 181.

29. Tillich, *Courage to Be*, 185.

The Art of Counseling

While still in his twenties, May was rapidly forming his understanding of this not-yet-accepted profession of counseling, an understanding that reflected both his pastoral work and his ministerial training and experience. Over time, he would come to see his life's arc in terms of the movement away from ministry and toward psychotherapy, and psychotherapy as the "royal road to true religion."[30] Out of this would emerge *The Art of Counseling*.

The renowned existentialist psychiatrist Irvin Yalom, in an endorsement on the back of the 1989 edition of *The Art of Counseling*, references it as a "once and future classic . . . an extraordinarily penetrating account of the source and amelioration of human suffering." Nine years previously, Yalom had written the introduction to Rogers's *A Way of Being*, in which he describes another of Rogers's books, *Counseling and Psychotherapy*, as being "destined, along with Rollo May's book *The Art of Counseling*, to play a significant role in the birth of clinical psychology and to shape the future of a humanistically oriented therapeutic approach."[31] Yalom, born in 1931, had been much influenced by the humanist movement in psychology, noting the interpersonal work of Erich Fromm, along with that of Karen Horney and Harry Stack Sullivan, as "eminently sensible."[32] The web of connections that formed between the broad humanistic and existentialist movements was strong and mutually enhancing.

As noted earlier, May wrote a revised edition to *The Art of Counseling* fifty years after the first, which, in the preface, he describes as almost a complete revision. Some changes are obvious, such as references to events that occurred after 1939 and modernizations such as the use of "his or her" rather than the male pronoun. Others can be discerned through readings of his later works: his spiritual insights near the end of the book approach those in *Paulus*, which reveals May at his spiritual maturity, suggesting that some of his more mature learnings found their way into the 1989 edition, as we would expect.

Biographer Clement Reeves, who was writing well before the 1989 revision, summarizes the book's purpose as the examination of "the relationship of personality development, problems, and adjustment to affirmation of 'the ultimate meaning of life.'"[33] Biographer Robert Abzug, writing well after the 1989 edition, describes it as "perhaps the first work to merge a spiritualized

30. Abzug, *Psyche and Soul*, 79.

31. Irvin Yalom, "Introduction," in Rogers, *Way of Being*, ix.

32. Yalom, *Becoming Myself*, 101.

33. Reeves, *Psychology of Rollo May*, 253.

psychotherapeutic vision of human personality with an intimate account of the encounter between counselor and client."[34] Today, *The Art of Counseling* is considered a classic in the field, one that addressed both the essentials of effective counseling and, through its focus on the importance of ultimate concerns to personality development, the interconnection of psychotherapy and spirituality. This latter accomplishment would signal the beginning of the development of counseling as a field unto itself, one that recognized the spiritual component of the work while declaring complete independence from the pastoral counseling offered by the various churches.

May wrote *The Art of Counseling* for those who were untrained as professional psychotherapists but who would benefit from a treatise on the rudiments of counseling, a readership that included college counselors, physicians, social workers, and ministers. This is not a book about depth psychology; it is about the fundamentals of effective counseling. For our purposes, it serves as both a primer on the counseling art and an entrée to May's developing spirituality, particularly in its third and final part, titled "Ultimate Considerations."

May opens by identifying the underlying principles of counseling, referencing personality theory, an understanding of self and spirit, and the importance of empathy, the last of which he considers the most critical. He notes that empathy reveals itself through our words, that "one could measure the degree of empathy of the minister with the congregation or the teacher with students by their ability to speak the other's language."[35] Given his early emphasis on empathy as a key component of counseling, we might wonder who more influenced whom, Rogers or May, regarding the place of that essential element in the therapeutic encounter.

While first giving a nod to the European preference for the word *soul*, May identifies the word *personality* as that which best describes the essence of the human person, defining it as "an actualization of the life process in a free individual who is socially integrated and is aware of spirit,"[36] neatly connecting four fundamental humanistic themes: self-actualization, personal freedom, social interest/engagement, and spirituality. He pays homage to Freud, recognizing his genius and the work he produced as representing "a watershed in the history of our endeavor to understand ourselves."[37] He provides a helpful summary of Freud's contributions, emphasizing his work on exposing the unconscious to the light of consciousness and demonstrating

34. Abzug, *Psyche and Soul*, 106.
35. May, *Art of Counseling*, 65.
36. May, *Art of Counseling*, 14.
37. May, *Art of Counseling*, 14.

that our moral struggles cannot be addressed through repression but must be brought to light and faced directly. Where he faults Freud is in his deterministic inclinations; May, always true to his own brand of existential humanism, prefers to highlight instead the importance of freedom and personal responsibility, adding that the surrender of freedom is characteristic of the neurotic state, words that Erich Fromm would certainly appreciate.

May introduces four principles of personality, which he offers as encouragement to counselors struggling to work more effectively with their counselees, *counselee* being his preferred term for the person on the other side of the therapeutic relationship. They are as follows:

- Freedom of the person, which emphasizes personal responsibility and creativity in response to one's hereditary and environmental influences
- Individuality in personality, which highlights the role of the counselor in helping the counselee become the person that destiny intended; in discussing personality, May references Aristotle's classic acorn-to-oak-tree metaphor as a helpful guide and reminds counselors to integrate the unconscious and be observant of projections of the self
- Social integration, in which May credits Alfred Adler, who emphasized courage, social interest, and cooperation, virtues that "mark healthy individuals who realize and cheerfully accept social responsibility"[38]—all neatly summed up by Adler's neologism *Gemeinschaftsgefühl*[39]
- Source of spirit, wherein May emphasizes the dynamic, creative dimension of personality in adjusting one's internal tensions in order to transform potentially destructive conflicts into growth opportunities

In this fourth point, which serves as a summary or transcendence of the other three, May is not arguing for the elimination of tensions. There is no state of permanent bliss to which the person might aspire, a point that he would often make in criticizing overzealous pronouncements by other proponents of humanistic psychology. Neither is he advocating for the removal

38. May, *Art of Counseling*, 33.

39. Alfred Adler might well deserve the honorific "secular patron saint of social justice" for his passionate advocacy of efforts to address social inequality. An example of this passion for social justice comes from *Understanding Human Nature*, written almost a hundred years ago: "All our institutions, our laws, our morals, our customs bear witness to the fact that they are determined and maintained by privileged males for the glory of male domination, thus creating the appearance of 'masculine privileges.' These institutions reach out even into the nursery and have far-reaching influence upon the child's psyche" (Adler, *Understanding Human Nature*, 101). Including social integration, à la Alfred Adler, in his principles of personality suggests that May resonated deeply with Adler's progressive, even revolutionary, sentiments.

of guilt; rather, he argues for its acceptance as the "perception of the difference between what a thing is and what it ought to be"[40] and what one wants to do and what one ought to do. May calls the principle of personality that makes this possible *spirit*, that aspect of the person that distinguishes him or her from the rest of the animal kingdom, for whom guilt, stress, and regret have no place. May closes his explication of the four aspects of personality by enjoining the counselor to help the counselee accept with courage the spiritual tension inherent in life, the "creative adjustment to the Ultimate"[41] that is at the heart of what it means to be human.

May emphasizes that the tension between what one is and what one ought to be is an ever-present reality for the person, and the response to that tension is one of internal adjustment. May is using the word *adjustment* here in a critically different manner from that of Fromm, who used it negatively, in terms of the alignment of oneself to another's code of behavior or to societal norms—the submission of one's freedom to an external authority. For May, it refers to an inner adjustment of the self to one's own higher values, a reordering of character, even if that results in one's living out of harmony with society. Granting that the person is continually acting within the environment, May emphasizes that the critical area of focus in responding to these tensions is nonetheless *within* the personality—with which, of course, Fromm would heartily agree. What happens outside of us is important because it relates to the personality tensions within, and the counselor's role is to help the counselee shift responsibility from the environment to the self, helping him or her accept responsibility for the needed internal adjustment. May sees the readjustment of personality tensions as "nature's greatest gift to humanity . . . synonymous with creativity."[42]

Moving into the realm of spiritual encounter, May speaks of a spiritual closeness, a dropping of boundaries that results in an encounter at the soul level, a "'nakedness' in the presence of the other . . . psychological nakedness,"[43] and he wonders if this is what Jesus meant by purity of heart. He is referencing here that rarely experienced intimacy between two people colloquially suggested by the simple Middle English word *get*, as in "she gets me," the feeling that the other has truly listened, heard your story, felt what you feel, and is willing to walk the path with you. Ultimately, it's about letting oneself "go into the other person with a willingness to be changed

40. May, *Art of Counseling*, 36.
41. May, *Art of Counseling*, 40.
42. May, *Art of Counseling*, 58.
43. May, *Art of Counseling*, 74.

in the process,"[44] one of the purest expressions of spiritual intimacy in the humanistic literature.

May observes that through the experience of empathy we open ourselves to the other's influence, and he entertains the question of why we are drawn to one source of influence, one experience, rather than another. Why does this specific person or experience elicit in me an empathic response? He suggests that this is an active, not passive, process, regardless of whether that other be a person, an idea, a media campaign, or any other influencing agent. Out of the infinite number of agents that impinge on a person's psyche, "the person *selects* these items . . . by a very creative and mostly unconscious process"[45] and makes that selection less in terms of the objective truth value presented by the influencer than in accordance with one's goals, one's striving for power, one's lifestyle—words that are strikingly Adlerian.

Ego striving has a direct relationship to one's willingness to be influenced by another or by another's ideas, and May, writing in 1939 but in words most contemporary, references the frightening effects of this in fascist countries wherein "[groups] are able to make themselves believe almost any piece of nonsense if it is in line with their ego striving."[46] Today, in a world plagued by intentional and imagined "fake news," his words are prescient. May concludes this section on empathy with words of encouragement to the counselor, quoting Swiss psychiatrist and "doctor of the soul" Carl Jung's words to therapists (and Gandhi's often-quoted admonition to us all) to be the change you wish to see in the world, to be the person you wish others to be.

May intended *The Art of Counseling* to be a practical book for clinicians, and he addresses this how-to approach in the second part of his work. He observes that assessing another's personality is a multifaceted affair, involving the consideration of birth order and the family constellation, early childhood memories, Freudian slips of the tongue, forgetfulness, and more, all designed to enhance understanding of the counselee's lifestyle. May understands lifestyle, a classic Adlerian concept, as something larger than personality style. It is the lens through which each of us fashions our own subjective meaning, our own personal belief system, and it functions as road map, compass setting, and GPS, providing direction, purpose, and a continuing sense of a unified personality throughout one's life.

In discussing the elements of the counseling session, May references the interview (the counselor's questions regarding what brings the client

44. May, *Art of Counseling*, 79.

45. May, *Art of Counseling*, 76 (emphasis in original).

46. May, *Art of Counseling*, 76.

to therapy) and the confession (the counselee's description of his or her concerns)—two words, *interview* and *confession*, happily no longer in general use in counseling. The interview and confession are followed by the interpretation, the joint effort of the counselor and counselee to identify the counselee's lifestyle, wherein may be discovered the source of what needs internal adjustment.

May's approach in counseling, unlike Rogers's, is direct, and he has no hesitancy to ask leading questions or offer suggestive insights. However, he mentions by way of clarification (and perhaps as an apologetic nod to Rogers) that "true counseling and the giving of advice are distinctly different functions,"[47] adding that he sees the giving of advice as a violation of the autonomy of the personality. What he wants for the client is the same as what Rogers wants: as he tells one client in a transcripted interview, "[It] is more a matter of relaxing the artificial tensions and giving your creative abilities a chance."[48] Of course, Rogers would have found ways to impart that through the often-wordless communication of congruence, unconditional positive regard, and empathic understanding.

For May, the final stage in counseling is the transformation of the personality, and he indicates several factors that contribute to a successful process. He references, by way of example, the offering of suggestions, and as in his discussion of influence referenced earlier, he wonders why one would be open to one suggestion rather than another. The counselor's role is to offer helpful ideas and insights, and the counselee's is to move in the direction of the offering that he or she sees as meeting the desired goals. May observes that perhaps just the right "suggestion from the environment may be the touch needed to loosen one of these tendencies which is already strong within the individual."[49]

A second factor in transforming personality is the creative function of understanding that takes place through the process of confession and interpretation. May references the neurotic function of self-deception and advocates that it be brought to light so that "the ego will be forced to relax its self-defeating training formula and direct itself into socially constructive forms of behavior."[50] Understanding, the result of the unconscious becoming more conscious through the miracle of the "talking cure," releases the creativity needed to free the self and identify the necessary changes. To May,

47. May, *Art of Counseling*, 117.
48. May, *Art of Counseling*, 108.
49. May, *Art of Counseling*, 119.
50. May, *Art of Counseling*, 120.

the counselee's inherent creativity is key, and the counselor's role is to serve as midwife for its release.

May returns to his discussion of empathy in his third factor affecting the transformation of personality or character, observing how empathy makes it possible "for the patient to identify with the therapist's positive will . . . thus taking on extra strength to triumph over his or her own negative will."[51] Herein we see further evidence of the difference between May and Rogers. Rogers understood empathy in terms of creating the conditions through which the client might experience being listened to, heard, and deeply understood and therefore being a person of value, resulting in the client's increasing ability to get in touch with his or her own internal strengths. May, in contrast, emphasized the client's ability to experience the *therapist's* strength and positive orientation and thereby overcome his or her hurdles thanks to this additional, borrowed strength. Both men, well immersed within the humanistic tradition, want their clients to grow in consciousness of their value and potentiality, but one believes it can be accomplished directly and the other in a somewhat vicarious manner.

A fourth factor in the transformation of character is the effective use of suffering, one that Viktor Frankl, who famously found meaning through suffering in the concentration camps of World War II, understood well. The presence of suffering, and its necessity in character transformation, is central to May's existential form of humanism: "A human being will not change his or her personality pattern . . . until forced to do so by suffering."[52] Suffering is also central to May's personality, his self-understanding, his sense of self. As biographer Abzug observes, May lived a life of "mordant introspection,"[53] and throughout his biography he describes May with words such as *struggled, tortured, overbearing, diffuse apprehension, untamed demons, self-consumed, self-interested, self-contempt, relentless work ethic, insatiable appetite for work*, and *private drama*.

May notes that the ego fears the insecurity that accompanies a change in one's life circumstances, even a positive change, and that many who are in the grip of neurosis will cling to the known suffering and resist that which might attend to the unknown. Many would rather endure their current pain than face the uncertainties of change. Fortunately, May observes, "the wheels of life do grind relentlessly on and bring a just portion of suffering as a penalty for every neurotic attitude."[54]

51. May, *Art of Counseling*, 121.
52. May, *Art of Counseling*, 123.
53. Abzug, *Psyche and Soul*, 60.
54. Abzug, *Psyche and Soul*, 123.

May sees the counselor's role not in relieving the suffering of the counselee but in redirecting it toward constructive purposes, and he is less interested in the counselee leaving the office happy than in leaving courageous and determined to lead a life of authenticity. For May, it is about transformation of the personality, and if this is taken seriously, suffering will accompany that process—"when life in its own good time has piled upon this individual the suffering egocentricity merits, the counselee will humbly make the change."[55]

May closes his discussion of personality transformation by noting that after all is said and done there remains some element of change that we don't understand, some change agent that can't be adequately categorized. He refers to this as "the mysterious creativity of life,"[56] in the face of which the counselor is called upon to stand humbly aside and to acknowledge gratefully and respectfully that which is beyond one's grasp.

May titles the third and final part of the book "Ultimate Considerations," signaling his intention to move more deeply into that "mysterious creativity of life"; he will take this deeper still in *Man's Search for Himself*. He begins by asking what factors go into the making of a good counselor, noting the importance of training but adding that "protracted work in experimental psychology as it is at present taught would not necessarily fit one for effective counseling—and might even unfit one."[57] Any counselor who has spent time working at a clinic that overly uses words like *testing* and *measurement* and *data-driven approaches* has experienced what experimental psychology hath wrought. May would likely argue that a strong dose of Freud would serve as an antidote to that experimental psychology, and he references the master's teaching regarding the importance of exploration into the deeper layers of the self, thereby bringing to light one's own prejudices. Failure to do so, he added, is "the worst stumbling block in the personality of the counselor."[58] Rogers's person-centered counseling would likewise serve as an alternative to experimental psychology, as well as any approach that focuses on the growth of the whole person—the interconnecting composite of the physical, psychological, emotional, spiritual, and interpersonal dimensions that defies testing, measurement, and data-driven assessments.

For the purpose of providing examples, May discusses his own work with religious workers from his days as director of men's studies at Michigan

55. Abzug, *Psyche and Soul*, 125.

56. Abzug, *Psyche and Soul*, 126.

57. Abzug, *Psyche and Soul*, 132.

58. Abzug, *Psyche and Soul*, 133.

State. He found them to be hardworking, conscientious, responsible, goal-oriented, fearful of failure, ambitious, and, in a word often used to describe Maslow and Fromm, messianic, which he describes as seeing one's work as indispensable to humanity and involving a potentially dangerous sense of one's importance. He also references difficulties in sexual adjustment among religious workers, noting that the sexual scandals of prominent Protestant preachers during the 1980s could have easily been predicted. Had May lived to witness the sexual scandals in the Catholic Church that have surfaced within the past thirty-plus years, he would no doubt have characterized them as just as predictable.

May expresses concern that when ego strivings surface in the moral realm, they tend to result in the moral elevation of the self and the corresponding depreciation of others. He cautions against moral judgments in counseling, the frequency of which in religious counselors he decries, and he recommends empathic understanding as essential to the esteeming, appreciating, and accepting of the other. He adds that the "ability to 'judge not' is the watershed between authentic religion and egocentric religiosity,"[59] something Pope Francis, who has placed mercy and forgiveness as central to his ministry, would much appreciate.

May identifies as the counselor's first responsibility the acknowledgement of what form the neurotic pattern takes in his or her own personality and developing the "courage to be imperfect," as Adlerian psychiatrist and child advocate Rudolph Dreikurs often championed—the courage to act out of who one is, rather than in response to cultural norms, and with the willingness to embrace whatever consequences ensue. He further encourages the counselor to enjoy the process of living itself, to identify and work to eradicate all-or-nothing thinking, and to become truly interested in people for their own sake, not simply for God's sake. In short, he is advising counselors to be sure to do their own inner work.

May defines morality in Aristotelian terms as the response to the question *How should I live the good life?*, and he discusses the creative personality in terms of the ability to respond courageously to situations that demand a moral response. Employing Freudian terminology, he calls not for the suppression of potentially harmful urges but their recognition as drives from the id that need guidance by the ego into creative channels. He calls for the healthy expression of our instinctual urges through *spontaneity*, a word which to May signifies a unified response of the conscious and the unconscious with the former in the lead, the experience of "speaking from

59. Abzug, *Psyche and Soul*, 142.

the depths of one's personality."[60] Rather than about impulsivity, spontaneity suggests authentic self-expression.

To put a human face to all this, May presents the case of Harold K., a young minister who was on the verge of a nervous breakdown due to a long-standing sense of personal inferiority. In response to that, Harold compensated by assuming an air of moral superiority, which took the form of religious obsessiveness and the renunciation of pleasure of all kinds. This in turn led to his assumption of an egocentric style of life that included the reduction of his fiancée to the singular role of servant—both to his ministry and to himself. In his efforts to overcome his feelings of inferiority, Harold had made of religion a barrier between himself and others. Religion, notes May, becomes neurotic whenever "it cramps and impoverishes life, thus destroying the possibility of living abundantly."[61] This was certainly the case with Harold. And perhaps for May himself: biographer Robert Abzug observes that his case histories tended to be autobiographical.[62]

Freud, of course, went further than identifying a specific form of religion as neurotic; he identified *all* religion as neurotic. May concedes that there is much truth in Freud's words, yet he avoids the reductionist temptation to discard all religion by observing that what Freud is attacking is not religion itself but its abuse. May differentiates authentic religion, which he describes as affirming the meaning of life and emphasizing "the uniqueness of individuals rather than focusing on the collective 'saving of souls,'"[63] from false, neurotic religion, as Fromm does throughout his works. He sees religion, when properly understood and practiced, as an aid in turning our neurotic tendencies toward creative activity and emerging with trust, confidence, and courage.

A graduate-level history professor of mine, a Holocaust survivor, would occasionally observe that if you take any academic discipline to its deepest level, you will cross the threshold into philosophy, and if you grapple with the deepest questions of philosophy, you will soon encounter theology and the question of God. May echoes those words in regard to his own discipline by noting that "the deeper one's thought penetrates in the field of psychotherapy, the closer one comes to the realm of theology."[64] Beginning with the problem of helping the sufferer overcome his or her neurosis, the therapeutic encounter naturally evolves into questions of meaning and

60. Abzug, *Psyche and Soul*, 155.
61. Abzug, *Psyche and Soul*, 161.
62. Abzug, *Psyche and Soul*, 109.
63. Abzug, *Psyche and Soul*, 39.
64. May, *Art of Counseling*, 167.

purpose (often the gateway to spirituality, if not theology), as well as to the tension between what is and what ought to be or, in theological terms, between vice and virtue. He references grace and *clarification*, a word that he understands as a psychotherapeutic cognate of grace, the light that makes it possible for us to see more clearly and express our creativity more directly. In words that recall the twelve steps of Alcoholics Anonymous, he advocates for the acceptance of a power or force greater than the self, a curative power that overrules the egocentric.

May understands this curative power as ever available to us, coming to our rescue when we surrender to the meaning or structure of the universe. Comparing it to grace, he observes that it arrives when we are able to say *no* to the self and *yes* to "the divine logos of meaning [wherein] there are purposes which swing in arcs greater than our own, and we will aim to put ourselves in harmony with them."[65] He hastens to add that this is not about "being saved," as if it were a unique, singular event. Rather, it is an adjustment that must be made and remade in each moment of life. Our guilt is not eradicated by grace or clarification; rather, grace/clarification opens the door for the acceptance of guilt and of the reality of the human situation. We then see ourselves and the world more realistically, more honestly, and are able "to walk the knife-blade edge of insecurity and to affirm truth and goodness even though truth is on the scaffold and goodness is never perfectly achieved."[66] We are now free to face the world with courage, hopefulness, and authenticity.

Years of Growth and Change

May received his bachelor of divinity degree from Union Theological Seminary in 1938 and for several years thereafter served as an ordained minister in the Congregational Church. Like Rogers, May experienced discouragement in his parish work, finding the answers that the church offered his parishioners unsatisfactory—unsurprising for an existentially oriented intellectual. His developing interests eventually led him away from ministry and toward pursuit of a doctorate in clinical psychology at Columbia University, the first doctorate in that field to be awarded by Columbia. That same year, he married Florence De Frees, with whom he had three children, a son and twin girls. Their relationship, which ended in divorce thirty-one years later, is described by biographer Abzug as tempestuous: "Whether due to unresolved neurotic tendencies, a basic mismatch, or a combination of

65. May, *Art of Counseling*, 170.

66. May, *Art of Counseling*, 171.

the two . . . [it] rarely attained a semblance of harmony . . . it was a disaster."[67] May married a second time at age sixty-one to a woman a quarter century his junior, a relationship that it would not be unfair to dismiss as a somewhat postponed midlife crisis; it lasted just a few years.

May's second book, *The Springs of Creative Living*, followed his first by only a year. Biographer Reeves states that it was quite similar in all respects to *The Art of Counseling* with the notable exception being "that it links more specifically May's conception of personality health and his Judeo-Christian beliefs."[68] Reeves further notes that May refused to allow this book to be republished, offering no explanation. Could it be that May's spiritual development had begun to outpace his attachment to traditional Christianity at that stage of his life and that he no longer saw himself constrained by a specific tradition? May makes only veiled reference to a role for Christianity in his thinking in *Man's Search for Himself*, published in 1953, and it is to a Christianity that could be said to have transcended its particularity, one interested less in discussions about the tenets of the faith (such as the divinity of Jesus) and more on the values espoused (such as love and universality), an advanced stage of faith response in James Fowler's classic faith development schema.

During the 1940s, May worked as a counselor at the City College of New York and studied psychoanalysis at the William Alanson White Institute, which was notable in its day for allowing the use of a variety of psychotherapeutic approaches, including psychoanalytic, existentialist, and humanistic. It was there that he befriended Harry Stack Sullivan, Erich Fromm, Frieda Fromm-Reichmann, and Clara Thompson. Shortly thereafter, May was invited to join them as a fellow faculty member at White. In addition, in 1946 he opened a private practice in New York City. It was a busy time for counseling, which had mushroomed in the years following World War II due to "the alarming number of soldiers suffering from combat stress."[69]

May completed his doctoral dissertation in 1949 and published it the following year as *The Meaning of Anxiety*. He defined two kinds of anxiety: normal, which emerges from life's realities and which can energize and motivate, and neurotic, which results from not having worked through and dealt with the normal anxiety of everyday life and which is manifested by negative symptoms, such as the moral superiority and religious obsessiveness noted in his client Harold. Although *The Meaning of Anxiety* has not

67. Abzug, *Psyche and Soul*, 123.

68. Reeves, *Psychology of Rollo May*, 255.

69. Abzug, *Psyche and Soul*, 175.

received the level of attention his other books have, May received the highest compliment on it from Paul Tillich, who told May that he wrote his own classic, *The Courage to Be*, "as an answer to *The Meaning of Anxiety*."[70]

May's decision to concentrate on anxiety in his doctoral dissertation was more than a purely academic one. It is fair to say that he was plagued by anxiety throughout his life, a disquieting angst that went to the core of the man he was—to his dark and introspective personality, deep inferiority complex, and his "tortured self-consciousness."[71] Combine all this with a Maslovian "sense of specialness and mission [that] had been fostered from birth"[72] and you've got a recipe for lifelong stress, struggle, and disappointment. Further, May's occasional moral transgressions exacerbated his feelings of guilt and personal failure, feeding the cycle of despair.

The defense mechanism May used to compensate for all that was to work relentlessly—teaching at various universities, holding official positions at the White Institute and the New York State Psychological Association, accepting speaking opportunities throughout the United States, championing and proclaiming the value of both existentialism and, increasingly through the years, humanistic psychology, serving as "America's minister" and "public intellectual," and, of course, counseling.

Also around this time, May contracted tuberculosis, an experience he draws on to explain his ideas about freedom within the many limitations life presents. In *Man's Search for Himself*, he references a hypothetical situation in which one might experience an absence of control, specifically referencing tuberculosis as an example, and then relates several attitudes people might take in response: giving up on life and forsaking the prescribed medical procedures, following the procedures but resenting them, or accepting the illness and using it as a time for reflection, to allow for the inner work so essential to living an authentic life.

Man's Search for Himself

Man's Search for Himself was published in 1953, about halfway between the initial publication of *The Art of Counseling* and its reprint in 1973, and well before its revision in 1989. It serves as a helpful window into May's thoughts in the middle years of his life. *The Art of Counseling*, first published at the dawn of counseling itself, focused on the therapeutic relationship in both its practical and spiritual dimensions; comparisons to Rogers's work

70. May, *Meaning of Anxiety*, 23.

71. Abzug, *Psyche and Soul*, 76.

72. Abzug, *Psyche and Soul*, 76.

are frequent. *Man's Search for Himself* is a thematically different book, one more in keeping with the social and psychological stirrings of the times and revealing May as a humanistically oriented existentialist.

In the former book, we see his debt to Alfred Adler; in *Man's Search for Himself*, his circle of mentors has expanded to include Fromm, Freud, Tillich, and Otto Rank, an Austrian psychoanalyst and confidant of Freud's. *Man's Search for Himself* is a message book, more in the style of Fromm's works. In addition, like in so much of Fromm's work, religious and spiritual questions abound, as in the final pages of *The Art of Counseling*. Biographer Abzug notes that *Man's Search for Himself* was honored for its "sheer wisdom . . . persuasive clarity . . . [and as] a companion volume"[73] to Tillich's *The Courage to Be*. At the very least, it advanced May's presence as America's purveyor of wisdom, as its public minister.

May opens with reference to what he sees as the overarching problems faced by Americans in the post-World War II era. He identifies three: an emptiness of desires and feelings related to a sense of powerlessness; loneliness, resulting from the loss of a sense of self and leading to increasing attempts to pursue social acceptance through conformity rather than individuality; and anxiety, which he understands as both cause and effect of the traumatic upheavals and changes taking place at that time. A person steeped in the arts, well versed in the classics of literature, and deeply appreciative of the liberal arts tradition, May sets the stage for his approach to addressing these ills by decrying what he sees as a modern-day rejection of the accumulated wisdom of the past—an inheritance he identifies with the Judeo-Christian tradition in its intersection with a humanism that stretches from the Greeks and Romans, through the late Middle Ages and Renaissance, and into modern times.

Somewhat parenthetically, May regrets the loss of a sense of enchantment—the magical, fantastical, mysterious, nonrational dimension of life so essential to a fuller understanding of the unconscious dimension of the self. In a charming commentary on mid-twentieth century life, he applauds that we have rid ourselves of a belief in witches and therefore no longer burn them at the stake, while regretting that we have also rid ourselves of "fairies, elves, trolls, and all of the demicreatures of the woods and earth,"[74] the result of which is a disenchanted world and a humanity out of touch with both nature and itself. One wonders if he had read *The Hobbit*, published sixteen years previously, and if the wondrous world created by J. R. R. Tolkien raised his consciousness about the loss of enchantment in our over-rationalized

73. Abzug, *Psyche and Soul*, 188.

74. May, *Man's Search for Himself*, 63.

world. *The Lord of the Rings* trilogy arrived just a year or two after publication of *Man's Search for Himself*, as if to underscore May's words.

May turns his attention toward the development of self-consciousness, or self-knowledge, "the most radical and important emergence so far in evolution,"[75] a proposition frequently referenced by biologist Julian Huxley as central to his own worldview. This emergence of personhood, of a sense of identity, of "I," allows for our ability to see ourselves as others do and opens the door to empathy—though at the price of anxiety, which often manifests from struggles with self-love as we grow in self- and other-awareness. Following Fromm, May distinguishes between self-love and selfishness, the former referring to the healthy experience of one's own worth.

In addressing the Oedipus complex, May interprets it, much as does Fromm, as "simply the sexual physical symbol of being turned inward on the family, and of being unable, correspondingly, to 'love outwardly' . . . [to] cut the 'psychological umbilical cord.'"[76] He interprets Jesus's words about setting children against their parents as a statement "in the most radical form that spiritual development is *away* from incest and *toward* the capacity to love the neighbor and stranger."[77] Later in the book, he references Freud's identification of the centrality of the Oedipus myth in human development as a mark of genius because it highlighted the pain and conflict that attends to the discovery of truths about ourselves, as Oedipus discovered to his profound regret. In seeking truth, which requires a level of self-awareness that is gained through greater access to the unconscious, we risk discovering what we don't want to know; it is a risk that requires confidence in oneself, one's ultimate values, and one's inner wisdom. And, as Tillich would remind us, the courage to be. But the risk is worth the effort: as Scripture assures us, "the truth will set you free" (John 8:32).

In a chapter on values, ethics, and religion titled "The Creative Conscience," one pivotal to an understanding of his approach to the place of religion in one's life and in society, May refers to the human person as "the 'ethical animal'—ethical in potentiality, even if, unfortunately, not in actuality."[78] Like freedom, this capacity for ethical judgment is dependent upon our developing self-consciousness and, like every step in our self-development, is achievable only through inner conflict, with its inevitable attendant anxiety.

75. May, *Man's Search for Himself*, 73.
76. May, *Man's Search for Himself*, 115–16.
77. May, *Man's Search for Himself*, 116.
78. May, *Man's Search for Himself*, 150.

Engaging a theme he will develop more in his later writings, May discusses two myths, the Judeo-Christian creation story and that of Prometheus, the Greek god of fire and champion of humanity. The former he interprets in terms of the development of self-consciousness and the latter in terms of creativity. Both myths speak to "the age-old conflict between entrenched authority, as represented by the jealous gods, and the upsurging of new life and creativity."[79] And both confront the authoritarian dimension that manifests in all religions and that sees itself in conflict with ethical insights that interpret morality in terms other than obedience to church, state, or society.

May recognizes the Jewish prophets as teachers of those newer ethical insights, noting that they transcended the codified ethical system into which they were born. He references Jesus's frequent use of the expression "you have been told, but I tell you," suggesting tension between those tethered to an institutional understanding of the moral code (external) and those who call for an approach based more on humanistic ethics (internal). He predicts that in the future "the main insights of both Freud and Nietzsche will be absorbed within the ethical-religious tradition and religion will become the richer and more effective for their contributions,"[80] thereby creating a larger place for contemporary philosophical and psychological thought in the formation of ethical principles.

May emphasizes that religion itself neither enhances health nor leads to neurosis. Rather, it is the *nature* of the specific religion and how it is conducted that matters. When discussing religion within the broad humanistic psychology movement, emphasis is consistently placed on the extent to which it fosters the development of the person through encouragement and support and the degree to which it sees its mission as prophetic, that is, as calling the world to reformation. Distinctions between, say, the professed beliefs of Jews and Christians are less relevant than the degree to which each religion promotes the self-actualization of the person within the community, serves as a font of meaning and purpose, affirms one's dignity and worth, and assists the person in developing his or her full potential through freedom, responsibility, and love. Erich Fromm would use the word *authentic* to describe such a person. May would second that and add the word *existential.*

Looking more deeply into the effect of religion on the development of personality, May notes the distinction between the aspects of religion that assist in the discovery of one's personal values and those that do not,

79. May, *Man's Search for Himself*, 160.

80. May, *Man's Search for Himself*, 164–65.

a frequent reference in the humanist literature. By way of example, he indicates two opposing character styles among people from religious backgrounds. On the one hand, he observes more zest for life, more desire to respond to one's problems, and a greater sense of meaning and purpose. On the other hand, he references an attitude of entitlement that leads to the expectation of never-ending success and happiness, as if in divine gratitude for their obedience to parents and parent figures. He adds that this second characteristic of religious persons leads to the expectation of never-ending success and happiness, as if in divine gratitude for their obedience to parents and parent figures. The former aspect is the healthy side of religion; the latter, the neurotic.

May calls upon churchgoers to have the courage to confront their anxiety and despair; to see virtue as its own reward (instead of expecting continual parental and parent-figure accolades for doing right); to accept the challenge to move toward greater freedom and personal integration; and to relate to each other through productive, creative work and love. He knows there is something beyond the negative caricature of religion, and, after establishing the importance of personal independence, he encourages his readers to take a second look at their faith tradition from a position of ego strength and develop a more creative relationship with it.

Rollo May was an American philosopher in the broader, etymological sense of the word—a true lover of wisdom, wherever it might be found. Particularly in *The Cry for Myth*, published in 1991, he displayed a breadth of knowledge rivaling the best of the classical, liberal tradition. He was fluent in the works and wisdom of Plato and Aristotle, Aeschylus and Sophocles, Goethe and Dostoyevsky, Kierkegaard and Spinoza. But he cautioned that to benefit fully from that wisdom, one must engage those teachers not as purveyors of a dead tradition (an occasional criticism of the "great books" approach to education) but in terms of one's own life experiences. It is through one's personal integration of the classics that the truth therein can transform and lift one to greater heights of self-knowledge and ethical responsibility.

Like both Fromm and Tillich, May questions the practice of making the subject of God's existence central to the discussion of religion, interpreting that approach as making of God "an entity, a being over against other beings, located in space heaven only knows where,"[81] and he references Tillich's argument that God is Being itself, not a being among others. He defines religion in terms of the personal identification of meaning and purpose in life: "Religion is whatever the individual takes to be his ultimate

81. May, *Man's Search for Himself*, 180.

concern,"[82] and it takes shape at the point at which one identifies that there are values in life worth living and dying for. He notes the importance of identifying how those beliefs and values are congruent with other truths, recalling Maslow's recognition that the universal values can be defined only in terms of each other. Truth builds upon truth.

May discusses conscience as an active process of introspection through which we confront the moral quandaries and decisions of life, using both our religious tradition and our own experiences as guides. He emphasizes that all have the power to affirm values for themselves, the power, we might say, to *valuate*, or to identify one's own values. Whereas Maslow focused on the identification of universal human values wherever he might find them, as if in anticipation of a new set of commandments by which we could align our lives, May, the existential humanist, emphasized that each of us must start from our own ethical awareness, our own ability to valuate in the sense noted above and face the world alone, if necessary.

Rather than concern himself with lists, May emphasizes the promotion of the creative, dynamic act of choosing, and he observes that the potentialities within us for health are released when the conscious decision is made to take action. He stresses that the ethical act is one that must be chosen by the person doing it, one expressive of his or her internal motivation, and he closes with the reminder that Jesus shifted the emphasis away from the external rules of the Ten Commandments toward more internal motivations, adding that that is what he meant by his exhortation to be pure of heart.

In *Man's Search for Himself*, May established himself within the camp of humanistic psychology as that tradition has confronted the place of religion and spirituality in our lives. To that he added a uniquely existentialist tone that emphasizes freedom with responsibility and the importance of choice, with the self—the inner core, the heart, the soul—as the locus of decision-making and values formation. His stated goal in writing *Man's Search for Himself* was to explore how the individual might achieve inner freedom and personal integrity through greater self-awareness. To the degree to which one can accomplish that, he or she can be said to be fulfilling what it means to be human, to be a self-actualized person—the most foundational emphasis in humanistic psychology. In May's later years, he would claim humanistic psychology as "the movement with which he most identified."[83]

In his closing words, May references a dialogue between Socrates and Glaucon in Plato's *Republic* about the possibility of the attainment of a "City of God" on earth in which Glaucon observes that whether or not we might

82. May, *Man's Search for Himself*, 180.

83. Abzug, *Psyche and Soul*, 305.

be able to experience such a state of existence, "the wise man will live after the manner of that city . . . and in so looking upon it, will set his own house in order."[84] From his first book to his last, May enjoined us to first set our own house in order.

Closing Years: The Emergence of America's Public Minister

During the second half of the 1950s and into the 1960s, May busied himself with a multitude of pursuits, including lecturing at the New School for Social Research in New York; teaching at New York University, Harvard, and Princeton; and continuing his work with the William Alanson White Institute. He later added Brooklyn College, Yale, and the University of California Santa Clara to his list of teaching posts. He was, as biographer Abzug aptly observes, "a man of almost boundless energy" with "an insatiable appetite for work" who "ran himself ragged."[85]

During those years, May's work gravitated more and more toward the existential, as evidenced by the publication of *Existence: A New Dimension in Psychiatry and Psychology*, which gave impetus to the development of American phenomenological existentialism by incorporating European thinkers into the conversation; *Existential Psychology*, which included essays by Maslow and Rogers; and *The Discovery of Being: Writings in Existential Psychotherapy*, a compilation of radio lectures he presented through the Canadian Broadcasting Corporation.

May is credited with having introduced existential psychotherapy to an American audience,[86] thereby providing another alternative to Freudianism and behaviorism besides Maslow's "third force" psychology. His best-known work, *Love and Will*, which became a national bestseller and was chosen as a Book of the Month club selection, was published in 1969. Its success suggests what America was hungry for at the time: an authentic, humanistic response to the cultural upheavals and consequent uncertainties of the 1960s. In 1973, May wrote *Paulus*, his intimate biography of Paul Tillich, in which both Tillich and May are revealed in the fullness of their humanity.

May was consistently progressive in his religious and political views throughout his life, having been influenced early on by the Christian social consciousness taught at the YMCA. He was appalled by the stultifying consumerism and conformity of the 1950s; energized by the election of the youthful John Kennedy and the civil rights movement; and shocked by the

84. May, *Man's Search for Himself*, 236.

85. Abzug, *Psyche and Soul*, 138, 199, 244.

86. Abzug, *Psyche and Soul*, 205.

assassinations of President Kennedy, presidential candidate Robert Kennedy, Martin Luther King, and others. Further, he actively supported initiatives to address poverty and fervently opposed the American war in Vietnam, even participating in a sit-in at the Capitol in 1972. Among those he honored as "exemplary rebels"[87] were the Catholic priests Daniel and Philip Berrigan, most known for their opposition to nuclear proliferation. May was instrumental in pushing the Association for Humanistic Psychology toward more engagement in the various social and political issues of the day.

During his final years, May wrote more about myth and symbolism, entering territory that was at times more Jungian than humanistic. In *Love and Will*, "a kind of intellectual collage,"[88] he expounded at length on the *daimon*, a word that signifies a guiding spirit or spiritual power, a concept more at home in a Jungian world that would find further expression in *The Cry for Myth*, published in 1991. No doubt influenced by his relationship with Georgia Lee Johnson, a Jungian therapist whom he married in 1988, as well as by the pioneering work of the great mythologist Joseph Campbell, *The Cry for Myth* is a panoramic study of themes as diverse as Freud's Oedipus complex, the frontier in American mythology, Grimm's fairy tales, the Great Circle of Love, and Dante's *Divine Comedy*, all of which reveal much about the "public intellectual" persona of Rollo May.

Rollo May died in 1994 at age eighty-five of congestive heart failure. At his bedside was his wife, Georgia, and Irvin Yalom and his wife, Marilyn. Yalom, today the most renowned existentialist psychiatrist in America, was tasked with officially pronouncing May dead. At the time of his death, May was living in Tiburon, California, having moved to the Bay Area in the late '70s, leaving the East Coast behind for good. In the history of humanistic psychology, all roads seemed to lead to California, after a sufficient number of years paying one's dues in New York City.

Where does May fit into the larger story of humanistic psychology? Earlier in this chapter, reference was made to Jessica Grogan's comparison of Rogers and May, the former being largely unconnected to the world of religion and the latter intimately so. May, like Fromm, could not help but engage religious questions, his perspective of course being Christian while Fromm's was Jewish. But to reduce either May or Fromm to an identification with the religion of his birth would be inaccurate; each responded to his respective religious inheritance from the perspective of a humanistic ethos that highlighted the authentic, life-affirming dimension of the tradition while leaving what was unwanted behind.

87. Abzug, *Psyche and Soul*, 293.

88. Abzug, *Psyche and Soul*, 270.

In his early years, May was more a practitioner than an academic, more a counselor than a philosopher. As the years passed, however, he revealed more of his philosophical, theological, and literary sides while advancing his own brand of humanistic psychology, one that emphasized being a person in touch with one's center of strength and acting with freedom and responsibility out of that center. In Grogan's apt phrase, he was America's "public minister," poised to heal the spiritual, philosophical, and psychological wounds of the world.[89]

Unlike Maslow, who was euphoric about the future of his third force movement as a personal and societal change agent, and Rogers, whose optimism about the process of personal affirmation through authenticity, unconditional positive regard, and empathic understanding knew no bounds, May was the gimlet-eyed skeptic on the side, looking askance at the occasional overzealous generalizations and simplifications of the broader humanistic psychology movement and the life decisions that were sometimes associated with it. Maslow, Rogers, and Fromm would see much hope in that humanistic approach. But May—who looked at life through a less rosy lens—might hesitate, advocating with the others for ongoing efforts to make changes both individual and societal but tempering hope with an existential hardheadedness, always reminding us of the need to embrace our anxiety, to make meaning of it, almost to celebrate it as concomitant with our humanity. He was the skeptic, ever ready to temper grand dreams with the hard reality of an existentialist perspective on the world. Yet he was also deeply attuned to the idea of a "City of God," a humanistic society in which all could strive to fulfill their potential within social constructs characterized by healthy, life-affirming values. He knew what we needed; he was just a little more cautious in declaring that we were on the brink of accomplishing it.

89. Grogan, *Encountering America*, 74.

Chapter 7

Science, Religion, and the Future of Homo Sapiens

The Evolutionary Humanism of Julian Huxley

The central belief of Evolutionary Humanism is that existence can be improved, that vast untapped possibilities can be increasingly realized, that greater fulfillment can replace frustration, initiating a new type of society, a "Fulfillment Society"—a new step in psychosocial evolution.

—Julian Huxley, *The Humanist Frame*

In 1957, Abraham Maslow assembled a diverse group of fifteen notable academics and other professionals in their respective fields under the auspices of the First Scientific Conference on New Knowledge in Human Values. Held at the Massachusetts Institute of Technology, its purpose was to discover "a validated, usable system of human values . . . that we can devote ourselves to because they are true."[1] These values are true, they proposed, not because they have been handed down from an external authority, human or supernatural, but because they have been validated through science. As noted in the chapter on Maslow, the speakers and writers who addressed this need represented a multiplicity of fields, from psychology and theology to architecture and economics. The book that followed the conference,

1. Maslow, *New Knowledge*, viii.

published in 1959 and titled *New Knowledge in Human Values*, provides an invaluable historical record of that watershed moment in the developing prominence of humanistic psychology. Due to the energy and enthusiasm of Abraham Maslow, the need for a universal approach to values became a key plank in the humanistic psychology platform.

In 1961, over three thousand miles away in London, evolutionary biologist Julian Huxley invited twenty-five scholars, also representing a wide range of interests including psychology, education, sociology, medicine, and economics, to join him in producing a compendium titled *The Humanist Frame*. Two years after Maslow proposed a need for "a validated, usable system of human values" and a "scientific ethics, a natural value system, a court of ultimate appeal for the determination . . . of right and wrong,"[2] Huxley proposed "a science of human possibilities to help guide the long course of psychosocial evolution that lies ahead."[3] Although Huxley's work was not presented at a conference, the articles suggest that scholars on both sides of the Atlantic were looking to humanistic thinking as a blueprint for the world's healing. And it was much in need of healing—only sixteen years after the close of the Second World War, and still sorting through the chaos of its aftermath, the world was confronting the specter of two superpowers teetering on the brink of nuclear destruction.

I have found nowhere in Huxley's books or Maslow's, or in any of the writings or biographies of other humanistic psychologists I have studied, any indication that they knew of each other's work or that they even knew of each other. Their life spans overlapped—Maslow's from 1908 to 1970 and Huxley's from 1887 to 1975—but they grew up an ocean apart and, more so, worlds apart: Maslow was a Brooklynite, raised by uneducated Russian Jewish émigrés whose own personal history was one of suppression, alienation, religious superstition, and the struggle for survival. On his celebrated hierarchy of needs, his family labored for years on the lower tiers, eventually succeeding in building a cooperage business that would lift them out of poverty—the stereotypical American immigrant story. Abraham spent a lifetime seeking and identifying mentors outside the family as he made his own personal ascent toward self-actualization.

Huxley, in contrast, was the scion of one of England's most respected families. His grandfather was Thomas Henry Huxley, noted defender and promoter of Charles Darwin; Aldous Huxley of *Brave New World* fame was his brother. Julian was born with the proverbial silver spoon well in place,

2. Maslow, *Toward Psychology of Being*, 15.
3. Huxley, *Humanist Frame*, 34.

entering a world of social privilege, of intellectual and cultural pedigree, of noblesse oblige. Of the two scholars, he had the far greater advantage in life.

Maslow, however, had fire in the belly; the prototypical American immigrant child's drive for excellence; the experience of anti-Semitic prejudice throughout his life, which he successfully channeled into an Adlerian-style striving for mastery; and a messiah complex that convinced him that he needed to get his message out—now. Maslow and Huxley, though one in their humanistic orientation, were likely much too far apart in upbringing and status to connect—but what intellectual fireworks they would have ignited together!

Julian Huxley, Man and Mission

Julian Huxley was a biologist who championed evolutionary humanism, the understanding that the continuing evolution of Homo sapiens would no longer manifest in the biological realm but in the psychosocial. Although denying the existence of a personal, transcendent God, he advocated for a place for a humanistic religion. His leadership in the field of biology and his unique evolutionary vision provide a larger perspective for us as we assess the humanistic psychology movement, particularly as it relates to the spiritual domain, of which the universality of values is a critical component.

Huxley was born in London and educated at Eton and Oxford. Upon graduation, he conducted research in marine biology and in 1912 was offered the opportunity to found the biology department for the recently created Rice Institute (now Rice University) in Houston, Texas. He returned home in 1916 to serve in the British Intelligence Corps during the war. Other appointments included a professorship in zoology at King's College, London, where he both conducted research and taught; a tenure as secretary of the Zoological Society of London; and appointment as first director-general of UNESCO, which he used as a fitting platform for his humanist agenda. In addition to *The Humanist Frame*, he published several other works, most notably *Religion without Revelation*, *Evolutionary Humanism*, and *The Uniqueness of Man*.

What was Huxley's understanding of the response of humanism to the problems of contemporary society? An evolutionary biologist, he understood science as both the servant of humanity and the means through which humanity would fulfill its mission as guardian and director of evolution. He championed the full integration of evolutionary thought into modern science and, significantly, its application to social policy, something of a heresy in both religious and scientific circles. Like Maslow, he advocated for a universal ethics, verifiable through observation and experimentation.

As a biologist, Huxley was a product of Great Britain's nineteenth-century fascination with the observation and classification of the natural world. It was a world that created Alfred Russel Wallace, Thomas Henry Huxley, Herbert Spencer, and Charles Darwin, a time when any proper Englishman of means was getting his hands dirty in the soil and differentiating the various plant and animal species—and discovering new ones. England in the nineteenth century was awash in both professional and amateur naturalists. Having a special interest in ornithology, Huxley, early in his career, wrote a paper titled "The Courtship Habits of the Great Crested Grebe," which was later turned into a book. Two chapters in *Evolutionary Humanism* are titled "Birds and Science" and "Riches of Wild Africa." His signature approach to humanism developed not from the world of psychology but from within the context of his biological studies.

As both a biologist and a humanist, Huxley advocated for the role of Homo sapiens as evolution's director and caretaker, which he addresses in *Evolutionary Humanism*: "Man is not merely the latest dominant type produced by evolution, but its sole active agent on Earth. His destiny is to be responsible for the whole future of the evolutionary process on this planet."[4] In *The Farther Reaches of Human Nature*, published posthumously in 1971, Abraham Maslow echoed Huxley's sentiments by noting that "we have come to the point in biological history where we now are responsible for our own evolution. We have become self-evolvers. Evolution means selecting and therefore choosing and deciding, and this means valuing."[5] It is interesting that in the index to that book, Maslow references Aldous Huxley and Aldous's wife, Laura. But no mention is made of Julian.

Julian Huxley drew a binary distinction between the competing ideas of external revelation and organic evolution, between "an interventionist notion of an outside power source . . . and an intrinsic model of emergent life based upon internal processes."[6] In the Huxley model, there is no "God in the gaps": the unknown can and does become known over time through science. He noted that religion calls for a theology (beliefs), a morality (ethical code), and rituals (enduring practices), and he proposed evolutionary biology as both the belief system and the process through which an ethical code can be agreed upon and altered as needed. As for rituals, Huxley was confident that these would emerge organically within communities and

4. Huxley, *Evolutionary Humanism*, 121.

5. Maslow, *Farther Reaches*, 10–11.

6. Morgan, *In Absence of God*, 64.

end up looking quite similar to some that are common in our contemporary religions. In this transformation from theistic religion to evolutionary humanism, nothing would be lost: "Meditation and self-examination will continue in place as awe, wonder, and reverence remain."[7]

Huxley trained his lens on humanity's responsibility to advance the evolutionary process for the betterment of all and the protection of the natural world, and he charged his readers with the task of creating and advancing a new meaning-system, a new way of understanding ourselves and others within the worldview of evolutionary science. As Huxley scholar John Morgan affirms in his collection of essays on secular spirituality titled *Post-Biblical Religion*, "We are in charge and are likewise charged with the responsibility for every decision and every outcome."[8] What we are learning today about the effects of our lifestyle choices on climate change and its impact on humanity across the globe serve as a timely reminder of what the wisdom of nature teaches us about ethical choices.

For Huxley, the new humanist religion is one that is consonant with the new science and any emerging science; it is evolution-centered rather than God-centered, responding to life with a sublime admiration for the resources and possibilities of Homo sapiens. Salvation in this approach is not otherworldly but present-worldly. It is about a deepening sense of commitment to the physical and psychological environment, "an investment by the human community in the perpetuity of the world rather than a personally enduring self."[9] As Steven Nadler writes in his study of Spinoza, referenced earlier, salvation for the humanists is more about the attainment of "virtue, happiness, and well-being in *this* world,"[10] not in some other world.

A Religion of Evolutionary Humanism

A look at Huxley's own contribution to *The Humanist Frame*, the compendium he produced two years after Maslow published his record of the MIT conference, will shed more light on his unique approach to the role of humanistic thinking in confronting the world's challenges. In the book's preface, he defines its goal as that of presenting humanism as an all-encompassing system of ideas, a new paradigm through which to understand the world. He proposes a "continued effort to extend the concept of evolution

7. Morgan, *In Absence of God*, 88.
8. Morgan, *Post-Biblical Religion*, 85.
9. Morgan, *Post-Biblical Religion*, 120.
10. Nadler, *Book Forged in Hell*, 74–75 (emphasis added).

over the widest possible range of phenomena"[11]—somewhat reminiscent of Rogers's efforts to extend his own foundational principles of personal authenticity, unconditional positive regard, and empathic understanding to all dimensions of life.

With this emphasis on an all-encompassing system of ideas, Julian Huxley channels the spirit and energy of his grandfather Thomas Huxley, whose passionate defense and advocacy of Darwin resulted in his earning the moniker "Darwin's bulldog." If Thomas Huxley's self-appointed role was to advance Darwinian thought in its infancy, Julian's was to shepherd it through adulthood—and declare it a new religion. In addition, as John Morgan argues in *Naturally Good: A Behavioral History of Moral Development*, Julian helped establish the "modern synthesis" of natural selection, "an updated version of Darwinism incorporating Mendelian genetics and the latest findings in all biological fields."[12]

In the opening chapter of *The Humanist Frame*, Huxley presents a wide-ranging treatise on humanism, religion, and the future of Homo sapiens. He begins with a restatement of his conviction that the world is experiencing the emergence of a new system of thought, what he often refers to as an "idea-system," a worldview that transcends both the magic-dominated tribal and the external theocentric systems. He calls for a humanism that embraces the twentieth century's explosion of knowledge and is organized around the central truth of the evolutionary process, without dependence upon a transcendent deity.

Huxley describes this humanism as unitary (noting the interconnection of body and mind), universal (relating to all life on earth and to earth itself), naturalistic (its spirituality emerging from within itself, not externally), global (speaking to all of humanity), and directional rather than static (oriented toward the future). Referencing the publication date of *The Humanist Frame* as marking the centennial of the publication of *On the Origin of Species*, he emphasizes the psychosocial dimension of evolution, the continuous enhancement of the species through humanity's focused mental processes in conjunction with existing cultural patterns.

For Huxley, evolution in the present day has transcended the biological phase and entered the ideological; human progress itself is now the focus of evolution. In this new system, "man's destiny is to be the sole agent for the future evolution of this planet."[13] We are called to use our minds in the service of "knowledge and reason, imagination and sensitivity, capacities

11. Huxley, *Humanist Frame*, 5.
12. Morgan, *Naturally Good*, 234.
13. Huxley, *Humanist Frame*, 17.

for wonder and love, for comprehensiveness and compassion, for spiritual aspiration and moral effort"[14]—with no need for outside assistance in the form of the supernatural.

Huxley confronts the loneliness and alienation that humankind might face in a world without a transcendent God by reminding the reader that we are not alone as a type, as a species. We are not alienated from the rest of the natural world but are "linked by genetic continuity with all the other living inhabitants of [our] planet."[15] We have the strength of ourselves and the knowledge of the legacy we will leave behind to draw upon.

Channeling Huxley's sentiments, existential psychiatrist Irvin Yalom, in *Staring at the Sun: Overcoming the Terror of Death*, offers what he refers to as "rippling," referring to the circles of influence that each of us leaves behind after we have passed on. Writing in 2008 when he was seventy-seven years old, Yalom observed that the "idea that we can leave something of ourselves, even beyond our knowing, offers a potent answer to those who claim that meaninglessness inevitably flows from one's finiteness and transiency."[16] Appropriately, given their shared affinity for humanism and existentialism, the back cover of *Staring at the Sun* carries a tribute by Rollo May to Yalom's contributions to the field of psychotherapy.

Huxley emphasizes the relative recency in evolutionary time of this psychosocial state, one with the emergence of Homo sapiens, some 200,000 years ago. He makes note of the horror and evil that has taken place during much of that time, from prehistory into the historic era, and he references the previous fifty years of world wars, genocide, targeted destruction of civilian populations, and the unleashing of atom bombs, noting that "our feet still drag in the biological mud, even when we lift our heads into the conscious air."[17] But he sees hope on the horizon in the form of a new unifying pattern of thought and belief that is evolution-centered (with the mind now understood as the principal factor in evolution), future-directed, knowledge-oriented rather than dogma-oriented, firmly grounded in the scientific method, and focused on advancement through the embrace of new discoveries, even as these conflict with older, established ways of thinking.

Demonstrating the social commitment of humanism, Huxley calls for population control. He advocates for an emphasis on the *quality* of human life rather than on the biblical injunction to increase and multiply, a directive that, Huxley would argue, has long outlived its relevance. Emphasizing

14. Huxley, *Humanist Frame*, 18.
15. Huxley, *Humanist Frame*, 19.
16. Yalom, *Staring at the Sun*, 83.
17. Huxley, *Humanist Frame*, 20.

this point in his 1964 collection of essays titled *Evolutionary Humanism*, he calls for policies on both the national and international levels to address it: "Man's dominant aim must be increase in quality—quality of human personality, of achievement, of works of art and craftsmanship, of inner experience, of quality of life and living in general."[18] Like Fromm, he criticizes the culture of materialism, marketing, advertising, and resource exploitation and advocates for "the qualitative satisfaction of real human needs, spiritual and mental as well as material and physiological."[19]

Throughout his writings, Huxley emphasizes a novel approach to religion, a psychosocial approach that addresses the destiny of humanity and that promotes a renewed sense of the sacred and ethical, as well as the creation and enjoyment of beauty, the experience of inner peace and harmony, the undertaking of grand projects, and the exploration of the mind. He shares his concerns about how religion is currently understood and practiced, while expressing hope that it could become a positive force in humanity's future as it takes note of the latest scientific knowledge and embraces the sacred as found in nature, art, love, and intellectual pursuit. He sees in evolutionary truth both a path to freedom from fear of the unknown and the supernatural and an invitation to focus on the identification of the possibilities that lie before us.

Huxley understands the humanistic emphasis on values as part of "one really major problem now before science—the problem of relating mind and mental activities to the rest of the phenomenal universe in a single scientific picture."[20] In this enterprise, he sees science not as the enemy of religion but its ally, providing a "'scientific' theology, a scientifically-ordered framework of belief, to whatever new religion emerges from the present ideological disorder."[21] Science, he observes, has expanded its influence over the years to include the newer fields of psychology and sociology; why would it not also be able to expand to include theology? Theology, which has progressed beyond both polytheism and monotheism, is now ready, in Huxley's vision, to enter a new phase, one that is scientific and evolution-centered.

Completing his argument against a supernatural theology, Huxley calls for aspirational prayer instead of the petitionary variety; concern directed to this world rather than another; and an end to the focus on original sin, damnation, and the patriarchal attitude of female inferiority. While calling upon religion to evolve, Huxley encourages it to maintain its sense of sacred

18. Huxley, *Evolutionary Humanism*, 246.
19. Huxley, *Humanist Frame*, 25.
20. Huxley, *Humanist Frame*, 37–38.
21. Huxley, *Humanist Frame*, 38.

mystery and the understanding of right and wrong. He affirms the continuing place of mystery in a nontheistic world, noting specifically the question of the very existence of the universe: *Why is there something rather than nothing?* And he consistently affirms the permanence of awe, wonder, and reverence in this new religion.

Taking a broader perspective, Huxley refers to religion as "applied spiritual ecology,"[22] ecology understood as the science of the interrelationships of humans with nature, with others, and with their communities. As suggested by those words, Huxley's religion is profoundly activist; its purpose, like that of science itself, is to advance humanity, to promote human fulfillment. He understands the universe as a unitary, evolutionary process with humans occupying that part of the process that is "capable of effecting its further course on earth and perhaps elsewhere."[23] Ultimately, he proposes science itself—with its openness and its ability, through the scientific method, to self-correct—as a model for religion.

Huxley recognizes the inhibition of many in the world of science to embrace a role for their discipline in areas traditionally outside the range of scientific inquiry, an inhibition he feels a responsibility to challenge. Toward that end, he directs a significant portion of his work toward broadening the scope of the scientific method, specifically by bringing it more into the psychosocial sphere and including within its purview values, ethics, art, socioeconomic organization, and religion. Religion's role must also change to meet the demands of evolutionary humanism as envisioned by Huxley: it must continue to provide for life's traditional, ceremonial markers, such as birth, marriage, and death, but as represented in the spirit of this new vision. He sees these efforts to broaden the scope of both science and religion as humanism's grand task, its ultimate challenge.

Huxley observes, as did Freud and many of those within the humanistic camp, that what is referred to as God is better understood as a symbol or metaphor upon which humanity has projected its own qualities of power, agency, and capability, resulting in the creation of a power greater than the self that is centered in a superpersonal being who can intervene in human affairs and alter the course of events. He notes that the qualities of power, agency, and capability are real—but not as attributions of the workings of an external God. Huxley acknowledges the debt the world owes to Christian ethics but wishes to relocate ethics within an evolutionary context, emphasizing the continuing accumulation of experience that is the hallmark of scientific progress.

22. Huxley, *Humanist Frame*, 43.

23. Huxley, *Humanist Frame*, 43.

Huxley confronts the challenge, frequently addressed in humanist and existentialist literature, of the individual's need to replace imposed authority systems (parental and societal) with ones freely and consciously developed. He argues for the replacement of the fall of man/original sin paradigm with a new humanistic ethic, one influenced more by humanity's own experiences than by an external thought system handed down through the ages.

Significantly, Huxley does not dismiss experiences typically understood as belonging exclusively to the province of theistic religion. He references, for example, "communion with some higher power, or inspiration from outside the personality, or a sense of transcendent power or glory, or sudden conversion, or apparently supernormal beauty or ineffable sacredness, or the healing power of prayer or repentant adoration."[24] Rather, he sees these experiences as "the outcome of human minds in their strange commerce with outer reality and in the still stranger and often unconscious internal struggle between their components."[25] He understands these eternal human strivings as real and valued, though often misdirected toward an external source, and he offers evolutionary humanism as its corrective.

Framing humanity's destiny in terms of the increasing actualization of its potential through evolution, with religion understood as that within the person that is primarily concerned with the experience of the sacred, Huxley calls for "a thorough investigation of man's inner world, a great project of 'Mind Exploration' which could and should rival and surpass 'Space Exploration' in interest and importance."[26] Echoing Maslow's forays into transpersonal psychology, he speaks of a "new realm of being . . . a realm of mental realities, built on but transcending the realm of material realities,"[27] and he adds that we all get occasional glimpses of this through love, mental exploration, poetry, and mysticism.

For Huxley, life itself, the natural world all around us, provides a sense of the divine; in Rogerian terminology, we might say that life itself serves as the necessary and sufficient requirement for encountering the transcendent. Cognizant of the conflicting ideologies that frustrate progress toward a unified approach to ethical development, Huxley recommends transcending them via a new evolutionary ecology, "a new pattern of our relations with each other and with the rest of our environment, including the mental environment which we both create and inhabit."[28]

24. Huxley, *Humanist Frame*, 45.
25. Huxley, *Humanist Frame*, 45.
26. Huxley, *Humanist Frame*, 46.
27. Huxley, *Humanist Frame*, 46.
28. Huxley, *Humanist Frame*, 47.

Evolutionary humanism provides a road map for the continuing enhancement of the human species for Huxley. To facilitate that process, he calls for the replacement of the idea of the welfare state with a more humanistic emphasis on the "Fulfillment Society," a social system organized in such a way that each individual's personal fulfillment could be attained: "a new type of society, a new step in psychological evolution [that addresses the] central belief of Evolutionary Humanism . . . that existence can be improved, that vast untapped possibilities can be increasingly realized, that greater fulfillment can replace frustration."[29] And like Maslow, Huxley betrays no doubt that this imagined future will occur.

Science Meets Theology: Julian Huxley and Pierre Teilhard de Chardin

The history of the modern humanist movement is dotted with examples of mutual admiration and support among theistic and nontheistic thinkers. We observed it in Maslow, with his reference to the scientist and the theologian who, united in their humanism, are separated at the close of life, one destined to a purely natural end and the other to a supernatural one with an afterlife and a transcendent God. We saw it in the mutual esteem between the nontheistic Carl Rogers and Brian Thorne, cofounder of the Norwich Centre in England, as well as that between Rogers and Martin Buber. We will find it again in the final chapter in reference to Daniel Siegel, UCLA-based psychiatrist and foremost spokesperson for the new field of mindfulness-based therapy, and the late John O'Donohue, poet, philosopher, author, and Catholic priest. Through his friendship with O'Donohue, a door was opened for the nontheistic humanist Siegel to grow in acceptance of the spiritual dimension of life, a process we have already observed in the lives of Maslow, Rogers, Fromm, and May. This model of theist and nontheist working together on behalf of humanistic values is no aberration.

Pierre Teilhard de Chardin (1881–1955) was a French paleontologist who participated in the discovery of the Homo erectus fossils popularly known as Peking Man during the 1920s. He was also a Catholic priest of the Jesuit order and in several critical respects held quite different views about "ultimate concerns" from that of the nontheistic Huxley. Yet in their appreciation and respect for scientific knowledge, evolutionary thinking, broadness of vision, the centrality of personhood, and the advancement of humanistic goals, Huxley and Teilhard were kindred souls, and their

29. Huxley, *Humanist Frame*, 48.

friendship proved that there is often far more of that which unites us than that which tempts us to withdraw into separate corners.

What drew Huxley to Teilhard? How did he come to see this priest/scientist as a fellow traveler and dear friend? Huxley was, as we have seen, decidedly nontheistic, yet he wrote the preface to Teilhard's *The Phenomenon of Man*, a profoundly spiritual work written in the 1930s but not published until 1955 due to opposition by both the Catholic Church and the Jesuit order. What united the two men was nothing less than a shared vision of humanity, one that highlighted the stages of evolution from the inanimate to the animate and on to the conscious mind, wherein the responsibility emerges within Homo sapiens to become director of the evolutionary process itself.

Since the characteristics we most admire in another are typically projections of characteristics we ourselves share, we can learn much about a person from the people he or she most esteems. A look at Huxley's introduction to Teilhard's classic work will shed light on the person of Huxley as well as that of Teilhard, just as Rollo May's *Paulus*, his personal biography of Paul Tillich, revealed the heart of Rollo May as much as it did that of Tillich. Indeed, it is occasionally unclear in both May's and Huxley's writings whether they are speaking about themselves or of Tillich or Teilhard, respectively.

Huxley opens the introduction with an immediate indication of how he sees both the man and the book: "*The Phenomenon of Man* is a very remarkable work by a very remarkable human being."[30] Referencing a tripartite synthesis effected by Teilhard—"of the material and physical world with that of mind and spirit, of past with future, and of the variety within creation with its fundamental unity, the many with the one"[31]—he commends Teilhard's evolutionary perspective and his attention to process.

Of his first meeting with Teilhard, in 1946, Huxley recalls that "he and I were on the same quest, and had been pursuing parallel roads ever since we were young men in our twenties."[32] Defining that quest, Huxley restates his foundational insight that evolution has reached a critical point of separation, with Homo sapiens proceeding on the convergent path of species enhancement while the merely biological continues on its divergent path of species multiplication. He posits his own drive for a universal approach to the world's ills, which he championed through UNESCO, as a practical manifestation of convergence toward species enhancement, a theme that

30. Huxley, "Introduction," 11.
31. Huxley, "Introduction," 11.
32. Huxley, "Introduction," 11.

resonates throughout the greater humanist movement, and he sees Teilhard's goals as equally convergent.

In *The Heart of Matter*, Teilhard's last published work, he references "the reality and spiritualizing value of the new form of 'cosmic sense' aroused in modern Man by the evidence that Science provides of his belonging to a convergent-type universe."[33] Teilhard emphasizes that the spiritual process he imagines will eventuate only from within the process of evolutionary humanism, although he expresses doubt that this can result in "the sort of religion that has been foretold with such warmth and brilliance by my friend Julian Huxley."[34] He adds that he embraces both "contemporary neo-Christianity and contemporary neo-Humanism"[35] and presents, intentionally written in poetic form, a mystical summary of his theology:

> It is Christ, in very truth, who saves,
> —but should we not immediately add that at the same time it is
> Christ who is saved by
> Evolution?[36]

The philosophy that most profoundly united Huxley with Teilhard was the mutual understanding that the universe in its totality must be understood as "one gigantic process of becoming, of attaining new levels of existence and organization, which can properly be called a genesis or an evolution."[37] In describing these new levels of existence and organization, Teilhard found it necessary to create new words or use old ones in novel ways, as many innovators are prone to do. Unlike many of Teilhard's followers who agonized over the numerous neologisms he employed to discuss his unique understanding of evolution, Huxley applauds them: *noogenesis* (referring to the evolution of mind), *cosmogenesis* (which places emphasis on the universe in process of continuous becoming), *hominization* (the process of becoming more truly human through the realization of one's potential, a pervasive theme in humanistic psychology), and *ultra-hominization* (the imagined future stage in which Homo sapiens will have so far transcended itself as to require new nomenclature).

On the other side of the Atlantic, Abraham Maslow was thinking similar thoughts with his reference to a possible fourth force in psychology, beyond the humanistic, that he called transpersonal psychology, wherein the

33. Teilhard de Chardin, *Heart of Matter*, 91.
34. Teilhard de Chardin, *Heart of Matter*, 91.
35. Teilhard de Chardin, *Heart of Matter*, 92.
36. Teilhard de Chardin, *Heart of Matter*, 92.
37. Huxley, "Introduction," 13.

person would experience a level of transcendence in which newer, higher needs would emerge, *metaneeds*, which would attend to the spiritual domain. Huxley takes this a step further: even the cultural distinctions of previous generations are being rapidly replaced by "cultural convergence . . . the union of the whole human species into a single interthinking group based on a single self-developing framework of thought (or noosphere)."[38]

Huxley references Teilhard's word *complexification*, referring to the increasingly elaborate organization of the universe from mere subatomic particles to Homo sapiens. Complementing that with his own term, *convergent integration*, he places emphasis on the role of the human mind in directing present and future change, and with the confidence that characterized much of his life, predicts what this will look like: "In the process of convergence and coalescence . . . the psychosocial temperature rises. Mankind as a whole will accordingly achieve more intensive, more complex, and more integrated mental activity, which can guide the human species up the path of progress to higher levels of hominization."[39]

In discussing Teilhard's spirituality and his use of the word *Christogenesis* (the understanding that Christ is the Alpha, the Omega, and the unifying element of the evolutionary process), Huxley observes that although he and many other scientists "find it impossible to follow him all the way in his gallant attempt to reconcile the supernatural elements in Christianity with the facts and implications of evolution, this in no way detracts from the positive value of his naturalistic general approach."[40] Huxley would no doubt applaud—with the same caveat noted above—the work being done today by Catholic scholars such as Elizabeth Johnson in *Ask the Beasts: Darwin and the God of Love*, Elia Delio in *The Emergent Christ*, Thomas Berry in *The Dream of the Earth*, and John Haught in *The Cosmic Vision of Teilhard de Chardin*, all of whom, in the spirit of Teilhard, point toward a broader, more cosmic spirituality. It must be noted, however, that each of these, like Teilhard, experienced resistance to their writings from within their own Church.

By way of defense against those in the humanist community who criticized him for his support of the Catholic priest Teilhard de Chardin, Huxley focuses on the centrality of personhood in the Jesuit's writings. He observes that Teilhard's notion of what he called the Omega point (wherein the noosphere, the sphere of mind, achieves a suprapersonal, divine organization) evolved out of his core humanism. And he applauds Teilhard's vision that

38. Huxley, "Introduction," 14.

39. Huxley, "Introduction," 17.

40. Huxley, "Introduction," 19.

the "developed human being . . . is not merely a more highly individualized individual . . . [but] has crossed the threshold of self-consciousness to a new mode of thought,"[41] one characterized by a higher degree of conscious integration of self and of self with others. In this vision, the person has transcended mere individuality and achieved personality, the becoming of a person, which Carl Rogers celebrated in his own more down-to-earth manner.

Huxley is fulsome in his praise for Teilhard's efforts to attempt an integration of Christian theology and evolutionary biology, to relate the facts of his religious experience and his understanding of Christology to those of natural science. Huxley strove to understand *all* experience within an evolutionary framework, and, in the spirit of William James's *The Varieties of Religious Experience*, he recognized religious phenomena as no less worthy of integration than any other experience. He honors Teilhard for combining a broad scientific knowledge with deep religious feeling and values, and he observes that in the light of Teilhard's insights, "it is no longer possible to maintain that science and religion must cooperate in thought-tight compartments or concern separate sectors of life; they are both relevant to the whole of human existence."[42]

Huxley closes his introduction to *The Phenomenon of Man* by reemphasizing his foundational insight that in Homo sapiens organic evolution has entered a new stage, now becoming "a psychosocial process based on the cumulative transmission of experience and its results . . . characterized more by cultural than by genetic or biological change,"[43] leading to newer and higher levels of organization and patterns of thought. He identifies areas needing progress: "global unity of mankind's noetic organization or system of awareness, but a high degree of variety within that unity; love, with goodwill and full cooperation; personal integration and internal harmony; and increasing knowledge,"[44] and he concludes with the testimony that the world's future is conditional upon the increase in knowledge and love called for by Teilhard de Chardin in *The Phenomenon of Man*.

Religion, Science, Philosophy, and Values

Julian Huxley and Pierre Teilhard de Chardin provided a model for the cooperation, even friendship, that is possible between nontheistic persons

41. Huxley, "Introduction," 19.
42. Huxley, "Introduction," 26.
43. Huxley, "Introduction," 27.
44. Huxley, "Introduction," 28.

of science and those for whom the place of God and religion are central to their lives. The questions they addressed are as applicable in the twenty-first century as they were during the early and middle years of the twentieth. In our own day, the many scientists, philosophers, and theologians who have weighed in on the issue from various perspectives include biologist and entomologist E. O. Wilson, neuroscientist Sam Harris, paleontologist and biologist Stephen Jay Gould, and Carnegie Mellon philosopher Andy Norman, as well as the previously referenced academic theologians Elizabeth Johnson of Fordham and John Haught of Georgetown.

Of the scientists referenced, Stephen Jay Gould merits further attention for his efforts to propose a practical working solution to problems related to the intersection of science and religion, particularly regarding the temptation to overreach in either of those two domains and dismiss the legitimacy of one or the other. In *Rocks of Ages: Science and Religion in the Fullness of Life*, Gould proposes what many tout as a workable, respectful pathway toward honoring both the scientific and religious perspectives, something we saw challenged first in these pages in Freud's *The Future of an Illusion* and *Civilization and Its Discontents*.

For Freud, religion and science are incompatible, and religion is a psychological problem to be dealt with through psychoanalysis and something that humanity will eventually outgrow. Carl Rogers, Abraham Maslow, Erich Fromm, Rollo May, and others featured in this work frequently addressed and challenged the role of religion from the perspective of their humanistic outlook on life, specifically in Maslow's *Religions, Values, and Peak-Experiences* and Fromm's *Psychoanalysis and Religion*. May's books abound with religious references, both complimentary and critical, and, as we recall, Rogers opened himself to the spiritual realm late in life after many years of spirited opposition. As much as they criticized what they saw as inauthentic examples of religion and held ideas about God certainly outside conventional theological understanding—God as the ground of being (Paul Tillich and Rollo May) or "the connectedness of all reality" (Erich Fromm and Julian Huxley)[45]—they often spoke respectfully about the spiritual domain, frequently describing it as that which elicits awe, reverence, and mystery in the face of life's many wonders.

How to speak respectfully about both religion and science while holding honest dialogue related to those two domains is the challenge set forth by the humanist Gould in *Rocks of Ages*. He encourages us to look upon science and religion not as enemies but as *non-overlapping magisteria* (NOMA), and he calls for "respectful non-interference—accompanied

45. Morgan, *Post-Biblical Religion*, ix.

by intense dialogue"[46]—quite the opposite of Martin Buber's model of two spheres that penetrate each other, work together, and are so centrally related that each could serve as the foundation of the other, as quoted in the chapter on Rogers. Recognizing that although religion and science work best when they stay within their respective magisteria, Gould is cognizant of the fact that they will certainly bump into each other, encroach upon each other, and spill over into each other's terrain from time to time.

Gould understands religion (broadly speaking about ethics, the search for meaning, the *why* of life) and science (reason, factual inquiry, the *what* and the *how* of life) as two separate and equal domains, one engaging the empirical realm (science) and the other the behavioral (religion). Religion is "a ground for moral contemplation . . . [not] a set of dogmas accepted without questions"[47] for Gould, and he quips, channeling Galileo, that "while science studies how the heavens go, religion shows us how to get to heaven."[48] And he applauds Charles Darwin's advocacy of that same approach a century and a half ago.

Gould, who was raised in a nonpracticing Jewish household in Queens, New York, explains that he "is not a believer [but] . . . an agnostic in the wise sense of T. H. Huxley," Julian's celebrated grandfather, adding that "I shared the enormous benefit of a respect for learning that pervades Jewish culture, even at the poorest economic levels"[49]—benefits likewise enjoyed by Maslow, Fromm, Fromm-Reichman, Frankl, Adler, and even, in spite of himself, Freud. In Gould's experience of Judaism, emphasis was placed on social justice and practical action, not on theology, superstition, or irrationality. Also, like Maslow and Fromm, he recognizes a clear distinction between affirming, encouraging, inclusive religion that seeks common ground and that advocates for moral and ethical principles, on the one hand, and religion that places priority on the "truth" of doctrinal statements, focusing on differences and distinctions, on the other. For Gould, the "enemy [of science] is not religion but dogmatism and intolerance,"[50] what Fromm called "inauthentic religion." Further, he does not hesitate to point out the overreach of both domains, chiding, for example, religionists who would deny the evolutionary record and seek to impose their will on school science curricula and the "militant atheists,"[51] science's own fundamentalists,

46. Gould, *Rocks of Ages*, 5.
47. Gould, *Rocks of Ages*, 42.
48. Gould, *Rocks of Ages*, 6.
49. Gould, *Rocks of Ages*, 8.
50. Gould, *Rocks of Ages*, 149.
51. Gould, *Rocks of Ages*, 68–69.

who argue that moral and ethical concerns have no place in the discussion of, for example, the uses of technology.

The facts of science should not be questioned on the basis of religious "truths," nor should religious concerns about moral principles be dismissed because they lack a scientific foundation—"The moral meaning of life [does not] lie exposed in nature's factuality,"[52] Gould asserts. Barbara J. King, an evolutionary biologist who promoted Gould's nonoverlapping magisteria paradigm in her fascinating study of the evolution of religion, *Evolving God*, seconds his approach with her observation that "matters of faith are not amenable to scientific analysis."[53] And, quips John Morgan, with a finality that settles the debate, "there is no faith-based science."[54]

Rounding out the discussion, Gould hastens to add that just as religionists must yield to men and women of science in matters fully within the scientific magisterium, scientists need persons with a religious sensitivity to help them maintain a focus on the role of values in deciding what should be done. Maslow's critique referenced earlier regarding valueless science making "possible in theory at least the Nazi physician 'experimenting' in the concentration camps, or the spectacle of captured German engineers working devotedly for whichever side happened to capture them" stands as a reminder that, though separate, neither domain can act without regard to the other. To the degree to which we succeed in this honoring of the separate domains of religion and science, Gould promises, the result will be an increase in wisdom, which itself will lead to the advance of healthier, more humanitarian versions of both religion and science.

Philosopher Andy Norman, director of the Humanism Initiative at Carnegie Mellon University and author of *Mental Immunity: Infectious Ideas, Mind-Parasites, and the Search for a Better Way to Think*, introduces a third factor into this science/religion debate: a unique perspective from the discipline of philosophy. Recognizing that philosophy is distinct from science, Norman nonetheless observes that its historical trajectory, encompassing numerous scientifically oriented thinkers such as Plato, Aristotle, Descartes, and Spinoza, "has always been quasi-scientific."[55] Norman is an epistemologist, a philosopher who trains his lens on the process of knowing—how we know, how reasoning works, how we distinguish knowledge from mere belief. While science accomplishes "knowing" through observation and experimentation, the tools of epistemology include reasoning, the

52. Gould, *Rocks of Ages*, 181.

53. B. King, *Evolving God*, 9.

54. Morgan, *Post-Biblical Religion*, 22.

55. Norman, *Mental Immunity*, 22.

testing of hypotheses, and the Socratic dialectical method, which he insists is not to be used as a cudgel by which to beat down the opponent but as a legitimate quest for wisdom and truth.

As in science, all philosophical truth is provisional—as strongly as we may support our present conclusion, new information might one day surface that will force a change in position. Consequently, rather than insist on achieving absolute certitude in determining philosophical truth—frequently, if not always, impossible—Norman is satisfied with what he refers to as *reasonable belief*, judgment that is backed by solid reasoning and that withstands reasonable challenges that genuinely *arise*—that is, arise because they are truly germane to the issue at hand. Challenge for the sake of challenge itself is counterproductive, as is the practice of stubbornly holding on to beliefs that crumble under relevant and well-founded challenges. *We must always be willing to yield to the better reason* is Norman's mantra. Just as Maslow and Huxley were drawn to the task of identifying healthy values to address post-World War II-era ills, so is Norman for our own day. A look at how he approaches that task will shed further light on the larger issue of religion and science, or faith and reason.

Demonstrating kinship with the humanistic psychologists' differentiation between authentic and inauthentic religion, Norman observes that "a misleading picture of responsible belief is holding us back; it excuses irresponsible believing and disrupts our reason-giving practices."[56] The good news is that "irresponsible believing" can be identified and effectively countered, a major theme of Norman's work. As a philosopher, he looks at values from the broad perspective of religious and secular disputes throughout the ages, and asks: *Who may weigh in on values—science, philosophy, or religion? Is there room for all three, and perhaps other academic disciplines, or are values the exclusive domain of one or another?* Both the religious fundamentalists and the "militant atheists" that Gould referenced will, of course, promote a narrow approach to this, the former proclaiming the infallibility of Scripture and the latter the absolute supremacy of the scientific method.

Most decidedly not a relativist, Norman employs the immunology metaphor to advance his thesis that there are healthy beliefs, ideas, and values and unhealthy ones, and that the distinctions between the two are both identifiable and verifiable. He proposes a pathway through which we might achieve some degree of immunity from pernicious thinking, just as today we have made progress toward COVID-19 immunity. And he offers a new discipline in the larger scientific world, *cognitive immunology*, through which we could address the "ideological pathogens" that bedevil us.

56. Norman, *Mental Immunity*, 14.

As Norman describes it, cognitive immunology is not values neutral. It unapologetically values "function over dysfunction,"[57] personal and societal well-being over unhealthy living, and the scientific method over religious belief—"healthy is better than sickness . . . shared well-being is better than shared suffering."[58] One in spirit with Huxley, Maslow, and all those who contributed to their respective values initiative projects, Norman recognizes that values come in both healthy and unhealthy varieties, and he celebrates reason, a somewhat revised Socratic method, a collaborative inquiry style, and "a general sense of right and wrong" as antidotes.[59]

Like Gould, Norman is no enemy of religion per se. He affirms that both religion and science "contain a piece of a larger truth"[60] and sees it as one of his goals to "bridge the divide between the secular and religious worldviews"[61] by ferreting out the difference between good ideas and bad ones. He challenges head-on the Enlightenment doctrine that everyone is entitled to his or her opinion, noting that ideas, beliefs, and opinions have consequences that affect all and that it is our moral responsibility to adjust our beliefs as evidence to the contrary presents itself. We can all readily identify beliefs and belief systems that directly lead to horrific violence and suffering, and we are not absolved from the responsibility of doing so. Norman positions himself within a larger tradition that includes Alfred Adler, who famously advanced that there is a belief behind every behavior, and the basic thesis of cognitive psychology that as goes our thinking, so too go our behaviors.

How does Norman propose to increase the level of mental immunity throughout the culture? Although his book should be read by all who are concerned with the prevalence of toxic ideas in American culture and throughout the world, to get into the details of his thesis would lead us too far astray from our purpose here, and this brief review falls well short of doing justice to Norman's masterful and important work. Suffice it to say that he advocates for an updated Socratic method that focuses on "the way of inquiry" or "collaborative inquiry" as opposed to closed-mindedness, the appeal to authority, or the a priori approach of "arm-chair philosophizing: a process of questioning and introspection that is little constrained by observation."[62] Collaborative inquiry is the search for truth wherein all par-

57. Norman, *Mental Immunity*, 10–11.
58. Norman, *Mental Immunity*, 75.
59. Norman, *Mental Immunity*, 145.
60. Norman, *Mental Immunity*, 17.
61. Norman, *Mental Immunity*, 111.
62. Norman, *Mental Immunity*, 162.

ties agree to change their minds in the face of incontrovertible evidence—a process quite distinct from debate, the purpose of which is to win rather than seek truth through honest reasoning.

Closing his book, Norman offers twelve helpful and practical steps toward achieving cognitive immunity, ranging from opening the self to new ideas and recognizing the relationship between beliefs and behaviors to engaging with others in a community of inquiry (rather than one based on mere belief). Last but certainly not least is putting our thoughts and ideas into positive action.

Andy Norman, while always advocating respectful dialogue in the debate between faith and reason, between religion and science or philosophy, is clearly more at home in the latter. Echoing Maslow's frequently messianic tone and the fervent aspirations of both Julian Huxley and Pierre Teilhard de Chardin, he speaks of science as representing "nothing less than the path to collective salvation,"[63] and he asks, "Why are there many competing religions but only one science?"[64] In a nutshell, he argues that we need to yield to the better reasons that science and philosophy—the search for wisdom, the relentless pursuit of truth—provide. More will be said about Norman in our final chapter, which looks at indications of a reemergence of humanistic psychology today.

A Summary of the Religion vs. Science Question: Three Contemporary Approaches to Determining Values

Broadly speaking, three positions have been delineated by the various commentators referenced in this chapter—from Huxley and Teilhard de Chardin to Stephen Gould and Andy Norman—concerning the respective societal roles of religion and science (or philosophy):

1. Religion as sentry vis-à-vis science, allowing only that which it deems to be in accord with its doctrines and precepts.

We have seen in a previous chapter how Baruch Spinoza was victimized by religious authorities in seventeenth-century Amsterdam for his efforts "to demonstrate the independence of intellectual matters from religious affairs and to defend the freedom of philosophy from political and religious

63. Norman, *Mental Immunity*, 165.

64. Norman, *Mental Immunity*, 164.

encroachment."[65] In our own times, we have witnessed the efforts of religious fundamentalists of various denominations interfering in science and history curricula and, on a much more frightening level, wreaking physical violence against "unbelievers" and "infidels." The position of religion as strict gatekeeper of science, contributing little toward the goal of healthy dialogue between the two, will likely be with us forever.

2. *Science (or philosophy) as sole determiner of human values, obviating the need for contributions from the religious community.*

Commentators advancing this position deny any meaningful role for religion in society beyond the ritual and ceremonial. E. O. Wilson in *On Human Nature*, for example, argues for human values based entirely on what is good for the natural world, a species-centered values system that denies a role for those who believe in the supernatural. Observing the world through the lens of sociobiology, which emphasizes the role of genetics in animal and human behavior, Wilson argues that "it lies with the human person and the human community, rationally and without any sense of an outside spiritual force, what should and should not be done, what is right and wrong, and what is good or evil."[66] John Morgan, an enthusiast of Wilson's approach to values and ethics, refers to it as an "if it's good enough for the cosmos, it's good enough for me" philosophy of life and calls for "*a religion which matches our science!*"[67]

Sam Harris echoes this approach in *The Moral Landscape*, wherein he argues that "right and wrong are a matter of increasing or decreasing well-being"[68] and that science can point the way to a moral code "linked directly to the facts about the happiness and suffering of conscious creatures."[69] In the process, religion, or at least religion's claim to be the adjudicator of values and ethics, will become obsolete, replaced by natural science. And striking a progressive pose, Harris translates his scientific humanism into political action: "We must build our better selves into our laws, our tax codes, and institutions."[70] Like Maslow and Huxley, Harris argues persuasively for the identification and promotion of healthy values, but unlike those two humanistic psychologists, he excludes those with a religious perspective from

65. Nadler, *Book Forged in Hell*, 74.
66. Morgan, *Post-Biblical Religion*, 101.
67. Morgan, *Post-Biblical Religion*, 101 (emphasis in original).
68. Harris, *Moral Landscape*, 43.
69. Harris, *Moral Landscape*, 64.
70. Harris, *Moral Landscape*, 70.

the discussion. In spite of differences large and small among the thinkers we've lumped together here, they would all agree that "we have a moral imperative to nourish and promote the well-being of [our] species."[71]

3. Science and religion as separate, autonomous, yet cooperative realms working within a climate of mutual respect and appreciation, while encouraging healthy and spirited dialogue.

As noted earlier, Julian Huxley praised Teilhard de Chardin in the introduction to *The Phenomenon of Man* for combining broad scientific knowledge with deep religious feeling and values, concluding that "it is no longer possible to maintain that science and religion must cooperate in thought-tight compartments . . . they are both relevant to the whole of human existence." With those words he anticipates the spirit of Gould, who would likewise honor both domains and respect their different gifts. Unlike Morgan, Harris, and Wilson, the humanist Gould is less sanguine about allowing science free reign here—just as he would rail against religion having veto power over science, so too would he oppose any attempt by science to discard the sociocultural role of religion. Gould's position is admittedly a broad one with many nuances, and it would include Maslow, Rogers, May, Fromm, Huxley, and Barbara J. King, who reminds us that "matters of faith are not amenable to scientific analysis";[72] they are separate domains.

When Julian Huxley observed, as quoted earlier, that although he, like many other scientists, was not in complete accord with Teilhard de Chardin's efforts to reconcile the supernatural elements in Christianity with the facts and implications of evolution and that "this in no way detracts from the positive value of his naturalistic general approach," he was demonstrating non-overlapping magisteria at their best. Science has its place and so too does religion, and neither has as its mission the subsuming of the other under its magisterium—they are separate. Further, each is to be respected, valued, and credited for its contributions to learning, culture, and society.

Huxley's worldview was one that did not include a place for a personal God. Nor did Gould's. But it did recognize that others—men and women of reason and values—do see the realm of the supernatural, with an understanding of God at its center, as one that offers a troubled world a moral compass by which to find its way. Both Huxley and Gould strove to honor that.

71. Morgan, *Post-Biblical Religion*, 99.

72. B. King, *Evolving God*, 9.

Over half a century ago, a physician, a man recognized in the community as a person of erudition and wisdom well beyond his chosen field, told me at the close of our appointment that his generation (the "Greatest Generation" or the "World War II Generation") had made it possible through advances in science for me to live to be one hundred. He then added, with the appropriate pause for effect, that it is now up to my generation to make that worthwhile. In so doing, he was honoring what Gould would describe some thirty years later: two domains, each having its place and purpose. Science can help all of us live longer, healthier lives; and authentic religion, healthy spirituality, and the world of values and ethics can help us be the kinds of persons who will make living all those years with each other a more humane and pleasant experience.

Huxley's Legacy

Julian Huxley lived a long and prolific life; he died in 1975 at the age of eighty-eight in the city of his birth, London. His marriage to Marie Juliette Baillot in 1919 produced two sons, Anthony Julian and Francis, who followed in their father's footsteps by becoming biologists. Among the numerous awards Huxley received in recognition of his achievements were the Darwin Medal of the Royal Society in 1956, the Darwin-Wallace Medal of the Linnean Society in 1958, and Humanist of the Year in 1962. In 1958, he was knighted by Queen Elizabeth II.

In addition to his prominence as an evolutionary biologist and humanist, Huxley gained both acclaim and notoriety as a proponent of eugenics. Springing from a passion for the continuing improvement of the human species, along with a Malthusian fear that population growth would outpace the world's limited resources, many in the scientific community championed some form of eugenics as a rational societal response. But following Nazi Germany's profane and barbaric use of eugenic practices against the Jewish people and others, any status it might have enjoyed before the 1930s quickly dissipated.

John Morgan, Sir Julian Huxley Professor of the History and Philosophy of Education during his years at Cloverdale College, treats this sensitively in *Understanding Ourselves*:

> Though wrongfully and, by his critics, unfairly criticized for his early musings regarding the future prospects of modern science rationally addressing the complex issues regarding eugenics, Huxley never believed that the human community, driven by a biologically mandated impetus for survival, would employ

> genetic engineering to our own detriment. Trusting in the rational utility of scientific knowledge, Huxley pled for an intentionality of genetic research designed for not merely survival but improvement of human life.[73]

Morgan, a humanist in the Quaker tradition, distinguishes between research into the improvement of Homo sapiens and the uses to which that research is directed. He references the benefits for humanity that could have been made through wise genetic research and admonishes its critics for their shortsightedness, noting that to "use Nazi research practices as an argument against scientific research is no less unreasonable than using obesity as an argument against eating."[74]

In addition to shedding light on the distinction between research and its uses, the story of the eugenics movement serves as a cautionary tale regarding the contrast between policies that promote and those that proscribe. From a broad etymological perspective, the word *eugenic*, which comes from the Greek words for "well" or "good" and "birth," might signify that which promotes the continuing health and growth of the species. We could imagine, from a humanistic perspective, the use of that word to designate various policies fostering a host of prosocial initiatives, such as wellness programs, prenatal and postnatal care, enhanced educational opportunities, expansion of mental health resources, efforts to reduce the wealth gap, and so on.

We know today that a healthy lifestyle—improved nutrition, for example—positively affects gene expression, so initiatives directed toward the promotion of healthier genes might well focus on improving living standards. Unfortunately, in addition to those and similar policies, some in the eugenics movements that arose in Europe and America during the early years of the twentieth century focused their energies on proscriptive approaches, such as marriage regulation and forced sterilization of people who were determined to be detrimental to the healthy continuation of the species.

Scholar and social justice advocate Dorothy Roberts, in her chapter on race in Nikole Hannah-Jones's monumental *The 1619 Project*, makes reference to just one of many egregious examples of eugenics practices, noting that "between 1933 and 1976, the Eugenics Board of North Carolina approved the involuntary sterilizations of more than 7,500 people—affecting Black people at a disproportionate rate—on the grounds that they were

73. Morgan, *Understanding Ourselves*, 183.

74. Morgan, *Understanding Ourselves*, 183.

mentally defective."[75] The racist theories that underlie those efforts were deplored by Huxley, and he personally "contributed to a pair of influential United Nations statements that debunked the pseudoscience of racial superiority."[76] Nonetheless, according to Michelle Nijhuis in *Beloved Beasts: Fighting for Life in an Age of Extinction*, which includes a chapter on Huxley and his contributions to species preservation, Huxley harbored the naïve, egotistic, and overly optimistic belief "that society should be informed by science and managed by scientists, forgetting that scientists were as capable as anyone else of abusing unbridled power."[77] Science itself may be values neutral, but scientists come with all the prejudices that the rest of us do.

Humanistic psychologists like those studied in this work believed fervently in the improvement of the species, but through the encouragement of person-centered interactions and the promotion of prosocial policies, not through the proscriptive arm of the state. Abraham Maslow, who was prone to utopian thinking and fanciful imaginings of a future status of humankind, a logical development from his work on self-actualization, occasionally caused eyebrows to rise in this matter. He never advocated for a proscriptive approach to the advancement of humanistic goals—his basic humanity would have prevented that—but he did occasionally employ verbiage that could be interpreted as advocating for the development of an elitist class of the highly self-actualized. Carl Rogers was quick to call him out on this by pointing out the potential danger of such words, on at least one occasion in person.[78]

From the perspective of our study of the intersection of spirituality and humanistic psychology, what does Julian Huxley have to offer? Returning to our definition of humanistic psychology noted in the first chapter—a holistic, health- and growth-oriented approach to working with and learning about persons in their unique, subjective, experiencing states that has as its goal the promotion of innate potential and the identification of the values essential to supporting that work, and that inspires us to take action for the greater good—I suggest the following:

1. *A growth orientation*—Carl Rogers's description of the potato plant shoots reaching toward the sun's dim rays through the dark cellar window and the plant's surviving in spite of that less-than-optimum environment remains a rich, descriptive metaphor for humanistic psychology's emphasis on innate potential and the promotion of factors

75. Roberts, "Race," 55.
76. Nijhuis, *Beloved Beasts*, 133.
77. Nijhuis, *Beloved Beasts*, 134.
78. Kirschenbaum, email to author, May 23, 2018.

supporting growth and health. Huxley, as a hands-on evolutionary biologist, understood well the instinctual striving in all living things toward survival and growth, and he never ceased to champion policies that supported the development of both the person and the species.

2. *A unique biological perspective*—In his earlier years, Huxley was a professor of zoology and physiology, and he later served as secretary of the Zoological Society of London. In addition, he was a founding member of the World Wildlife Fund. He had the biologist's keen, intuitive sense of the natural, organic evolution of the species that well paralleled humanistic psychology's foundational emphasis on the self-actualization of the person. To the psychological insights of Maslow, Rogers, Fromm, and May, he added the biological.
3. *An evolutionary perspective focusing on cultural rather than strictly biological factors*—In addition to Huxley's contributions to the "modern synthesis" of natural selection incorporating the new understanding of genetics noted earlier, he championed societal recognition and action to advance the next, post-biological stage of human evolution, the sociocultural. As other species continue to multiply through natural selection, forming new species just as they have through the ages, Homo sapiens, instead, is poised for continual growth and development—species enhancement rather than species multiplication; cultural rather than biological evolution.
4. *Religion as deserving a place at the table of societal improvement, even in a post-supernatural world*—Huxley's respect for religion, even as he denied the necessity of a theistic element, allowed him to walk with intellectuals from that world, most notably Pierre Teilhard de Chardin. In so doing, he aligned himself with humanistic psychology's emphasis on the distinction between authentic, person-centered religion, on the one hand, and that which projects an institutional and proscriptive presence, on the other, emphases advanced most notably by Erich Fromm, Rollo May, and Abraham Maslow, as well as Stephen Jay Gould, Barbara J. King, and Andy Norman. Huxley was, in John Morgan's words, "the quintessential proponent of religious humanism."[79]
5. *The focus on values as a legitimate area for scientific study*—As noted in the opening to this chapter, while Abraham Maslow was establishing the identification of universal values as his life task in America, Julian Huxley was gathering together like-minded thinkers toward that pursuit in London. The centrality of values in humanistic psychology

79. Morgan, *Beyond Divine Intervention*, 37.

cannot be overstated; Huxley demonstrated that they are likewise central to evolutionary biology.

6. *A broader vision of our responsibility to the world*—As we have seen, humanistic psychology did not limit itself to the study of the person. Its fundamental emphases on health, growth, self-actualization, and values inevitably led to its embrace of a larger perspective, one that addressed familial, societal, national, and global issues. Huxley engaged this broader humanist perspective—his UNESCO leadership providing an obvious example—adding his own passionate emphasis on the enhancement of the species.

Finally, in addition to the preceding, the friendship that Huxley maintained with Teilhard de Chardin serves as a living, working example of the intersection of humanism and spirituality. By offering a model of how persons with differing beliefs about God and religion can unite in common cause on behalf of humankind and the future of the planet, their friendship stands as a sharp counterpoint to a world fractured by religious strife. We need more examples of the mutual admiration and common scholarship represented by those two men.

In *Rocks of Ages*, Stephen J. Gould relates the story of Charles Darwin's burial in Westminster Abbey, in spite of the self-effacing Darwin's desire to be laid to rest in his own local churchyard. That effort was spearheaded by none other than Thomas Henry Huxley, foremost promoter of Darwin and Julian's grandfather, who argued that in spite of Darwin's nontheistic view of the world, and in addition to his unquestioned renown, he was a man of kindness and charity demonstrated both on the individual and societal levels throughout his life. Gould takes this a step further by suggesting that Huxley's initiative was "prompted by a spirit of reconciliation, and by the strong and positive symbol represented by a revolutionary man of science, and at least an agnostic in personal belief, lying in the holiest of Christian holies because he had not feared to seek knowledge and understood that whatever he found could not confute a genuine sense of religion."[80]

On June 15, 2018, 136 years after the death of Darwin, the *Dallas Morning News* published an Associated Press article about the burial of physicist Stephen Hawking's ashes at Westminster, appropriately between the graves of Charles Darwin and Isaac Newton. The burial was officiated by the Very Rev. John Hall, the dean of Westminster. How could Hawking, a self-proclaimed and highly public atheist, be interred at an Anglican cathedral? Said Rev. Hall, "My position is quite simply this: Whether a person

80. Gould, *Rocks of Ages*, 44.

believes in God or not, if someone is achieving extraordinary things, then I believe that God is in that process."[81] I suspect that the Catholic priest Pierre Teilhard de Chardin and the nontheistic evolutionary biologists Thomas Henry Huxley and Julian Huxley would smile at those words.

81. Associated Press, "Hawking Buried."

Chapter 8

The Spiritual Path

James Fowler's Stages of Faith Development

The Quakers call it the Light Within. I don't think it matters a bit what you call it. Whether you call it God or Jesus or Cosmic Flow or Reality or Love, it doesn't matter what you call it. It is there. And what you learn directly from that source will not tie you up in creeds that separate you from your fellow man.

—QUOTED BY JAMES FOWLER, *STAGES OF FAITH*

NO ONE COULD HAVE predicted that out of the humanistically oriented stirrings in the psychological world during the 1950s would emerge a new way of thinking about religion and spirituality. As we have seen, what motivated those who would come to represent the new direction in psychology and psychotherapy was the need to identify an alternative to the sterility of the behaviorists and the pessimism of the Freudians. They sought an alternative that moves attention away from the fixation on id, ego, and superego or measurement and control of behavior and toward "the farther reaches of human nature," the title of one of Maslow's books. That new approach would soon embrace the title *humanistic psychology*, signaling a connection to the larger philosophical movement of humanism and, consequently, bumping up against humanism's typically nontheistic view of life and occasional ant-religious proclivities. None of that was on Abraham Maslow's mind when he led the charge for a third force in the world of psychology. Nor was it on the minds of Rogers, May, or Fromm.

None of those studied in this book would have been called devout practitioners of their respective faith traditions. Their spiritual paths were marked by years of outright rejection of formal participation, with Rollo May alone appearing to have reconciled with his religious roots and returning to the practice of Christianity in his final years through the influence of his wife, Georgia, a Jungian therapist. There is no evidence that Maslow and Fromm, though born into and immersed within a Jewish worldview, ever saw the inside of a synagogue in their adult years, although both wrote stirring and timeless books on religion and spirituality, *Religions, Values, and Peak-Experiences* and *Psychoanalysis and Religion* respectively. Nonetheless, it would be difficult, if not impossible, to understand each without reference to the Judaism that, at least in part, fueled their spiritual activism. Rogers, in spite of the efforts of his friend and biographer Brian Thorne, never returned to the Christianity of his youth, although he did experience what we can only describe as a spiritual awakening late in life, albeit a spirituality devoid of religious content. As for Julian Huxley, he continued in the tradition of his family, remaining agnostic—a word coined by his grandfather, Thomas Henry Huxley—throughout his life.

Yet, as we have seen, these men spoke often of matters spiritual and religious. Although not traditional, their journeys were often transcendent, as Rogers's reference late in life to the possibility of an afterlife demonstrates. Transcendent also were Rogers's understanding that the person was "a continuing spiritual essence lasting over time, and occasionally incarnated in a human body," as noted previously, and Maslow's exploration through his own transpersonal psychology of the "farther reaches of human nature."[1] Whether they were aware of it or not, they were carving out a spiritual space within the larger world of psychology, one that proudly referred to itself as humanistic.

How can we best understand how the spiritual journeys of the five chosen representatives of humanistic psychology and the larger humanist world evolved? Did they follow pathways that are common and recognizable to us all? Can their spiritual journeys serve as models for others, particularly those whose life vocation involves the academic discipline of psychology or the practice of psychotherapy, wherein the spiritual dimension occasionally surfaces? Do the lessons derived from their faith experiences have anything to offer those in ministry, for whom counseling or spiritual direction might feature prominently in their work?

1. Thorne, *Carl Rogers*, 92; Maslow, *Farther Reaches*.

To address these questions, we could do no better than turn to *Stages of Faith: The Psychology of Human Development and the Quest for Meaning*, James Fowler's seminal work on the six stages of faith development published in 1981. Fowler (1940–2015) was a United Methodist minister, professor of theology, and director of the Center for Ethics at Emory University in Atlanta. His developmental approach to faith parallels in importance the work of Lawrence Kohlberg, Carol Gilligan, Erik Erikson, Jean Piaget, and other pioneers in developmental psychology, whom he references throughout *Stages of Faith*. Fowler was a researcher who approached his work through the classic inductive method: he and a team of assistants observed, asked questions, recorded interviews, transcribed what they learned, and developed the stages of faith out of their discoveries.

The core of Fowler's book is, as the title promises, an identification and explication of his six stages of faith. Before delving into them, however, he focuses first on how to understand the word *faith* itself, which he interprets as a way of providing meaning and purpose for our lives and not necessarily as religious in content—as a source of personal guidance and direction, not as a compilation of beliefs to which we profess assent. He understands faith as inherent to our humanity, an integral dimension of what it means to be a person. And he speaks of faith in relation to "ultimate concerns," Paul Tillich's term for values that center and motivate.

Fowler sees the development of faith as universal and antecedent to the embrace of a religious tradition, and he locates it within our earliest relationships with our caregivers: "We all begin the pilgrimage of faith as infants."[2] As Erik Erikson pointed out in his celebrated eight stages of psychosocial development, the infancy years are about trust and fidelity. To Fowler, they are about "trust in the caretakers and the environment they provide; trust in the self, its worthiness and its being at home; trust in the larger world of meaning inchoately surrounding the infant and caretakers."[3]

In defining faith in terms broader than the specifically religious, Fowler signals a clear distinction between the spiritual striving that faith entails and religiosity, an understanding with which we've become familiar through the journeys of the theorists studied. For Fowler, religion is defined in terms of a cumulative tradition and faith as "the person's or group's way of responding to transcendent value and power as perceived and grasped through the forms of the cumulative tradition."[4] Faith is about a relationship, "an

2. Fowler, *Stages of Faith*, 119.
3. Fowler, *Stages of Faith*, 121.
4. Fowler, *Stages of Faith*, 9.

alignment of the heart or will, a commitment of loyalty or trust."[5] Although distinct, faith and the specific religious tradition enjoy a reciprocal relationship: faith is nurtured by the religious tradition, and the tradition is enriched through the faith of its adherents. With that as background, we can now look at the six stages and discuss how the faith journeys of the five theorists studied can be better understood in the light of Fowler's schema.

Stage One—Intuitive-Projective Faith

After discussing an infancy pre-stage, a stage of undifferentiated faith characterized by the degree of development of trust and mutuality, Fowler introduces the first stage, that of intuitive-projective faith, during which the child uses speech and symbolic representation to organize and make meaning out of sensory experiences. At this stage, which corresponds to the preschool years, the child assumes that whatever is being experienced or perceived is universally experienced or perceived; there is as yet no imagining of different perspectives. Uninhibited by logical thought, the child's imagination develops freely. At the same time, the child's inability to differentiate between reality and fantasy carries the potential danger of "exploitation of her or his imagination in the reinforcement of taboo and moral or doctrinal expectations."[6] Stage 1 is characterized by perceptual openness—the child as sponge, absorbing everything indiscriminately—and the long-term result is a host of childhood images and feelings, both positive and negative, that have taken shape within the unconscious and remain well hidden from view.

Freud and others have highlighted the effect of our first two years (Fowler's pre-stage) and our early childhood years (stage 1) on personality development. Maslow's lifelong rift with his mother was due in large part to her harsh, superstitious approach to the religion of her ancestors, as well as to her apparent cruelty. Could Maslow have experienced and internalized during those early years images of God or God-substitutes that were so terrifying that they turned him away from all associations with organized religion for life? His lifelong antipathy toward his mother suggests such a possibility. Biographical indications about the earliest years of Rogers, Fromm, May, and Huxley, unlike those of Maslow, suggest minimal disruption to the trust and mutuality necessary for the formation of healthy faith responses in the pre-stage and the development of imagination in stage 1.

5. Fowler, *Stages of Faith*, 11.

6. Fowler, *Stages of Faith*, 134.

Stage Two—Mythic-Literal Faith

In the first stage, fantasy, facts, and feelings tend to run together in the child's mind. In the second stage, that of mythical-literal faith, corresponding to the middle childhood years around ages six to twelve, the sorting out of what is real from what is not begins. Fantasy is assigned to the world of play, while in the real world, the child seeks proof and life becomes more concrete and literal. The egocentric state of stage 1, characterized by an inability to understand differing perspectives, is replaced by the ability to contrast one's perspective with those of others and to create and share stories.

Fowler quotes a stage 1 child describing God with charmingly ethereal words—"God is like the air, he is everywhere"[7] or "[God] doesn't look like anything. He's all around you"[8]—expressions not too unlike those of the mystical theologian who might speak of God as "the circle whose center is everywhere and whose circumference is nowhere," a quote attributed to Augustine, among others. Might this mystical imagery, as occasionally presented through the innocence of a child's words, be what Jesus meant by his reference to becoming like little children in order to experience the kingdom of heaven?

In stage 2, children tend to see God in anthropomorphic terms. There is also a pronounced sense of fairness—reward for good behavior, punishment for bad—and reciprocity, often evidenced in prayer: I will pray for the door to open unto me, and you will make sure that it does. We can all appreciate the staying power of that need for reciprocity and have no doubt found ourselves, well into higher stages of faith development, mouthing reciprocity prayers (what the spiritual writer Anne Lamott purportedly calls "gimme, gimme, gimme" prayers) just in case—a Pascal's wager for the supplicant.

The stage 2 years must have been faith-formative ones for Rogers, who, as noted, was raised in a strict, moralistic family. We can imagine how the understanding of right and wrong took firm root in his moral consciousness and wonder how this affected his tenacious, almost obsessive research on what makes for effective counseling. His understanding of what falls under the category of right and what under that of wrong would change through the years, but the conviction of rightness remained strong. It was manifested, for example, by his never wavering from the three necessary and sufficient conditions for therapeutic change, which became for him the model for all interpersonal relationships. Further, a certain testiness and

7. Fowler, *Stages of Faith*, 139.

8. Fowler, *Stages of Faith*, 129.

impatience was noted in Rogers from time to time, perhaps related to his judgmental upbringing. When Rollo May confessed that although he loved Abe Maslow he never warmed to the aloof, and at times peevish, Rogers, as referenced earlier, he likely spoke for many.

Stage Three—Synthetic-Conventional Faith

Stage 3, or synthetic-conventional faith, beginning around age twelve, is characterized by a heightened interpersonal consciousness and the ability to introspect; it corresponds to Erikson's fifth stage, identity versus role confusion. God is seen in relational terms, as a friend, companion, helper, one through whom the self can be confirmed—*my friends may be mad at me, but I know God is there, and he always accepts and loves me.* Authority for stage 3 persons is about the expectations of others, and the values they choose tend to correspond to those that have been chosen for them by the significant people in their lives.

Many adults, perhaps most, could best be described in terms of stage 3 characteristics. Fowler refers to this stage as a tacit system, meaning unexamined, an approach to faith characterized by a deep emotional investment in the values and beliefs that surround us while lacking an appreciation that our set of values and beliefs is one of a potentially infinite number of faith systems. It is accepted as it is *because* it is; it is the stage of conventionality, of the prevailing view.

We can think of Carl Rogers at stage 3 before his China trip, which catapulted him into stage 4, the individuative-reflective stage, and Erich Fromm before his introduction to psychoanalysis. Fromm's partaking of leavened bread with Frieda Reichmann on Passover in his early twenties served as an intentional break from stage 3. Maslow, who fled his own bar mitzvah at age thirteen, might have been rebelling more against his mother's controlling and superstitious ways than signaling a shift to stage 4, but he too rejected conventional faith at a relatively early age. As for May, his movement through stage 3 and beyond was energized by his sojourn in Greece and eastern Europe after graduation from Oberlin. But unlike Rogers, May had the immense good fortune of encountering a spiritual guide and mentor in the person of Paul Tillich, who led the very willing May through a "spiritual odyssey," as Robert Abzug proclaims in the subtitle to his biography.

The stage 3 person is conventional, readily accepting of external authority, reluctant to question the teaching of his or her tradition, and comfortable with the values of the larger community, whatever that community might be. Faith for them is about identity and outlook: *I am Lutheran, so*

I believe such and such. (For a secular version of this, insert your favored political affiliation.) Stage 3 people serve as the cornerstone of their faith tradition; as Fowler observes, "[in] many ways religious institutions 'work best' if they are peopled with a majority of committed folk best described by Stage 3."[9] This stage becomes permanent for many; they are the majority of churchgoers everywhere and typically serve as the most active and involved members of their communities.

Each stage has its strengths and weaknesses, as well as its positive and negative stereotypes, and many critics of organized religion are thinking of the negative stereotype of the stage 3 person when they express their antagonism to all things religious. We can readily find this criticism in the writers studied, each of whom would be quick to point out, however, that he is not critiquing faith or religion itself, as did Freud, but authoritarian, psychologically unhealthy religion (Fromm); dogmatic, inauthentic religion (Maslow); religion that distracts from the challenge of facing freedom and responsibility (May); religion that places itself in opposition to science (Huxley); or any religion that mandates what one must believe (Rogers). "The enemy is not religion," observes Stephen Jay Gould in *Rocks of Ages*, "but dogmatism and intolerance, a tradition as old as humankind, and impossible to extinguish without eternal vigilance, which is, as a famous epigram proclaims, the price of liberty."[10] It is safe to say that although those studied passed through stage 3, they didn't stop off and spend much time there. They certainly didn't develop roots in stage 3.

Stage Four—Individuative-Reflective Faith

The shift from stage 3 to stage 4 is sometimes occasioned by an unsettling or traumatic event. To pick a contemporary example, news reports in recent years of Catholic priests who have sexually abused children have forced many throughout the Catholic world to question previously held assumptions about the holiness of the priesthood and the sanctity of the Church itself. In 2015, in the throes of ongoing reports of multiple cases of abuse in Ireland, the populace voted to legalize marriage for persons of the same sex, making Ireland the first nation to approve same-sex marriage by democratic vote—this in a country long perceived as firmly positioned on the conservative end of the religious spectrum and, of course, most decidedly Catholic. Then, three years later, the citizens of Ireland voted to liberalize their nation's strict anti-abortion law. Much of that dramatic shift on two core moral

9. Fowler, *Stages of Faith*, 164.

10. Gould, *Rocks of Ages*, 149.

stances of the Catholic Church can be attributed to anger and protest at what was perceived as the Church's betrayal of the people's centuries-long trust. But whatever one's opinion might be of the merits of those two votes, a case could also be made that it suggests, at least in part, a national shift in faith development from one described as accepting and conventional to one characterized by reflection and individuation.

Not all who are scandalized by their religious community move to stage 4. Some might join an alternative stage 3 level faith community; others might simply suppress the negative information and retreat into denial.Further, not all movements into stage 4 are occasioned by traumatic events. Chance encounters with persons holding distinctly different perspectives on matters of importance might open the door for a shift to stage 4. Falling in love with someone from a different faith tradition, culture, or political allegiance might also elicit a change. Experiences such as going away to college, joining the Peace Corps or the military, immersing oneself within a different culture—indeed, any experience that allows one to come face-to-face with an alternative worldview and begin to question one's received tradition—may occasion a shift to stage 4.

Stage 3 persons tend to see symbols and their meanings, as well as the rituals that express them, as inseparable. Communion, to pick an example familiar to the Christian world, might be narrowly and precisely defined by people in stage 3, with proscriptions concerning who may partake and who may not. In a recent conversation with a Methodist minister, someone whose ministry and life experiences have led him to appreciate the world through stage 4 or 5 thinking, feeling, and responding, I inquired about how his understanding of communion differs from the Catholic understanding, the one in which I was raised. He hesitated for what seemed like a full minute, his eyes half closed and his head gently nodding in my direction, then said, "Something happens. Something happens." For that minister, communion is about the awe, wonder, mystery, and reverence that is experienced in the moment; it is not up to him, or anyone else, to define its meaning for others.

In stage 4, symbols like the bread and wine of communion are set free from the tightly defined meaning found in stage 3, a process of demythologizing that is typically experienced as a threat to stage 3 persons. At the stage 4 level, different meanings may attend to the same symbol. Intercommunion—an agreement among the Christian churches to open reception of communion to all Christians regardless of the interpretation they might place on the meaning of the bread and wine—might serve as a practical example of the separation of meaning and symbol found in stage 4.

In *On the Brink of Everything: Grace, Gravity, and Getting Old*, the spiritual writer Parker Palmer discusses this distinction between symbols and meanings in reference to a quote from St. Paul: "We have this treasure in earthen vessels to show that the transcendent power belongs to God and not to us" (2 Cor 4:7). Understanding the earthen vessels as the means through which the treasure (the word of God to the religious person; the truth of a philosophical or scientific proposition to the secular one) is communicated, Palmer concludes that "every vessel we create to hold the treasure is earthen, finite, and flawed, and is never, ever to be confused with the treasure itself," adding that "when people of any tradition insist that the treasure cannot be carried except in *their* earthen vessels, they commit idolatry."[11]

As suggested by Palmer's commentary, which Fowler would certainly appreciate, the belief that one's religion is the "one true faith," that it has a lock on the rituals and their meanings, perhaps even sole possession of the "keys of the kingdom of heaven," represents a stage 3 approach to faith that falls by the wayside in stage 4. In the individuative-reflective stage of faith development, we notice the formation of something akin to an anthropological/sociological perspective, the idea that "ideologies have particular histories and that persons and groups have world views that grow out of their particular experiences and the conditions with which they have had to deal."[12] One's faith tradition begins to be understood less as the one true faith and more as the faith tradition that one belongs to because he or she was born and raised within it or, perhaps, has chosen it out of a sense of comfort and compatibility with what it has to offer. The stage 4 person begins to understand that one's faith tradition may have much less to do with possession of the truth than it does with the accident of birth and culture.

What matters for transformation to stage 4 is not so much the experience itself but the processing of that experience, the drawing out of the specific meaning it has for the individual. Discarding one exclusivist religious tradition and readily embracing another equally exclusivist one will not result in transformation; it signifies no more than a lateral movement from one faith tradition to another. But to reject reliance on an external source of authority and, in its place, embrace a personal, internal source would be transformational. As Fowler observes, "The tyranny of the 'they' . . . must be undermined [in the place of] an internal panel of experts who reserve the right to choose and who are prepared to take responsibility for their choices."[13] A stronger ego must emerge for stage 4 to take root, what Fowler refers to as an executive ego, an enhanced sense of internal motivation and locus of control.

11. Palmer, *On Brink of Everything*, 103–4.

12. Fowler, *Stages of Faith*, 177.

13. Fowler, *Stages of Faith*, 179.

Having embraced an inner-authority approach to faith, the stage 4 person focuses less on *What do I believe?* and more on *What does it mean to me?* Further, stage 4 opens the door to a metaphorical interpretation of matters of faith, one popularized in recent times by the late Marcus Borg, a prominent theologian and participant in the Jesus Seminar, a group of New Testament scholars who, beginning in 1985, have focused on the study of Jesus in his historical setting. Borg famously responded to questions of belief by shifting the emphasis to meaning: Believe what you wish about, say, biblical inerrancy or the divinity of Jesus, but what does that *mean* to you? This is a stage 4 response. The stage 4 faith approach typically arrives, if it does at all, in one's thirties or forties, a time when the importance of taking responsibility for one's own lifestyle, beliefs, and values emerges.

Stage Five—Conjunctive Faith

Although all of our faith travelers readily left stage 3 behind, none spent much time in stage 4 either, at least to the degree to which that stage typically suggests an identified religious tradition. It could be said that Maslow, Rogers, and Fromm took the exit ramp off the faith highway at stage 4 and settled comfortably into a nonreligious approach to life, one that would necessitate the gifts of old age to invite a shift to stage 5, conjunctive faith, wherein a new approach to the spiritual is often discovered.

After Rogers's break from his inherited religion during his later college years, he wanted nothing to do with things religious or spiritual, taking a fifty-year sabbatical before rediscovering spirituality in the final years of his life. Maslow found himself confronting spiritual questions as a result of his work with peak-experiences and Being-values, the values expressed at the level of self-actualization. As referenced earlier, he was on the brink of new spiritual discoveries that led to his movement beyond humanistic psychology to what he labeled transpersonal psychology when he died.

Fromm was the most articulate in his defining of authentic religion, and he may have been the most open to the mystical dimension, a stage 5 encounter, as well. May, with the tutelage and friendship of Tillich ever present to him, moved handily into stage 5; his spiritual journey appeared to be steady and intentional throughout, certainly in comparison to those of Maslow, Rogers, and Fromm. And Huxley, with his enticing insights about the evolution of Homo sapiens to a level beyond our current consciousness, found a welcome companion and guide in the person of Teilhard de Chardin, whose spiritual perspectives almost exhaust the profundity of stage 5 thinking.

Fowler begins his description of stage 5, conjunctive faith, by acknowledging his difficulty in describing it. One gets the sense in reading Fowler that he agonized over every word; he was both meticulous in his terminology and eloquent in his prose. His struggle to define stage 5 is a testimony to the seriousness with which he approached his work, both in understanding faith development and in articulating it in writing.

In stage 4, critical reflection takes precedence over loyalty to one's inherited faith tradition. Other ways of seeing the world, including alternative faith traditions, are made manifest, and the sense that one might actively choose a faith tradition becomes an inviting reality. However, in focusing on the rational *meaning* of a religious belief or liturgical event, rather than on its power to touch the heart and soul, symbolic power is threatened, potentially leaving the spiritual traveler with a faith drained of its soulfulness. The question *What does it mean?* focuses on the rational dimension of faith and, potentially, leaves the mythological and its power to speak to the believer's heart behind. In stage 4, there is the temptation to force symbolic representations and their enactments "to yield their meanings for translation into conceptual or propositional statements."[14]

Stage 5 persons, in contrast, know that the mythological cannot be separated indefinitely from the conceptual meaning; the symbol and the symbolized must be reunited, or the power of the symbol and the myth to transform will be lost. Where does this power of the myth come from? It derives from the unconscious, the archetypal world, the universal heritage of all humans out of which are born the great stories—about God, creation, peoplehood, identity—that better serve to communicate deeper, universal truths than the propositions they are often forced into. Consider, for example, the Christmas story. Through a wondrously enchanting mythology, including angels, shepherds, a child born of a virgin, and traveling wise men from the East, with a star fortuitously pointing the way, a deeper truth is revealed: God is present in the world, offering a vision radically distinct from that of power and wealth, strife and division—a promise of peace and goodwill for all.

In stage 5 faith, we observe a transcendence of the dialectic between the article of faith or liturgical experience and the myth or metaphor that encompasses it. Myth is reunited with belief; it is now understood as the great story that gives life to one's theology. The stage 5 person can now go home to his or her religious heritage, if desired, and enjoy its myths and traditions, experiencing no need to choose between an archetypal/mythical spirituality or a more meaning-based religiosity; the spiritualities can be

14. Fowler, *Stages of Faith*, 187.

appreciated together. The person of faith can accept both, understanding that the liturgies, ceremonies, creeds, myths, and metaphors of all religions provide pathways to truth and ethical responses to the world.

Still appreciative of the question *What does it mean?*, stage 5 persons are more interested in *How do these words speak to me, personally?* As an example of stage 5 spirituality, Fowler references the Ignatian exercises and the emphasis placed by that centuries-old spiritual practice on listening to the words of Scripture and discerning the Spirit's movements within the self: *What truth am I discerning within these words?*

Further, stage 5 people know that the doctrines and symbols of each group are "partial, limited to particular people's experience of God and incomplete."[15] They know that dipping into another's tradition can serve to complement and enliven one's own. A typical stage 5 response offered by an interviewee in Fowler's research sums this up well:

> The Quakers call it the Light Within. I don't think it matters a bit what you call it. Whether you call it God or Jesus or Cosmic Flow or Reality or Love, it doesn't matter what you call it. It is there. And what you learn directly from that source will not tie you up in creeds that separate you from your fellow man.[16]

The strength of stage 5 faith development, then, is to be at peace with one's faith tradition while recognizing that all faith traditions are "relative, partial and inevitably distorting apprehensions of transcendent reality."[17] Thomas Merton comes readily to mind, fully at home within his Christianity while at the same time having no difficulty engaging the truths of Buddhism. In our own day, Franciscan priest Richard Rohr, who offers an integral, universal, and often mystical message of spiritual healing through his New Mexico-based Center for Action and Contemplation, and Episcopal priest Cynthia Bourgeault, who places Jesus within the centuries-old wisdom tradition, might be fitting examples of stage 5 faith development.

By the end of their lives, all five thinkers had found a home in stage 5—Maslow through his foray into the mystical realm of transpersonal psychology, Rogers through his quite out-of-character musings about the spiritual and mystical during his final years, and May through the enduring influence and friendship of Paul Tillich. May's attainment of stage 5 faith development is particularly evident when he references the many lessons he learned from Tillich, which included: the focus on ultimate concerns; the

15. Fowler, *Stages of Faith*, 186.
16. Fowler, *Stages of Faith*, 192.
17. Fowler, *Stages of Faith*, 198.

existential significance of asking, *Why is there something rather than nothing?*; the formulation that "God does not exist. He is being itself, beyond essence and existence";[18] the readiness to find revelation in places other than Jesus (such as art, nature, social justice, and love); and the "steadfast refusal to accept any beliefs that produce a theology of exclusion."[19]

Fromm likewise had advanced to stage 5, but his often highly charged political orientation and socialistic inclinations added a unique seasoning to his faith development. His approach to life was more activist than the others, and his stage 5 at times bore much in common with the tendency to embrace a messianic posture occasionally observed in stage 6, universalizing faith, a characteristic likewise noted in Maslow. Huxley, too, exuded stage 5 sentiments, particularly when referencing his friend Teilhard de Chardin, whom he praised for his promotion of a convergent, evolutionary worldview.

Stage Six—Universalizing Faith

If the stage 5 person can be said to have grasped the central truth that all is one and that one can reach the ultimate through a multiplicity of spiritual traditions, stage 6 is where all that is put into authentic, existential, living practice—"a disciplined activist *incarnation*."[20] It is tempting here to provide examples of persons who might be representative of stage 6 faith development, people whose lives are characterized by the "inclusiveness of community, radical commitment to justice and love and of selfless passion for a transforming world."[21] But to identify a few would be a disservice to the many who live stage 6 lives in obscurity.

Think of those who "hunger and thirst for righteousness"; those who put their lives on the line for justice's sake; those who provide food to the hungry, drink to the thirsty, and clothes for the naked; those who welcome the stranger and visit the sick and imprisoned. We all know persons who live their lives through a stage 6 perspective of the world. They represent all faith traditions and no faith traditions at all, and their actions are daily reminders of our responsibility as humans to respond to each other's needs and to address the world's ills. Theologically, this stage is characterized by the belief that all forms of religious life are relative representations or responses to the ultimate, similar to stage 5.

18. May, *Paulus*, 86.

19. May, *Paulus*, 99.

20. Fowler, *Stages of Faith*, 200 (emphasis in original).

21. Fowler, *Stages of Faith*, 203.

In discussing this final stage, Fowler addresses the "absoluteness of the particular,"[22] which he posits as a third way, a transcendence, of those who would deny the existence of truth and absolutes and those who directly or indirectly make the claim that their faith community enjoys exclusive possession of the truth and that any who would contest that assertion are descending into relativism . . . or worse. This third way is the recognition that within the particular of each religion absolutes reveal themselves, but no religion can be identified as the sole possessor of those absolutes. The absoluteness he is referencing is that quality of the transcendent "that comes together in revelation, but not necessarily of the symbols, myths, propositions, or doctrines formulated to represent it or communicate it."[23] It is an inclusive absoluteness that can manifest through the many diverse forms and contexts of the world's religious communities. Fowler notes that this is most evident in interfaith encounters, "in our honest, unexaggerated and nonpossessive sharing of what we take to be the moments of absoluteness"[24] in our particular faith tradition. He closes with reference to the eschatological character of the reign of God—the redeeming, restoring, and fulfilling of all being in God—and enjoins us to "live as pioneers of the coming Kingdom,"[25] while giving a nod to stage 6 people as those who offer the most promise for the future. All five of the men reviewed in this work recognized and honored men and women at stage 6, which is about the closest the vast majority of us ever get to universalizing faith.[26]

22. Fowler, *Stages of Faith*, 208.

23. Fowler, *Stages of Faith*, 209.

24. Fowler, *Stages of Faith*, 209.

25. Fowler, *Stages of Faith*, 210.

26. For an alternative and complementary study of the stages of faith, see *Faith after Doubt: Why Your Beliefs Stopped Working and What to Do about It*, by spiritual writer Brian McLaren, published in 2021—thirty years after Fowler's book. McLaren proposes four stages: Simplicity (dualistic, "black and white," "us versus them," characterized by certainty and absolutism), Complexity (pragmatic, independent, success-oriented, characterized by a striving for effectiveness through mentors and coaches rather than authority figures), Perplexity (honest, authentic, curious, uncertain, characterized by critical thinking), and Harmony (unitive, harmonious, non-dual thinking, characterized by the search for meaning and purpose, Maslow-like experiences of awe and wonder, and revolutionary love). McLaren insists that it is doubt that fuels our progress through the stages—doubt that there is more to our faith journey than blindly following authorities, searching for the next best self-help book, or living in a perpetual state of questioning and uncertainty—and that our ultimate goal is to replace doubt with revolutionary love. *Faith after Doubt* is an encouraging, heart-warming, hope-filled, and beautifully written book destined to become a spiritual classic.

Can a Humanist Believe in God?

Missing so far in our exploration of the spiritual development of the theorists studied is discussion related to what, for many, is the central spiritual—and certainly religious—question: *Does God exist?* The words *atheist*, *agnostic*, and *nontheistic* have been used by multiple commentators to describe the worldviews of Maslow, Rogers, Fromm, May, and Huxley. Each of those theorists was proudly humanistic, a term often identified with atheism, particularly when preceded by the word *secular*. But are those descriptors accurate? Do they do those theorists justice?

Do you believe in God? The question is posed occasionally as an honest inquiry into another's understanding of the world beyond the physical, other times as a challenge to another's religion or spiritual path. For many, it's an easy question to address: Of course I believe in God. Or: No, I'm an atheist. Or: Not sure; I'm an agnostic.

But, argues Serene Jones, president of Union Theological Seminary, it's not so simple. "Do you believe in God?" might best be answered with "It depends." As she explains in *Call It Grace: Finding Meaning in a Fractured World*,

> If by God you mean an entity that hovers somewhere above us, watching all we do and constantly judging if we are doing right or wrong, then no. If you mean God as a being, like we are beings, or as any kind of an object, or even an essence, as we understand those terms, then also no. But if you believe that the universe is ultimately loved by a divine reality that is greater and more wonderful than we can begin to imagine, and that in this reality we find our ultimate destiny, the purpose of our existence, then yes.[27]

There are, to be sure, an infinite number of ways to respond to questions related to the infinite, including that of existence itself. It all depends upon what you mean by *God*. Like most of us, the five humanistic thinkers studied herein held ideas about God that changed throughout their lives. Did they believe in God? The short answer would be no. But as Jones's response indicates, to stop there would be to shortchange them.

Humanists in general appear to be largely, if not overwhelmingly, nontheistic. Google the American Humanist Association and you will find the following descriptors of humanism: "a progressive philosophy of life . . . without theism or other supernatural beliefs," "free of supernaturalism . . . from theological or ideological arbitration," "not theistic, and does not

27. Jones, *Call It Grace*, xvi.

accept supernatural views of reality," "a joyous alternative to religions . . . without belief in deities, transcendent entities, miracles, life after death, and the supernatural."[28] On the contrary, however, on the same American Humanist Association website, Joseph C. Sommer, a volunteer attorney and longtime member, offers that "because science cannot now and probably never will be able to explain the ultimate origin or destiny of the universe . . . reasonable people [can] hypothesize about the origin of the natural universe and life beyond this one"—a "life beyond this one" that would, presumably, entail the existence of God.

As we recall, Abraham Maslow's biographer described him as a "lifelong atheist who had always associated religion with dogma and superstition." Yet during the final year of his life, Maslow formulated, together with Stanislav Grof and Anthony Sutich, a response to life's questions that he called transpersonal psychology, which emphasized the conscious engagement of spiritual practices such as meditation. Maslow died at age sixty-two, just as he was formulating these new thoughts. Where would he have gone with them had he lived another ten or twenty years? Would God have been in that picture?

Carl Rogers turned his back on all things spiritual and religious in his early twenties. Yet, in his later years, he found himself engaging the spiritual world, even opening himself to the possibility of an afterlife, observing, as noted previously, that "I now consider it possible that each of us is a continuing spiritual essence lasting over time, and occasionally incarnated in a human body."[29] Was Rogers on the brink of accepting the existence of a transcendent God? As we have learned, Brian Thorne, friend and biographer, saw deep religious strivings in Rogers throughout his life and wondered what course his life would have taken had his family atmosphere been characterized by a more embracing theology and less separatist religious experience. If he had lived a few years longer, would he have experienced that "embracing theology" and found God?

Erich Fromm—whose writings occasionally exuded such a depth of spirituality that they merited the admiration of religious figures across the spectrum, including Pope John Paul II—was enamored of the mystical tradition from Isaiah to Jesus to Meister Eckhart. And none of those studied in these pages was more viscerally connected to his religious roots than Fromm—roots that were profoundly and intimately deistic.

Rollo May likewise could not fully shed his religious inheritance. An on-again, off-again minister, he became a regular churchgoer late in life

28. https://americanhumanist.org.

29. Thorne, *Carl Rogers*, 92.

through the influence of his wife, Georgia. The God he would come to believe in was the God that Paul Tillich believed in: the God who is Being itself, not a being among others.

From all indications, Julian Huxley was agnostic, if not atheistic, to the end. As noted earlier, his celebrated grandfather, Thomas Henry Huxley, coined that word *agnostic*, so it was in the family blood, and Julian was a scientist with little apparent interest in religion. However, as we have seen, that did not prevent him from befriending one of the most profound theologians of modern times, Teilhard de Chardin. Was God within Huxley's reach through Teilhard's musings on the transcendent? No doubt Teilhard's continuing reference to the Omega point—"a confluence of thought, the convergence of people at a higher collective level, the growth of superconsciousness, and ultimately the appearance of some 'ultra-human'"[30]—warmed Huxley's heart as much as it did Teilhard's. There is little doubt also that that formulation is as close as Huxley would ever be to the acceptance of a transcendent God.

So, can a humanist believe in God? I suggest that we can safely answer yes—but certainly not the god that Serene Jones rejects, which is also the god that Maslow, Rogers, Fromm, May, and Huxley would reject. The God that could be accepted by those with a humanistic orientation toward the ultimate questions is a larger God—larger perhaps than can be assumed by our current world religions. This is not a god that responds to prayers requesting random favors, that spares us from the destruction of floods and tornados, that blesses our arms in war, or that helps our favorite football team win the big game. Those gods are false gods, distractions to our spiritual lives. They do not exist.

But the God that James Fowler's higher levels of faith development point to, that transcends the limitations of every religious tradition, that millions of thoughtful believers honor as a source of love, that merits definition as "a divine reality that is greater and more wonderful than we can begin to imagine, and that in this reality we find our ultimate destiny, the purpose of our existence," in the words of Serene Jones,[31] and, of course, the God that the "believing humanist" Martin Buber acknowledges, does exist. That is the God that many who claim the descriptor *humanistic* could accept. And many do.

30. U. King, *Spirit of Fire*, 176.

31. Jones, *Call It Grace*, xvi.

Chapter 9

Still in the Air

The Resurgence of Humanistic Psychology

If we measure the extent to which the leading concepts of humanistic psychology have pervaded our culture, in fact, we might deem the movement a whopping success. The language of humanistic psychology is everywhere: Humanistic ideas of self, growth, individual potential, and relation are now woven into the very fabric of our thoughts and perceptions.

—Jessica Grogan, *Encountering America*

A fitting close to this study of the humanistic psychology movement is a discussion of its legacy: *What gifts did it leave us? Where do we find it today? Who are today's humanistic psychologists and psychotherapists, and what is the place of spirituality, however defined, in their worldview?*

In *A Way of Being*, published in 1980 with the golden age of humanistic psychology behind him, Carl Rogers wrote, "I am no longer talking simply about psychotherapy but about a point of view, a philosophy, an approach to life, a way of being, which fits any situation in which *growth*—of a person, a group, or a community—is part of the goal."[1] A finer statement of the legacy of humanistic psychology could hardly be made—it had become a way of life, so much permeating the culture, so much one with the spirit of the times, that it had become nearly invisible. As Jessica Grogan observes

1. Rogers, *Way of Being*, xvii.

in *Encountering America*, "If anything, it's the utter pervasiveness that has made evidence of its influence so elusive."[2] Carl Rogers's "way of being" had spread throughout American culture—not achieving the global transformation he and other humanistic psychologists might have envisioned but permanently affecting that culture nonetheless.

But not without challenge. In the early 1980s, the new managed care approach to providing mental health services posed a serious threat to the legacy of person-centered psychotherapy. Managed care demanded restrictions on the number of therapy sessions allowed for compensation, promoted cognitive behavioral approaches based on discrete presenting concerns (an affront to the integral approach of humanistically oriented therapists), and emphasized diagnoses based on the *Diagnostic and Statistical Manual of Mental Disorders* (*DSM*). The *DSM* follows a medical, pathology-based model rather than one that is holistic and health- and growth-oriented—fundamentally inconsistent with the approach begun by Maslow that emphasizes "the range of exalted emotions like awe, bliss, ecstasy, euphoria, reverie, and wonder," as quoted earlier.[3]

The managed care approach to therapy struck at the heart and soul of humanistic psychology. Gone, or so it appeared, was any reference to seeing the client as an integrated person—body, mind, heart, spirit—whose concerns could best be addressed through the personal identification of meaning and values, the embrace of one's personal freedom and consequent responsibilities, a healthy self-image, and engagement of the spiritual.

Today, humanistic psychology is more often than not ignored in textbooks or thrown together with a plethora of other approaches under the heading of "Other" or "Eclectic." Prominence is given to "data-driven" approaches, like cognitive behavioral and solution-focused therapies, which appease the minimalist allowances of the insurance industry. Nonetheless, humanistic approaches in counseling remain, for they have so permeated the cultural consciousness that not even managed care can completely overcome them. A personal story will illustrate.

In 2008, shortly after becoming a therapist following thirty-four years as an educator, I was invited into a study group of licensed clinical social workers, all deeply engaged in the diagnostic approach to therapy. Most worked within the managed care system, and all were well-versed in both cognitive-behavioral and psychoanalytic approaches. After a prolonged discussion of a particular case, during which focus was placed on identifying the correct diagnosis from the *DSM*, I ventured to ask (thereby revealing

2. Grogan, *Encountering America*, 310.
3. Hoffman, *Right to Be Human*, 289.

my rookie status), "Yes, but what do you *do*? What do you *say*? How do you specifically address the client's *concerns*? What words do you use to help the client *progress*?" One of the seasoned therapists in the group looked at me with a kindness that revealed a hint of exasperation, as if the answer were obvious, and said, "Oh, you know—you *listen*, you offer your full *presence*, you *empathize*, you *encourage*, you *value* the client . . ."

I didn't realize it then, but I do now: call it what you like and use whatever verbiage the managed care system demands, what most therapists offer today is some form of humanistically oriented, person-centered therapy that takes for granted the centrality of Rogers's triad of congruence, positive regard, and empathy. As Grogan observes, American therapists "tend to be nondirective, privileging meaningful subjective input from patients and relying on their active involvement in the counseling process."[4] Largely gone, too, are hierarchical distinctions, with most therapists today working on a first-name basis.

We can observe the presence of humanistic approaches—or at least signs of appreciation for the gifts of humanistic psychology—in academic and research circles as well. In his foreword to the 2001 edition of the *Handbook of Humanistic Psychology*, Mihaly Csikszentmihalyi, a leader in the positive psychology movement who passed away in 2021, notes that "the perspective on the human condition that humanistic psychology represents is too important to be ignored . . . now more than ever we need insights into psychology that the humanistic perspective can provide."[5] For years, leaders in the positive psychology movement denied all connection to humanistic psychology in spite of their own emphasis on the identification and promotion of human strengths—strengths that bear a remarkable resemblance to Maslow's B-values. The perennial disconnect between academic and research psychology, on the one hand, and the actual practice of psychotherapy in the counseling office, on the other, will likely remain, but Csikszentmihalyi's testament to humanistic psychology is a positive sign—and much appreciated.

Further, humanistic psychology continues to be referenced favorably in academic journals. In a 2018 edition of *The Behavioral Mind: A Journal of Personality Disorders*, Eric Shyman, associate professor of education at St. Joseph's College in New York, reviewed behavioral analytic interventions in the treatment of children with autistic spectrum disorder (ASD) from the perspective of Rogers's three conditions for change. He found them wanting and concluded that by "grounding its approach in the positivistic

4. Grogan, *Encountering America*, 310.

5. Csikszentmihalyi, "Preface," xvi.

medical model and addressing individuals with ASD as 'sick' and in need of 'treatment,' the behavior analytic approach appears to fall quite short of employing Rogers's Core Conditions."[6] Of particular interest for our study is that Shyman holds up humanistic psychology, particularly of the Rogerian flavor, as the standard by which to measure other psychotherapeutic interventions.

Shyman is an academic who is advancing humanistic psychology through his chosen field of education. He is not alone; today, numerous other professionals in various fields are promoting the vision of positivity; encouragement; self-actualization; innate potential; forward movement of the species; the interconnectedness of all humanity; the advancement of the greater good; spirituality; and the experiences of awe, wonder, and reverence that we have witnessed in our pioneering humanistic psychologists and the larger humanist movement. Three noteworthy professionals—Scott Barry Kaufman, Andy Norman, and Daniel Siegel—are promoting humanistic principles through the fields of psychology, philosophy, and psychiatry, respectively, through their writings, podcasts, workshops, and other activities, keeping the vision of Maslow, Rogers, Fromm, and May alive for contemporary audiences. A look at each of these contemporary humanists will further demonstrate the enduring presence of humanistic psychology today.

Humanistic Psychology for the Twenty-First Century: Scott Barry Kaufman and the New Science of Self-Actualization

In the chapter on Abraham Maslow, I asked what he might have accomplished had he lived beyond the paltry sixty-two years he was allotted. As we have seen, in the last year of his life he founded a new psychological approach, transpersonal psychology, that focused on "unitive consciousness, mystical experience, and cognitive blissfulness" and emphasized the conscious engagement of spiritual practices such as meditation.[7] Maslow was seeking higher levels of personal growth, beyond that of self-actualization itself—a state of being that transcended the ubiquitous pyramid of needs through which beginning psychology students are first introduced to Maslow.

Always thinking, always wondering, Maslow was striving to flesh out his thoughts related to the transcendent, and his last year of life was marked by "a continuing striving for transcendent experiences and transcendent

6. Shyman, "Normality, Pathological Orientation," 118.

7. Grogan, *Encountering America*, 250.

values."[8] Indeed, as psychologist Scott Barry Kaufman observes in his timely reintroduction of Maslow to contemporary psychologists and psychotherapists, *Transcend: The New Science of Self-Actualization*, during his final days "Maslow was working on a set of axioms and propositions that would lay the foundation for a humanistic revolution . . . [even] proposing the need for a fifth force in psychology—transhumanism—that would transcend human interests and focus on species-transcendent values."[9]

As a humanistic psychologist, Kaufman is a welcome presence in a world still largely characterized by behavioral approaches to studying and understanding the person. That in the year 2020, exactly fifty years after Maslow's death, he chose to publish a book centered on the life and teachings of the very embodiment of humanistic psychology—well, it warms the heart of many a lonely, diehard humanistic psychology practitioner today!

What might Maslow have accomplished had he lived beyond age sixty-two? Kaufman, too, has entertained that question, and the research he engaged in reveals Maslow as few have known him: a man whose ever-restless spirit imagined a realm of study pointing "beyond individual growth (and even health and happiness) and [that] allows for the highest levels of unity and harmony within oneself and with the world . . . [from] which we can view our whole being from a higher vantage point with acceptance, wisdom, and a sense of connectedness with the rest of humanity."[10]

Kaufman's book well merits the descriptor *comprehensive*. He confronts the full range of issues addressed in contemporary psychology—from attachment theory and the need for connection to self-esteem and personal growth—all from the perspective of a committed humanist and a practicing psychologist. On one level, it serves commendably well as an enlightened, "all you need to know about self-help" book. But it is so much more: it is a reimagining of what psychology could be within a humanistic frame. Like Maslow (and Fromm, who is liberally referenced), Kaufman unapologetically envisions a better world, one inspired by, enthused about, and imbued with humanitarian values. He is motivated by the question of "what makes human life valuable and significant to the individuals *who are actually living it* . . . how each and every one of us can *transcend* our parts—becoming something greater than the sum of our parts as we each deal with the givens of existence in our own style."[11] And he continually emphasizes

8. Kaufman, *Transcend*, 219.
9. Kaufman, *Transcend*, 251.
10. Kaufman, *Transcend*, xxxiv.
11. Kaufman, *Transcend*, xxxvii–xxxviii.

that "[personal] growth and humanitarian concerns tend to go together naturally"[12] within the humanistic psychology worldview.

Like many whom we've studied in these pages, Kaufman highlights the social justice perspective that is foundational to humanistic psychology. On the first page of his first chapter he references the "ten million Americans working full time . . . living below the official poverty line . . . despite the striking growth in incomes of the top 1 percent."[13] Further on in the book, he addresses this from a larger philosophical perspective, referencing "The Light Triad" of humanism, Kantianism, and faith in humanity, thereby defining and celebrating the commitment of humanists from both the psychological and philosophical perspectives to boots-on-the-ground responses to humanity's struggles. These three intersecting, interlocking, and enlightened worldviews promote innate potential, the development of self and others, the categorical imperative to live one's life in such a manner that could be expected of all, and to approach our fellow humans with a faith that assumes goodness and good intent.

As the book's title suggests, Kaufman understands Abraham Maslow's quest as pointing beyond self-actualization toward personal transcendence, represented by "higher ideals and values that go beyond the satisfaction of basic need and the fulfilling of one's unique self,"[14] the domain of self-actualization. During the last years of Maslow's life, transcendence displaces self-actualization in the hierarchy of values; indeed, it transcends the hierarchy itself.

What characterizes this new human striving? Central to Maslow's understanding of transcendence is the presence of plateau-experiences, which are characterized by enhanced encounters with the sacred in everyday life; more attentiveness to humanity's needs, both present and future; increased self-knowledge; the identification of and attention to species-transcendent values related to the health of the planet itself; greater attention to the ultimate values of truth, beauty, and goodness; and more. The words *more* and *greater*—change that is both quantitative and qualitative—are increasingly used by Kaufman to denote the difference between self-actualization and transcendence.

Like Rogers, Maslow saw it as his lifelong mission to extend the core principles of humanistic psychology into all dimensions of life, toward all human experiences. After his final chapter in *Transcend*, Kaufman channels Maslow's passion by offering something of a coda to the book, titled

12. Kaufman, *Transcend*, 79.

13. Kaufman, *Transcend*, 7.

14. Kaufman, *Transcend*, 220.

"Live More in the B-Realm," inspired by ideas Maslow was toying with during his final years. Maslow was busy: in Kaufman's rendering, there are some thirty-five entries, including a focus on ends, not just means (a clear transcendent approach to life); cultivating periods of quiet meditation; the by-now-familiar awe, wonder, reverence, and respect approach to life; opening oneself and others to the recognition of personal faults (what Carl Jung would call the shadow side); avoiding external signs of validation; living as if you had but one more year to live; transcending the ego; and many practices more common to spiritual direction than to psychology and philosophy. Kaufman clearly sees his own work as not only highlighting Maslow's mission but building upon it. His is a renewed and much appreciated humanistic psychology for the twenty-first century.

Humanistic Philosophy: Andy Norman and the Search for a Better Way to Think

What Kaufman does for humanistic psychology, Andy Norman does for humanistic philosophy: he reintroduces it to twenty-first-century students, both young and old, and explores its application to present-day concerns. For Norman, the Carnegie Mellon philosophy professor referenced previously in our chapter on Julian Huxley, *humanistic* is more than a descriptive adjective; it is a conscious, motivating philosophy of life. His Humanism Initiative, launched in 2013, approaches "humanism as an inclusive, value-centered philosophical outlook with which students can examine the human condition, scientific research, moral analysis, and more . . . [and that] will pursue community building, education, and research."[15]

Norman's goal of advancing humanism received a significant boost with the 2021 publication of his groundbreaking study of the effects of toxic thinking on society, *Mental Immunity: Infectious Ideas, Mind Parasites, and the Search for a Better Way to Think*. Employing the immunology metaphor throughout the book, he successfully demonstrates how we can protect ourselves from cultural pathogens, parasites that invade our minds, and become better and more collaborative learners through the perennial philosophical search for wisdom. His book could not be more timely as it directly confronts the current plague of ideologies, malevolent actors in politics and the media, the dark web, and destructive voices throughout the culture.

Fine-tuned through his many years engaging students in philosophical inquiry at Carnegie Mellon, Norman's work flows directly from a worldview that recognizes humanity's need to become a better and wiser version of

15. Posted at www.cmu.edu on Mar. 27, 2013.

itself through enhanced reasoning skills. He begins his study by addressing the present day's attack on truth and reason by powerful factions of the media, all of which is exacerbated by the internet, particularly in its darker recesses. He identifies the need for a "mind vaccine" against extremism and demagoguery, and he calls for a science of mental immunity, or cognitive immunology, just as we have a science of physical immunology against disease and a science of computer immunology that seeks to identify and neutralize malware. He is confident that a well-developed science of cognitive immunity can help to identify, expose, and root out the malicious ideas that wreak havoc in our lives and threaten our social, economic, and political infrastructure.

Norman appreciates all this as "the natural evolution of an ancient quest . . . [the] hunt for wisdom,"[16] the perennial philosophical pursuit. He observes that Socrates, whom he both reveres and critiques, "was martyred for the cause of bad idea removal,"[17] and he identifies "bad idea removal" as the first step in that wisdom quest. He assails the contemporary culture of cynicism that has given birth to cognitive epidemics such as "moral panics, conspiracy theories, science denial,"[18] and the blight of "willful unreason":[19] the stubbornness that occasionally frustrates healthy dialogue. Like many we have studied in these pages, he recognizes and encourages "the human need for transcendence and spiritual connection."[20]

Norman proposes a cognitive immunology toolbox that begins with the understanding, as did Maslow a couple of generations previously, that values cannot be dismissed as purely subjective, outside the purview of philosophical or scientific inquiry; there are both beneficial and harmful values—kindness is good and cheating is bad, for example. He observes that although we are born with the ability to screen out bad ideas, that ability can be frustrated over time by biases, cultural conditions, and psychological factors such as confirmation bias (wherein we are more attuned to noticing evidence that supports our ideas and ignoring that which opposes them) and belief persistence (when our beliefs tend to linger despite contrary evidence).

What then must we do? Norman's response, repeated frequently throughout the book, serves well as a mantra for our times: we must commit ourselves to yielding to the better reasons—to be willing to alter our

16. Norman, *Mental Immunity*, 18.
17. Norman, *Mental Immunity*, 20.
18. Norman, *Mental Immunity*, 33–34.
19. Norman, *Mental Immunity*, 56.
20. Norman, *Mental Immunity*, 36.

opinions in the face of contrary evidence. Norman refers to this as "the growth mindset . . . [which] promotes resilience, success in school, and better relationships,"[21] adding that the opposite of the growth mindset is a fixed and unmovable mindset, "a species of mental immune disorder."[22]

Norman takes his readers through a multitude of "cultural roadblocks" to the development of a healthy mental immune system: relativism regarding values and morality; philosophical attachments to the right to believe whatever one wishes, responsible or otherwise; identity politics, which helps to cement personal opinion in spite of the consequences of those opinions on others (think white supremacy); faith systems that take on "an identity-based unwillingness to follow the evidence";[23] and limiting theologies. Like all who merit the descriptor *humanistic psychologist*, Norman insists that all rights come with responsibilities.

Norman proposes a "collaborative inquiry" approach to idea testing that is designed to minimize the temptation latent within the Socratic method to descend into the bottomless pit of never-ending *why* questions, thereby making "skeptical debunking tragically easy"[24] and frustrating the building of commonly held knowledge. In Norman's approach, the questioner has both the *freedom* to ask why and the *responsibility* to ask only those questions that legitimately and naturally arise within the conversation. Cognitive immune health, insists Norman, requires a collaborative spirit, one of inquiry, not debate, suggesting that what he is advocating for is an approach to learning wherein "the *will to find out* predominates over *the will to believe*."[25]

Norman encourages us to think of our beliefs as houseguests—friends, yes, but friends that can overstay their welcome—and he adds that it is both healthy and helpful to open "a gap between your beliefs and your sense of self,"[26] as any good therapist would advise. He points a finger at ideologues who practice what he calls "the way of belief," wherein belief is immersed within identity, and advocates instead for his "way of collaborative inquiry," which makes possible "a hallowed space for minds to meet in understanding."[27] Rather than attacking those who parrot toxic ideas, he

21. Norman, *Mental Immunity*, 59.

22. Norman, *Mental Immunity*, 59.

23. Norman, *Mental Immunity*, 91.

24. Norman, *Mental Immunity*, 267.

25. Norman, *Mental Immunity*, 298 (emphasis in original).

26. Norman, *Mental Immunity*, 103.

27. Norman, *Mental Immunity*, 102.

calls for civility and patience, observing that "in most cases, irresponsible believing calls for patient instruction, not condemnation."[28]

Confronting the obstacles that faith-based systems might present to his call for collaborative inquiry, while at the same time recognizing the possible psychological and social benefits of religion such as comfort, hope, fellowship, and belonging, Norman enjoins men and women of faith to let go of any problematic belief elements and channel their energies more toward prosocial activities, what many would call social justice or the social gospel. Rather than concentrate on what he refers to as the upstream components of faith—its origins, which tend to be shrouded in myth and propagate belief in miracles that might frustrate collaborative inquiry—religious persons should focus on the downstream benefits—feeding the hungry, giving drink to the thirsty, clothing the naked. Observing that "highly religious societies tend to have *high* levels of social dysfunction,"[29] and adding that this correlation applies equally within the individual American states, he concludes with the admonition that "the fact that a belief is religious in no way exempts it from ethical review."[30] Belief systems were implanted in our minds long before we had the maturity to deal with them, Norman reminds us, adding that it is our moral responsibility to review and correct any falsehoods and submit to the evidence rather than persist in belief. For Norman, this submission to the force of the better reasoning is the essence of the scientific method properly understood.

In response to the inevitable question *To whose reasons are we to submit?*, he responds: *Our* reasons, good evidentiary reasons formed through our collaborative inquiry, the melding of our minds toward the creation of a world in which persuasion displaces coercion. "Thou shalt yield to the better reason" is his moral touchstone, and he proposes his own "epistemic golden rule: 'Observe the same standards of belief you would have others observe.'"[31]

In confronting infectious ideas and harmful beliefs, Norman is no utopian. When critiquing the moral incuriosity, rigidity, and backwardness that pervades much of our culture, he calls for a metaphorical "wisdom-inducing vaccine" in response. He is arguing not for a cure-all but only for a *better* understanding of what reason requires—that it be "clear, explicit, vetted, defensible, well-functioning, and shared"[32] and, of course, subject

28. Norman, *Mental Immunity*, 127.

29. Norman, *Mental Immunity*, 139 (emphasis in original).

30. Norman, *Mental Immunity*, 141.

31. Norman, *Mental Immunity*, 237.

32. Norman, *Mental Immunity*, 258.

to continuing review. This is philosophy's "wisdom quest," he reminds us, our human imperative.

Like Maslow before him, Norman calls for "a genuine *science* of right and wrong,"[33] adding that a helpful standard of discerning between the two is whether or not the beliefs in question promote flourishing, or well-being. In words reminiscent of the messianic spirituality of both Maslow and Teilhard de Chardin, he fleshes out the way of collaborative inquiry, through which that science of right and wrong will emerge: it is "an attitude fueled by wonder, one that strives for ecstatic but responsible communion with the real . . . a humble submission . . . [that] facilitates the noncoercive convergence of belief . . . [that] holds the key to building responsible, shared understanding of what *matters* as well as understanding of what *is* . . . the path to collective salvation."[34]

Norman closes his book with a practical twelve-step program through which each of us can work toward greater awareness of the presence of infectious ideas and mind parasites in our culture and develop greater cognitive immunity. It starts with the challenge to take ideas and opinions seriously: "Ideas can inspire, connect, and enlighten; they can also distract, disorient, and delude."[35] Do not take ideas for granted; rather, confront them, evaluate them, change them if needed.

Evaluate your belief systems, Norman encourages; check their downstream effects by asking: *How do my beliefs play out in the world?* Noting that learning is about subtraction as well as addition, he encourages us to be open to reasoned challenges to our beliefs and to let go of the troublesome ones: "Reasons and questions are like antibodies: Used properly, they hunt down bad ideas and neutralize them."[36] Further, he challenges us to let go of the relativistic thinking that all value judgments are subjective: kindness to others is objectively good; mean-spiritedness is objectively not so. In closing, he enjoins us to consider forming communities of inquiry rather than communities of belief. For Norman, mental immunity is first and foremost a collaborative responsibility.

In the introduction to *Mental Immunity*, Andy Norman referenced the attack on the Tree of Life synagogue in Pittsburgh on October 28, 2018, where his young son attended day care as of the book's writing. Eleven congregants were killed that day by an assassin motivated by the toxic belief that "all Jews must die." It was "the deadliest attack on Jews in American

33. Norman, *Mental Immunity*, 145 (emphasis in original).

34. Norman, *Mental Immunity*, 165 (emphasis in original).

35. Norman, *Mental Immunity*, 347.

36. Norman, *Mental Immunity*, 33.

history";[37] several Holocaust survivors were among the victims. Norman reminds us that a better way of thinking can reduce toxic beliefs and help create a more collaborative, tolerant world. What we believe truly does matter.

Daniel Siegel—Humanistic Psychiatry and Mindfulness-Based Psychotherapy

The legacy of humanistic psychology is observable in the contemporary psychiatric profession as well. Daniel Siegel, one of the authors most recently of *The Power of Showing Up: How Parental Presence Shapes Who Our Kids Become and How Their Brains Get Wired*, is a clinical professor of psychiatry at UCLA and perhaps America's foremost pioneer and advocate in the field of interpersonal neurobiology, an approach to working with people—patients and clients—that emphasizes the interrelational dimension of the mind.

Siegel describes the mind as "an embodied and relational process that regulates the flow of energy and information" both within and between persons,[38] and he discusses the self in terms of mind, brain (understood expansively as "the mechanism of energy and information flow in the extended nervous system distributed throughout the entire body"),[39] and relationships (through which we extend our influence to, and in turn are influenced by, each other). The widespread application of his work—which has been heralded in multiple fields, including counseling, parenting, education, relationships, and business practices—is reminiscent of the pervasive influence of Maslow, Rogers, Fromm, and May from the 1950s through the 1980s.

Siegel coined the term *mindsight* to distinguish the path he is charting in the larger field of interpersonal neurobiology. He defines it as

> a kind of focused attention . . . that helps us to be aware of our mental processes without being swept away by them, allows us to get ourselves off the autopilot of ingrained behaviors and habitual responses, and moves us beyond the reactive emotional loops we all have a tendency to get trapped in.[40]

Where Siegel particularly intersects with humanistic psychology is in his work on the components of optimum therapy discussed in *The Mindful Therapist: A Clinician's Guide to Mindsight and Neural Integration*, a book

37. Norman, *Mental Immunity*, 2.
38. Siegel, *Mindful Therapist*, 25.
39. Siegel, *Mindful Therapist*, xxii.
40. Siegel, *Mindsight*, xi–xii.

that could readily serve as a twenty-first-century complement to Rogers's *On Becoming a Person*, May's *The Art of Counseling*, Frieda Fromm-Reichmann's *Principles of Intensive Psychotherapy*, and Irvin Yalom's *The Gift of Therapy*. In *The Mindful Therapist*, Siegel focuses on three therapeutic behaviors—presence, attunement, and resonance—as critical to the creation of an environment in which therapeutic change can occur.

Presence entails being fully open to whatever the client may be expressing, to set aside any agenda other than that of the client, and to allow the client's inner and outer worlds to be the entire focus of the interaction—creating an "openness to the unfolding of possibilities"[41] within the counseling hour. Attunement is the ability to profit from that presence and "soak in the internal states of others as we pick up their signals and have internal shifts in our own state."[42] Finally, resonance, "a coupling of two autonomous entities into a functional whole,"[43] is the synergistic experience in which therapist and client become joined and experience a deep sense of being heard, understood, and truly felt. The legacy of Rogers's necessary and sufficient conditions of therapeutic change is evident in Siegel's work, an encouraging sign for the future of person-centered counseling.

In addition to embracing a humanistic approach to therapy, Siegel found himself in the second half of life following a path that has become familiar to us—that of opening himself to the spiritual dimension through the experience of a close friendship based on common interests. As a result of their mutual interest and work related to the intersection of body, mind, and spirit, Siegel and John O'Donohue—mystic, poet, philosopher, Catholic priest, and author of the 1998 spiritual classic *Anam Cara* ("soul companion," in O'Donohue's native Gaelic tongue)—formed a working relationship in spite of foundational theological differences. Like Rogers before him, Siegel found himself confronted by something that would not fit neatly into his rational, scientific worldview—a spiritual vision that was leading to some of the same conclusions about the centrality of the interpersonal dimension as was his own scientific work.

Siegel's friendship with O'Donohue, who died in 2008 and whom Siegel would consistently reference as "dear friend," is a contemporary example of the intersection of the spiritual and the humanistic that we have observed throughout the story of humanistic psychology. Examples of these include: the affection between Julian Huxley and Pierre Teilhard de Chardin and between Carl Rogers and Brian Thorne, the honest search for mutual

41. Siegel, *Mindful Therapist*, 34.

42. Siegel, *Mindful Therapist*, 38–39.

43. Siegel, *Mindful Therapist*, 54.

understanding evidenced by the distinctly secular Rogers and the "believing humanist" Martin Buber, the attraction of men and women in ministry to the affirmational psychology of Rogers and of persons in positions of religious prominence to Erich Fromm's humanistic values, and even the relationship between Rollo May and Paul Tillich, whose connection in both their humanism and their spirituality was less about the discovery of a new way of thinking on May's part as it was a verification of the thoughts he was struggling to articulate. All these serve as enduring testaments to the ability of persons of good will to work together in spite of their differences. Recognizing their similar interests, particularly in the area of mindfulness studies and spirituality, Siegel, O'Donohue, and a host of others (including the mindfulness meditation guru Jon Kabat-Zinn and the Dalai Lama) have collaborated through the years on mind studies that would lead, in Siegel's case, to an unexpected opening to the spiritual domain.

Siegel's spiritual path serves as a two-generations-hence version of Maslow's, Rogers's, Fromm's, and May's. Ethnically Jewish, with roots traced to the Ukraine, Lithuania, and Russia, his family set aside traditional religious observance somewhere during their trek from eastern Europe to California. Raised as a member of the pacifist Unitarian and Quaker churches, which he would experience as teaching and embracing the presence of good in all religions, Siegel responded to a question about his spirituality by noting that he grew up "in a very logical, science-based, education-oriented family without any background in religion or spirituality." He added that

> [We] were very focused on improving the lives of others and were active in the civil rights movement. In that sense, if you define spirituality as living a life of purpose and meaning—of being connected to a larger whole than yourself—then, yes, that was a spiritual life. . . . And now I have a regular reflective practice to cultivate those ways of living each day, but I usually use the term integrative instead of spiritual.[44]

Many in the religious and spiritual sectors have found themselves attracted to Siegel's teaching, in which they see an affirmation of something beyond the material. When Siegel speaks of the mind as a process that monitors and moderates the flow of energy and information both within the person and between persons, many readily imagine a dimension beyond the physical, one of spirit or soul. When he speaks of the power of love communicated through the eyes, one person to another, literally affecting the neural structure of each other's brains, they see an image of the divine.

44. Mowe, "Q & A."

In 1999, Siegel had a personal audience with Pope John Paul II—at the pope's request. John Paul, who had read of Siegel's thoughts on the power of love transmitted from mother to child through the eyes, wanted to discuss the impact of his own mother's eyes, of which he had enduring memories, on his spiritual development. The mental image of these two men from widely divergent backgrounds and representative of two often-contesting worldviews engaged in dialogue about a mother's love—at the pope's request!—bodes well for the future of constructive dialogue between humanists and scientists, on the one hand, and men and women of religion, on the other. A credible claim could be made that Siegel's work in interpersonal neurobiology and his consequent celebration of presence, attunement, and resonance in the counseling office could well serve as a twenty-first-century incarnation of the humanistic psychology movement as it embraces the psychological and the biological, as well as, quite frequently, the spiritual.

Concluding Thoughts

Since the golden age of humanistic psychology—the 1950s through the 1980s—its influence has extended well beyond the fields of counseling and psychological studies. The impact of Rogerian influences on the field of education and parenting has already been referenced in the personal story that opens the chapter on Rogers. The learning I experienced through that training led to a fifteen-year commitment to leading parenting and teaching groups in the study and practice of interpersonal skills development, an experience that led directly to my decision to leave the world of education and become a counselor.

The effects of humanistic psychology can be observed in the world of pastoral ministry as well. The growing attraction of spiritual direction, for example, encouraged through Spiritual Directors International and its journal, *Presence*, is leading to a more humanistic approach to faith development that focuses less on creedal distinctions, as Maslow and Fromm encouraged, and more on personal journeys of faith and how they affect individuals and communities.

Businesses and health-care organizations often go out of their way today to address the personal needs and concerns of their employees and clients, and although the cynic might respond that humanistic approaches to management and worker relations are favored only so long as the bottom line increases, anecdotal evidence abounds that real changes are being made. Employee retreats and full employee participation in mission and vision formulations are becoming more common, even the norm. I once held a mission and vision workshop in a Dallas warehouse with thirty-five forklift drivers. Having never before been asked for their opinion regarding the direction the company should take, they embraced the opportunity to do so—with raucous, unabashed, Texas-style enthusiasm.

The effects of person-centered humanism can be discovered even in our criminal justice centers—although so much more remains to be done, as Bryan Stevenson, founder and executive director of the Equal Justice Initiative, has so eloquently argued in his bestseller, *Just Mercy*. A conversation I once had with a Missouri county sheriff suggests the potential for humanistic reform in that critical area. The sheriff shared with me his pride in a detention center under his jurisdiction, noting that wardens throughout the country would visit to learn his secret for the low rate of violence within its walls. He told me that it really wasn't much of a secret: "All we do is address each prisoner by name—Mr. Matthews, Mr. Lopez, Mr. Jackson. When you address people respectfully, they tend to feel better about themselves and offer respect back . . . and violence decreases." In that Missouri correctional facility, the detainees have become persons, and the spirit of Carl Rogers is no doubt smiling at that comment by a not-so-hardened officer of the law.

What, then, is the legacy of humanistic psychology? Jessica Grogan in *Encountering America* sums it up well:

> If we measure the extent to which the leading concepts of humanistic psychology have pervaded our culture, in fact, we might deem the movement a whopping success. The language of humanistic psychology is everywhere: Humanistic ideas of self, growth, individual potential, and relation are now woven into the very fabric of our thoughts and perceptions.[45]

Present-day psychotherapists who are inspired by humanistic psychology and the larger humanist movement have much to celebrate. The humanistic psychology movement left us with a philosophy of the person—an intrinsic, growth-oriented, holistic approach that values the person in his or her unique, creative, experiencing, self—and a revolutionary approach to healing—a person-centered approach that in its purest form finds expression in Carl Rogers and is lived out daily in its many modifications by the majority of therapists today.

It also brought existentialist approaches to counseling into the mainstream, largely through the efforts of Rollo May. Further, through the genius of the psychoanalytically trained Frieda Fromm-Reichmann, Freud's revolutionary insights were adapted and placed in the service of humanistic psychology—a humanistic psychoanalysis that offers the best of both

45. Grogan, *Encountering America*, 322.

traditions. Counseling was transformed by the humanists; in fact, as suggested throughout, a solid argument could be made that it was the humanistic psychologists who "invented" counseling as we know it today.

Abraham Maslow, Carl Rogers, Erich Fromm, Rollo May, and Julian Huxley have left us the legacy of an approach to working with and showing concern for people that champions the essence of what it means to be human—the striving to lead ethical lives in line with consciously identified values, lives that seek both our own personal fulfillment and that of the greater good. Coming from different perspectives and traveling their own unique paths, they celebrated the centrality of personhood with a spiritual maturity through which they could imagine a better world—and even, occasionally, a world beyond our own. Moreover, being largely nonreligious persons who were at the same time intensely values-oriented, they transcended the dialectic between the religious and the secular, proving there could be a third way. The search for and identification of humane values can be undertaken by all of us, whatever our faith tradition—or even if we have no faith tradition at all.

Postscript

In the introduction to this book, I referenced that it evolved out of my doctoral dissertation at the Graduate Theological Foundation, an educational institution that "serves those within faith communities who are engaged in the wide range of traditional and emerging forms of ministry as a way to strengthen their quest for a deeper sense of unity both among themselves and in their developing relations with other religious traditions and secular society."[1] During my defense of that dissertation, I was challenged to respond to the following question: "Erich Fromm and various other schools of thought share a common interest with religion as they deal with the human person—the soul, *anima*. Could you walk us through how these schools of thought contribute to the realization of the ultimate goal of religion, namely, the salvation of the soul (*salus animarum*)?"

Good question! And my response fits neatly into the subject matter of this book:

Two anecdotes spring to mind in relation to this important question, fundamental to an understanding of how humanistic psychology and the world of religion might find common ground. The first is from a brief exchange in the 1944 W. Somerset Maugham novel, *The Razor's Edge.* A central character in the novel has died, and a distinguished local cleric is present to administer the last rights. The narrator describes the scene as the cleric approaches the deceased gentleman's manservant, Joseph, who is not a man of faith:

> "You are a freethinker, my son?"
> I could see Joseph making an effort over himself.
> "Yes, Monseigneur."

1. www.gtfeducation.org.

> "Do not let it trouble you. You have been a good and faithful servant to your master. God will overlook the errors of your understanding."[2]

The second anecdote is Abraham Maslow's stirring metaphor near the close of *Religions, Values, and Peak-Experiences*, in which the minister of God and the nontheistic person of science walk arm and arm down the road of life, content that they have worked together to promote the good of humanity. Having reaching a fork at the end, one takes the direction leading to an afterlife with God, the other to an eternal sleep.

Will the manservant's soul in Maugham's novel be saved in spite of his absence of faith, as suggested by the cleric? Is there a place in heaven for "freethinkers"? In Maslow's parable-like story, is only one of the two souls saved? Did the one who went to an everlasting sleep lose his soul? If we can assume that he followed his conscience and led a life aligned with healthy values, is he nonetheless barred from salvation?

If the ultimate goal of religion is the salvation of the soul, how is that salvation to be understood? Through what means is that salvation achieved—what beliefs, behaviors, and activities and what level of acceptance, obedience, and submission are essential to it? Is salvation narrowly restricted to the requirements of a specific religion? Could it be available to all who lead lives of compassion and healing and love for their fellow humans?

The humanistic theorists studied were men who eschewed formal religion yet fully embraced and engaged the spiritual dimension as they understood it. Abraham Maslow is perhaps the best example of this. His celebrated hierarchy of needs, by which most outside the field know his name, received few references in his subsequent work after he homed in on the top of the pyramid, self-actualization. There he observed a correlation between psychological health and ethical living, wherein the peak-experiences of awe, wonder, mystery, reverence, and the sublime were more naturally and frequently experienced. To him, it was where heaven itself is experienced: Maslow understood heaven as always available, ever present, ready to be stepped into and experienced at a moment's notice.

Maslow, Fromm, Rogers, May, and Huxley spoke little of the traditional understanding of salvation. Yet each understood that by promoting humanity's healthy values in their respective fields they were helping others recognize and embrace their inner wholeness and goodness, thereby becoming persons who could better grasp what to do in the spheres of influence in which they might find themselves. For them, humanity's salvation

2. Maugham, *Razor's Edge*, 235.

would arrive through the active embrace and living out of humanistic values that speak to the essence, the Being, of the person.

Striving to articulate what authentic, healthy religion means, Erich Fromm defined it in terms of that which recognizes and promotes the freedom of the person, a freedom that he stressed was more about freedom *to* (to be the responsible person one is called to be, both individually and within the larger sociocultural milieu) rather than exclusively a freedom *from*. Writing in the shadow of Nazism and fascism, he knew well what violation of personhood means. For Fromm, salvation of the soul is about freeing the person from a life of slavish obedience and conformity to any system detrimental to one's humanity, be it consumerism, materialism, totalitarianism, hyper-nationalism, or any other worldview antithetical to the flourishing of the spiritual person.

Carl Rogers and Rollo May likewise promoted the sanctity of the person. Rogers did so through his work as a counselor and community developer, both on the micro level of the person-centered community and on the macro level through his hands-on efforts to promote peace in the world's trouble spots, such as South African and Northern Ireland. May promoted the sanctity of the person on a more philosophical and academic stage. For Rogers, salvation, both of self and others, emerges through the personal or group encounter, through which persons are heard, listened to, and understood. For May, salvation arrives through personal self-consciousness or self-knowledge; he took the Socratic "Know thyself" very much to heart.

Julian Huxley frequently spoke of a place for religion in his worldview. He saw salvation at work within the advancement of the human species itself. Evolution has arrived at a place at which the person is now both its highest achievement and its director, bearing responsibility for the promotion of values and actions that enhance all of life, particularly that of Homo sapiens. Therein lies humankind's salvation in Huxley's worldview: it is salvation for the species, and it is within our own hands.

How one views the soul might shed further light on how the theorists being studied imagined the person's salvation. What is the soul? My many years in Catholic schools have guided me toward a description of the soul as that which gives life to the body and that which perdures after the death of the body. (I will leave it to others to sort out what happens after the resurrection of the body.)

A memory from my early years—seventh grade, perhaps—is of the teacher explaining in religion class that the theory of evolution, including the evolution of the person, presents no problem in the Catholic worldview. The only requirement, he went on to say, is to understand that what separates the person from that from which it evolved is the presence of the soul. An image of God reaching out and touching that first evolving person, ensouling that person, remains etched in the memory bank of my mind. The point was made: the soul is divine, it is what separates us from the animal kingdom, it is the point in evolution at which the person evolved, and it endures for all eternity.

In the world of humanistic psychology, the soul is referenced in terminology other than the above. Rather than speak of the soul needing to be *saved*, humanistically oriented persons would more likely speak of the soul needing to be *healed*. A 2012 book about working with returning soldiers suffering from signs of PTSD might help us here. Titled *Soul Repair: Recovering from Moral Injury after War*, by Rita Nakashima Brock (no relation) and Gabriela Lettina, it suggests a more this-worldly (in the sense of being more present in the moment) focus than one directed toward the afterlife, a more temporal focus that sees a person in need of repair or healing at the deepest part of the self, the soul. The soldier, the authors argue, needs to be reconnected to that center of the self from which he or she is estranged due to having experienced the brutality of war. Brock and Lettina propose that reconnection with the deepest self, the soul, will help the soldier heal and begin to live a life that embraces a more eternal perspective, a life lived *sub specie aeternitatis*.

Are the two perspectives mutually exclusive? Is it either about saving the soul in a defined afterlife, or about repairing and healing the soul for life on this earth? I would argue not. None of the thinkers studied envisioned a personal God and a traditional afterlife. But they were all keenly focused on the salvation of the person, and as they understood the soul as the deepest part of the person, they were focused on its salvation as well. I suspect there is a place for them in the heaven they could not imagine.

Bibliography

Abzug, Robert H. *Psyche and Soul in America: The Spiritual Odyssey of Rollo May.* New York: Oxford University Press, 2021.

Adler, Alfred. *Understanding Human Nature.* Center City, MN: Hazelden, 1998.

Allport, Gordon. "The Emergence of Existential Psychology." In *Existential Psychology*, edited by R. May, 11–51. New York: Random House, 1966.

Associated Press. "Hawking Buried at Westminster Abbey." *Dallas Morning News*, 2018.

Bair, Deirdre. *Jung: A Biography.* New York: Little, Brown, 2003.

Bakan, David. *Sigmund Freud and the Jewish Mystical Tradition.* Mineola, NY: Dover, 2004.

Belford, Ann Elizabeth. "'Third-Force Psychologists' and Judaism's Shared Positive View of Humanity." *Foundation Theology* (2016) 1–15.

Berry, Thomas. *The Dream of the Earth.* San Francisco: Sierra Club, 1998.

Brock, Rita Nakashima, and Gabriella Lettina. *Soul Repair: Recovering from Moral Injury after War.* Boston: Beacon, 2012.

Buber, Martin. *A Believing Humanism: Gleanings.* New York: Simon and Schuster, 1969.

———. *I and Thou.* New York: Scribner Classics, 2000.

Bühler, Charlotte. *Values in Psychotherapy.* New York: Free Press, 1962.

Bühler, Charlotte, and Melanie Allen. *Introduction to Humanistic Psychology.* Belmont, CA: Wadsworth, 1972.

Burston, Daniel. *The Legacy of Erich Fromm.* Cambridge, MA: Harvard University Press, 1991.

Concord Media. "Carl Rogers Interviews: Richie." YouTube, 2014. https://www.youtube.com/watch?v=QyJ3mvQousc.

Csikszentmihalyi, Mihaly. "Preface." In *The Handbook of Humanistic Psychology: Leading Edges in Theory, Research, and Practice*, edited by Kirk J. Schneider et al., xv–xvii. Thousand Oaks, CA: Sage, 2001.

Delio, Ilia. *The Emergent Christ: Exploring the Meaning of Catholic in an Evolutionary Universe.* Maryknoll, NY: Orbis, 2011.

Dewey, John. *A Common Faith.* New Haven, CT: Yale University Press, 1962.

Donne, John. "No Man Is an Island." All Poetry, n.d. https://allpoetry.com/No-man-is-an-island.

Elkins, David N. *Beyond Religion: A Personal Program for Building a Spiritual Life outside the Walls of Traditional Religion.* Wheaton, IL: Theosophical, 1998.

Erikson, Eric H. *Insight and Responsibility*. New York: Norton, 1964.

Fowler, James. *Stages of Faith: The Psychology of Human Development and the Quest for Meaning*. 2nd ed. New York: HarperCollins, 1981.

Frankl, Viktor E. *Man's Search for Meaning*. 3rd ed. New York: Simon & Schuster, 1984.

———. *The Unheard Cry for Meaning: Psychotherapy and Humanism*. New York: Simon & Schuster, 1978.

———. *Yes to Life: In Spite of Everything*. Boston: Beacon, 2019.

Freeman, Lucy. *Freud Rediscovered*. New York: Arbor House, 1980.

Freud, Sigmund. *Civilization and Its Discontents*. New York: Norton, 1961.

———. *The Future of an Illusion*. New York: Norton, 1961.

———. *An Outline of Psychoanalysis*. New York: Norton, 1969.

Friedman, Lawrence J. *The Lives of Erich Fromm: Love's Prophet*. New York: Columbia University Press, 2013.

Friedman, Maurice S. *Martin Buber: The Life of Dialogue*. New York: Harper and Row, 1960.

Fromm, Erich. *The Art of Loving*. New York: Harper Perennial, 2006.

———. *Escape from Freedom*. New York: Holt, 1994.

———. *Psychoanalysis and Religion*. New Haven, CT: Yale University Press, 1950.

———. *The Revolution of Hope*. Riverdale, NY: American Mental Health Association, 1970.

———. *The Sane Society*. New York: Holt, 1990.

———. *To Have or to Be?* New York: Harper and Row, 1976.

Fromm-Reichmann, Frieda. *Principles of Intense Psychotherapy*. Chicago: University of Chicago Press, 1950.

Funk, Rainer. *Erich Fromm: His Life and Times*. New York: Continuum, 2000.

Gay, Peter. *Freud: A Life for Our Time*. New York: Norton, 2006.

———. "Sigmund Freud: A Brief Life." In *An Outline of Psycho-Analysis*, by Sigmund Freud, edited by James Strachey, vi–xx. New York: Norton, 1989.

Goble, Frank. *The Third Force: The Psychology of Abraham Maslow*. New York: Grossman, 1970.

Goldstein, Rebecca Newberger. *Betraying Spinoza: The Renegade Jew Who Gave Us Modernity*. New York: Schocken, 2006.

Gould, Stephen Jay. *Rocks of Ages: Science and Religion in the Fullness of Life*. New York: Ballantine, 1999.

Green, Hannah. *I Never Promised You a Rose Garden*. New York: Holt, Rinehart and Winston, 1964.

Grogan, Jessica. *Encountering America: Humanistic Psychology, Sixties Culture & the Shaping of the Modern Self*. New York: HarperCollins, 2013.

Haidt, Jonathan. *The Righteous Mind: Why Good People Are Divided by Politics and Religion*. New York: Vintage, 2013.

Harris, Sam. *The Moral Landscape: How Science Can Determine Human Values*. New York: Free Press, 2010.

Hartman, Robert. "The Science of Value." In *New Knowledge in Human Values*, edited by Abraham Maslow, 13–37. Chicago: Regnery, 1971.

Haught, John F. *The Cosmic Vision of Teilhard de Chardin*. Maryknoll, NY: Orbis, 2021.

Hoffman, Edward. *The Right to Be Human: A Biography of Abraham Maslow*. Los Angeles: Tarcher, 1988.

Holpuch, Amanda. "Stanford Apologizes for Limiting Jewish Admissions in the 1950s." *New York Times*, Oct. 13, 2022.

Hornstein, Gail. A. *To Redeem One Person Is to Redeem the World: The Life of Frieda-Fromm Reichmann*. New York: Other Press, 2005.

Huxley, Julian. *Evolutionary Humanism*. 2nd ed. Buffalo, NY: Prometheus, 1992.

———. *The Humanist Frame*. New York: Harper & Brothers, 1961.

———. "Introduction." In *The Phenomenon of Man*, by Teilhard de Chardin, translated by Bernard Wall, 11–28. New York: HarperCollins, 1958.

———. *Religion without Revelation*. 2nd ed. New York: New American Library, 1957.

James, William. *The Varieties of Religious Experience: A Study in Human Nature*. N.p.: Megaladon Entertainment, 2008.

Johnson, Elizabeth A. *Ask the Beasts: Darwin and the God of Love*. London: Bloomsbury, 2014.

Jones, Serene. *Call It Grace: Finding Meaning in a Fractured World*. New York: Viking, 2019.

Kaufman, Scott Barry. *Transcend: The New Science of Self-Actualization*. New York: Tarcher Perigee, 2020.

Kavanaugh, James. *A Modern Priest Looks at His Outdated Church*. New York: Pocket, 1968.

King, Barbara J. *Evolving God: A Provocative View on the Origins of Religion*. New York: Doubleday, 2007.

King, Ursula. *Spirit of Fire: The Life and Vision of Teilhard de Chardin*. Maryknoll, NY: Orbis, 2004.

Kirschenbaum, Howard. *The Carl Rogers Reader*. New York: Houghton Mifflin, 1989.

———. *On Becoming Carl Rogers*. New York: Delacorte, 1979.

Kirschenbaum, Howard, and Valerie Land Henderson. *Carl Rogers: Dialogues*. London: Constable, 1989.

Klingberg, Haddon, Jr. *When Life Calls Out to Us: The Love and Lifework of Viktor and Elly Frankl*. New York: Doubleday, 1996.

Kugelmann, Robert. *Psychology and Catholicism: Contested Boundaries*. Cambridge: Cambridge University Press, 2012.

Laggner, Thomas. "A Dialogue with Carl Rogers and Paul Tillich, Part 1: Saybrook University." Vimeo, n.d. https://vimeo.com/506139124.

Leslie, Robert C. *Jesus as Counselor*. Nashville: Abingdon, 1965.

Lundy, Janice. "The Art of 'Being With.'" Unpublished paper, 2022.

———. "Serving Spiritual Independents: Companionship without Bias." *Presence Journal* 24 (Sept. 2018) 18–25.

Maslow, Abraham. H. *The Farther Reaches of Human Nature*. New York: Viking, 1971.

———. "Letter to B. F. Skinner." In *Future Visions: The Unpublished Papers of Abraham Maslow*, edited by Edward Hoffman, 197–98. Thousand Oaks, CA: Sage, 1996.

———. *Motivation and Personality*. 2nd ed. New York: Harper and Row, 1970.

———. *New Knowledge in Human Values*. Chicago: Regnery, 1971.

———. *The Psychology of Science*. South Bend, IN: Gateway, 1966.

———. *Religions, Values, and Peak-Experiences*. New York: Penguin Compass, 1994.

———. *Toward a Psychology of Being*. Floyd, VA: Sublime, 2014.

Maté, Gabor, with Daniel Maté. *The Myth of Normal: Trauma, Illness & Healing in a Toxic Culture*. New York: Avery, 2022.

Maugham, W. Somerset. *The Razor's Edge*. New York: Vintage, 2003.

May, Rollo. *The Art of Counseling*. 2nd ed. New York: Gardner, 1989.
———. *The Cry for Myth*. New York: Norton, 1991.
———. *The Discovery of Being*. New York: Norton, 1983.
———. *Existential Psychology*. New York: Random House, 1961.
———. *Man's Search for Himself*. New York: Norton, 1953.
———. *The Meaning of Anxiety*. New York: Norton, 2015.
———. *Paulus*. New York: Harper & Row, 1973.
McLaren, Brian. *Faith after Doubt: Why Your Beliefs Stopped Working and What to Do about It*. New York: St. Martin's Essentials, 2021.
Morgan, John. H. *Beyond Divine Intervention: The Biology of Right and Wrong*. Lima, OH: Wyndham Hall, 2009.
———. *Clinical Psychotherapy: A History of Theory and Practice from Sigmund Freud to Aaron Beck*. Mishawaka, IN: Graduate Theological Foundation, 2017.
———. *The Damaged Self: Exploring the Psychopathology of a Diminished Life*. Levering, MI: Wyndham Hall, 2021. (Citations from unpublished proof copy.)
———. *Geriatric Psychotherapy: Essays in Clinical Practice and Counseling Psychology*. Mishawaka, IN: Graduate Theological Foundation, 2017.
———. *In the Absence of God: Religious Humanism as Spiritual Journey*. South Bend, IN: Cloverdale, 2006.
———. *Naturally Good: A Behavioral History of Moral Development*. Levering, MI: Wyndham Hall, 2021.
———. *Post-Biblical Religion: Essays in Secular Spirituality*. Mishawaka, IN: Graduate Theological Foundation, 2017.
———. *Understanding Ourselves: Essays in the History and Philosophy of the Social Sciences*. Mishawaka, IN: Graduate Theological Foundation, 2017.
Moss, Donald. "Roots and Genealogy of Humanistic Psychology." *The Handbook of Humanistic Psychology: Leading Edges in Theory, Research, and Practice*, edited by Kirk J. Schneider et al., 5–20. Thousand Oaks, CA: Sage, 2001.
Mowe, Sam. "Q & A with Dr. Dan Siegel." *Spirituality and Health*, July 7, 2014. https://www.spiritualityhealth.com/articles/2014/07/07/qa-dr-dan-siegel.
Nadler, Steven. *A Book Forged in Hell: Spinoza's Scandalous Treatise and the Birth of the Secular Age*. Princeton, NJ: Princeton University Press, 2011.
Nijhuis, Michelle. *Beloved Beasts: Fighting for Life in an Age of Extinction*. New York: Norton, 2021.
Norman, Andy. *Mental Immunity: Infectious Ideas, Mind-Parasites, and the Search for a Better Way to Think*. New York: HarperCollins, 2021.
O'Donohue, John. *Anam Cara: A Book of Celtic Wisdom*. New York: Cliff Street, 1997.
Palmer, Parker. J. *On the Brink of Everything: Grace, Gravity, and Getting Old*. Oakland, CA: Berrett-Koehler, 2018.
Perry, Helen Swick. *Psychiatrist of America: The Life of Harry Stack Sullivan*. Cambridge, MA: Belknap, 1982.
Rea, Shilo. "Carnegie Mellon's Dietrich College Launches Humanism Initiative." Carnegie Mellon University, Mar. 27, 2013https://www.cmu.edu/news/stories/archives/2013/march/march27_humanisminitiative.html.
Reeves, Clement. *The Psychology of Rollo May*. San Francisco: Josey-Bass, 1977.
Roberts, Dorothy. "Race." In *The 1619 Project: A New Origin Story*, created by Nikole Hannah-Jones and *The New York Times Magazine*, edited by Caitlin Roper et al., 45–62. New York: One World, 2021.

Rogers, Carl R. *Carl Rogers on Personal Power: Inner Strength and Its Revolutionary Impact*. New York: Delacorte, 1977.
———. *Client-Centered Therapy*. London: Constable & Robinson, 1951.
———. *On Becoming a Person*. New York: Houghton Mifflin, 1989.
———. *A Way of Being*. New York: Houghton Mifflin, 1980.
Rohr, Richard. "A Liberating Path." Center for Action and Contemplation, Jan. 6, 2023. https://cac.org/daily-meditations/a-liberating-path-2023-01-06/.
Rowan, John, and Dina Glouberman. "What Is Humanistic Psychology?" In *Humanistic Psychology: Current Trends and Future Prospects*, edited by Richard House et al., 17–33. London: Routledge, 2018.
Samuel, Michael Leo. "How Does One Build an 'I and Thou' Relationship?" Rabbi Michael Samuel, June 15, 2008. https://www.rabbimichaelsamuel.com/how-then-does-one-build-an-i-and-thou-relationship/.
Satir, Virginia. *The New Peoplemaking*. Mountain View, CA: Science and Behavior, 1988.
Schimmel, Noam. "Judaism and the Origins of Erich Fromm's Humanistic Psychology: The Religious Reverence of a Heretic." *Journal of Humanistic Psychology* 49 (2009) 9–45.
Shyman, Eric. "Normality, Pathological Orientation, and Power: Can Behavior Analytic Intervention for Individuals with ASD Qualify as Humanistic?" *The Behavioral Mind* 1 (2018) 103–20.
Siegel, Daniel J. *The Mindful Therapist: A Clinician's Guide to Mindsight and Neural Integration*. New York: Norton, 2010.
———. *Mindsight: The New Science of Personal Transformation*. New York: Bantam, 2010.
Siegel, Daniel J., and Tina Payne Bryson. *The Power of Showing Up: How Parental Presence Shapes Who Our Kids Become and How Their Brains Get Wired*. New York: Ballantine, 2020.
Sorokin, Pitrim A. "The Powers of Creative Unselfish Love." In *New Knowledge in Human Values*, edited by Abraham Maslow, 3–12. Chicago: Regnery, 1971.
Spinoza, Baruch. *Theological-Political Treatise*. Cambridge: Cambridge University Press, 2012.
Stevenson, Bryan. *Just Mercy: A Story of Justice and Redemption*. New York: Spiegel & Grau, 2019.
Sullivan, Harry Stack. *Conceptions of Modern Psychiatry*. Toronto: Norton, 1953.
Taylor, Eugene. *Shadow Culture: Psychology and Spirituality in America*. Washington, DC: Counterpoint, 1999.
Teilhard de Chardin, Pierre. *The Heart of Matter*. New York: Harcourt Brace, 1980.
Thorne, Brian. *Carl Rogers*. London, UK: Sage, 2003.
Tillich, Paul. *The Courage to Be*. New Haven, CT: Yale University Press, 2000.
———. "Is a Science of Human Values Possible?" In *New Knowledge in Human Values*, edited by Abraham Maslow, 189–96. Chicago: Regnery, 1971.
Westley, Dick. *A Theology of Presence: The Search for Meaning in the American Catholic Experience*. Mystic, CT: Twenty-Third, 1989.
Yalom, Irvin D. *Becoming Myself: A Psychiatrist's Memoir*. New York: Basic, 2017.
———. *The Spinoza Problem*. New York: Basic, 2012.
———. *Staring at the Sun: Overcoming the Terror of Death*. San Francisco: Jossey-Bass, 2008.

Index

About the Author

Mike Brock is a Dallas-area psychotherapist whose academic background includes degrees in philosophy, history, counseling, and psychology. He holds a PhD and a PsyD in clinical and pastoral psychotherapy from the Graduate Theological Foundation.

Mike spent the first thirty-four years of his professional life as a teacher and school principal in New York and Texas. After becoming a counselor, he set up a private practice in Dallas, which he continues to the present day. During much of that time, he also served as director of the counseling center at the University of Dallas. In addition to counseling in private practice, Mike teaches through the Graduate Theological Foundation, where he is the Carl Ranson Rogers Professor of Counseling Psychology.

Mike can be contacted through his webpage, www.mikebrock.org.

www.ingramcontent.com/pod-product-compliance
Lightning Source LLC
LaVergne TN
LVHW051051220926
848485LV00001BA/66
* 9 7 8 1 6 6 6 7 7 4 0 2 3 *